West Germany:
Politics and Society

DAVID CHILDS AND JEFFREY JOHNSON

ST. MARTIN'S PRESS NEW YORK

© 1981 David Childs and Jeffrey Johnson
All rights reserved. For information write:
St. Martin's Press, Inc., 175 Fifth Avenue, New York, N.Y. 10010
Printed in Great Britain
First published in the United States of America in 1981

Library of Congress Cataloging in Publication Data
Childs, David, 1933—
    West Germany, politics and society.

    Includes index.
    1. Germany, West — Politics and government. 2. Germany,
West — Social conditions.   I. Johnson, Jeffrey, joint author.
II. Title.
JN3971.A5C46 1981   320.943   80-16747
ISBN 0-312-86300-4

CONTENTS

TABLES

ABBREVIATIONS

ADF	Aktion Demokratischer Fortschritt
ARD	Arbeitsgemeinschaft der öffentlich-rechtlichen Rundfunkanstalten der Bundesrepublik Deutschland
BetrVG	Betriebsverfassungsgesetz
BP	Bayern Partei
BR	Bayerischer Rundfunk
BRD	Bundesrepublik Deutschland
BVP	Bayerische Volkspartei
CDU	Christlich-Demokratische Union
CSU	Christlich-Soziale Union
DAG	Deutsche Angestellten Gewerkschaft
DBB	Deutscher Beamtenbund
DDP	Deutsche Demokratische Partei
DDR	Deutsche Demokratische Republik
DFS	Deutsches Fernsehen
DFU	Deutsche Friedens-Union
DGB	Deutscher Gewerkschaftsbund
DKP	Deutsche Kommunistische Partei
DLF	Deutschlandfunk
DNVP	Deutschnationale Volkspartei
DP	Deutsche Partei
DRP	Deutsche Reichs-Partei
DVP	Deutsche Volkspartei
DW	Deutsche Welle
FDP	Freie Demokratische Partei
FRG	Federal Republic of Germany
FVP	Freie Volkspartei
GB/BHE	Gesamtdeutscher Block/Bund der Heimatvertriebenen und Entrechteten
GDP	Gesamtdeutsche Partei
GDR	German Democratic Republic
GVP	Gesamtdeutsche Volkspartei
HR	Hessischer Rundfunk
KPD	Kommunistische Partei Deutschlands
LPD	Liberal-Demokratische Partei Deutschlands
NPD	Nationaldemokratische Partei Deutschlands

NDR	Norddeutscher Rundfunk
SDR	Süddeutscher Rundfunk
SFB	Sender Freies Berlin
SPD	Sozialdemokratische Partei Deutschlands
SR	Saarländischer Rundfunk
SRP	Sozialistische Reichspartei
TVG	Tarifvertragsgesetz
WDR	Westdeutscher Rundfunk
Z	Zentrum
ZPF	Zweites Deutsches Fernsehen

PREFACE

There are at least several books which provide good coverage of various aspects of West Germany's institutions. Hardly any, however, attempt to be comprehensive. Our aim has been to provide such comprehensive coverage, emphasising those aspects normally neglected or omitted — the economy, social welfare, women, law and order, the mass media and the armed forces. Although the book is aimed, in the first place, at undergraduates, we hope it will also appeal to a wider audience, intrigued as we are by the re-emergence of this dynamic neighbour.

We would like to express our thanks to Professor Roger Morgan for giving us his advice on Chapter 11, Professor Kurt Sontheimer (Munich) for his comments on Chapter 3, and Dr Karl-Christian Kuhlo (IFO-Institute) for reading Chapter 4. All errors and opinions are the responsibility of the authors alone.

David Childs
Jeffrey Johnson

1 PARTIES AND ELECTIONS

New Beginnings 1945

Given the horrifying conditions which existed in Germany, and given the bitter legacy of the Third Reich, it is remarkable that so many Germans were prepared to become politically active so soon after the surrender in May 1945. The future looked black for Germany both materially and politically. The Allies — Americans, Russians, British and French — alone determined policy in their respective zones, leaving little scope for German initiative. Moreover, all political activity had to be sanctioned by the occupying power and any German bold enough to gain that sanction ran the risk of appearing a stooge of one or other of the victorious foreign powers. Yet even before the capitulation of the armed forces of the Third Reich, German political activity had started up again in Hannover — at a meeting held on 19 April, shortly after the town's capture by the Americans, by a group of Social Democrats led by Dr Kurt Schumacher (1895–1952).

It is significant that the Social Democrats were among the first on the post-war political scene, for they bore less responsibility for the disaster which had overtaken Germany than any other German political group. Set up in 1875 at Gotha, the SPD had campaigned for democracy and socialism in the Kaiserreich (1870–1918). The Social Democrats had played a decisive part in the establishing of the democratic Weimar Republic (1919–33) and had tried hard to make it a success. In 1933, they alone had voted in the German parliament or Reichstag against the Enabling Act, which was the legal facade of the Nazi dictatorship. Many Social Democratic activists, including Schumacher, had suffered in Hitler's concentration camps, been driven abroad or even murdered. Schumacher and many of his colleagues felt, therefore, that the SPD had the moral right to take the lead in building a new Germany.

Equally certain about their own leading role were the members of the Communist Party of Germany (KPD). Founded in January 1919 by Karl Liebknecht, Rosa Luxemburg and Wilhelm Pieck from a number of disparate radical socialist groups, the KPD became the most important Communist party outside the Soviet Union. It proclaimed its aim as a Soviet Germany and took its policy direction from Moscow. At the elections of November 1932 it gained 16.8 per cent of the vote as compared with the SPD's 20.4 and the Nazis' 33.1 (these were the three largest parties). It was the first party to be banned after Hitler became Chancellor. The Communist leader Ernst Thälmann was killed by the Nazis in a concentration camp and many KPD cadres suffered the same fate. Others died in Stalin's purges in the Soviet Union where they had sought refuge. Not so Walter Ulbricht. He headed a group of emigré Communists which arrived at the end of April 1945 from Moscow. Its tasks were to supervise any local Communist activity and, more importantly, set up local government administrations. It was in the Soviet Zone of Germany that German political activity was first permitted by the occupying power. This was on 10 June 1945. Within days the KPD and the SPD had been established. Two weeks later the Christian Democratic Union (CDU) was proclaimed. At the beginning of July the Liberal Democratic Party (LDP) followed. Thus the political tendencies which have dominated post-war Germany were born in Berlin in the summer of 1945.

The CDU was not merely the revival of a Weimar party. At its best it was an attempt by bourgeois and Christian democratic elements to learn from the mistakes of the Weimar period and come to terms with the likely reality of post-war Germany. But it was far from being just that. Neither the Catholic nor the Protestant Church had records they could be proud of in regard to the Third Reich. Yet the churches represented the one institution which went on virtually unhindered by the collapse of 1945. They retained their nationwide organisation and vast wealth. In the Western Zones they were respected by the occupying powers, in the Soviet Zone they were at least tolerated. More than the Protestants, the Catholics enjoyed excellent international contacts at high levels. Clearly, during this period when all Germans were regarded with suspicion by the victors, the imprimatur of the Catholic Church could work wonders in the Western Zones. An understanding of this fact is important to an understanding of the course the CDU took and its success. The CDU was part of an international trend; similar parties appeared in other West European countries, most successfully in Italy and Austria. Pope Pius XII had a tremendous fear of and hostility towards Communism (and socialism) which appeared on the verge of taking over Europe. He was therefore looking for new political forms, new alliances to avert this threat. The former Catholic indifference, if not downright hostility, to democracy was no longer acceptable. In addition, any new force would have to stress the social question if it were to have any appeal to the working classes.

Pius XII, himself the former Papal representative in Germany, showed his continued interest in Germany by elevating two German bishops into the College of Cardinals, and by being the first head of state to send a diplomatic representative to post-war Germany. He appointed the American bishop, Aloysius Muench, as Papal Nuncio, a powerful figure to intervene on behalf of the Germans with the Allies. This papal interest helped to establish the new party's credentials with the Americans, played a considerable role in determining its ideological framework, and helped to ensure that the Old Catholic Centre Party of Weimar was not resurrected. The Centre Party sought the allegiance of Catholics both in the Kaiser's Germany and in the Weimar period. In November 1932 it had gained 11.7 per cent of the vote.

Even if the Pope had been indifferent to a new non-socialist, Christian political movement, there were a considerable number of the surviving Weimar political elite who thought in such terms. They felt that the divisions among Christians before 1933 had made the victory of the 'anti-Christ' — Hitler — possible. If Germany were to survive, Christian principles in political life were more important than ever before. Some believed that one of the vices of the Weimar political system was the multiplicity of parties, making strong government impossible. A non-denominational, non-socialist, 'catch-all' party was therefore necessary to ensure the success of a future democratic German political system. Some saw socialism as inevitable but wanted to imbue it with Christian rather than Marxist assumptions. The Frankfurt group of Walter Dirks was prominent in this direction. On the other hand, there were those, no doubt, who simply calculated that if the propertied classes were to save anything of their wealth they needed to unite in a popular movement relying on the authority of the churches to rally support. More representative than Dirks and his group were the many former members of the German National People's Party (DNVP), the German Democratic Party (DDP) and, above all, the Centre Party. Among the latter were Dr Leo Schwering in Cologne and Doctors Andreas Hermes and Heinrich Krone in Berlin.

In Bavaria a quite separate Christian Social Union (CSU) was formed. In many respects this party drew on the traditions of the Bavarian People's Party (BVP) of the Weimar period. In North Rhine-Westphalia certain left Catholics reformed the Centre Party and gained ten seats in the first *Bundestag*. In the second *Bundestag*, due to their allegiance with the CDU, they were able to win two seats. Most of the leading members joined the CDU but the party retained a few political representatives in local government.

The fourth political trend which emerged in the summer of 1945 was that which wanted to carry on the traditions of German Liberalism. In Berlin two former ministers of Weimar Germany, Dr Eugen Schiffer and Dr Wilhelm Külz, set up the Liberal Democratic Party (LDP). The same trend appeared as the Free Democratic Party (FDP) in Bavaria, led by Dr Thomas Dehler. In Schleswig-Holstein it was called the Democratic Union and in Hamburg the Party of Free Democrats. In Hesse the same name was used as in Berlin. Of great significance for the future of West German Liberalism was the establishment of the Democratic People's Party (DVP), by Dr Theodor Heuss and Dr Reinhold Maier, in Württemberg. At the last free election in Weimar Germany, in November 1932, the two Liberal parties had only achieved about 2 per cent of the vote. In 1919 their vote had been nearer 23 per cent.

The Failure of Communism

The division of Germany had a fundamental impact upon the fate of the four political tendencies which had emerged in 1945. The first two parties to feel the impact of the Cold War, and the division of the country which resulted from it, were the Social Democrats and the Communists. Perhaps the majority of ordinary Social Democrats and Communists favoured the building of a united socialist party in 1945. They did so because they believed their earlier rivalry had opened the door to Hitler. By the time the Soviet military authorities pressed to bring this about in the first part of 1946 many Social Democrats had cooled their enthusiasm. Soviet policies in their occupation zone constituted the basic reason for this. Under Otto Grotewohl, the SPD in the Soviet Zone was nevertheless amalgamated with the KPD in April 1946. In the West the SPD continued its separate existence, formally electing Schumacher as its chairman at its Hannover conference in 1946. Schumacher then led the party until his death in 1952. The Western SPD acknowledged Marxism as a method, but rejected any dogmatic reliance on Marxist texts. It advocated widespread public ownership for reasons of social justice, because of the involvement of many big industrialists with the Nazis, and because it believed speedy German economic recovery required it. It vigorously upheld German unity, rejecting any dismemberment of the pre-1938 Reich. Later it rejected West German membership of NATO and the EEC because it felt this would make agreement with the Soviet Union over German reunification more difficult. As the Cold War intensified, West Germany recovered and the SPD lost elections, the Social Democrats modified their line, drawing nearer to that of the CDU. This is not to say that the SPD changed its position merely as the response to electoral defeat. The SPD's evaluation of the performance of the centralised, state-owned, East German economy led it to the conclusion that a free market economy offered the best prospects for economic and social progress. The experience of German Social Democratic refugees with the less ideologically based working-class movements of Scandinavia and Britain, on the one hand, and the *Weltanschauungsparteien* of Stalin's Russia and Hitler's Germany, on the other, constituted another major factor in the change. Willy Brandt lived in Scandinavia during the Nazi period. Erich Ollenhauer, SPD Chairman (1952–63), spent this time in Britain. Herbert Wehner was able to contrast life in the USSR with that in Sweden. Fritz Erler, another influential Social Democrat, remained in the Third Reich. Electoral defeat made it easier for these and other Social Democrats to persuade their party that change was necessary. The new line found expression in the Bad Godesberg Programme of 1959.

The new programme proclaimed the virtues of the free market economy and private initiative but called for a just distribution of incomes and wealth. It came out strongly in favour of national defence but rejected West German possession of nuclear weapons. It called for co-operation between the churches and the SPD but warned against the misuse of religion for political purposes.

Though it held office in a number of the *Länder*, notably Bremen, Hamburg, Hesse, Lower Saxony and West Berlin, the SPD was excluded from the federal government until it joined a grand coalition with the CDU in 1966. After the election of 1969, its candidate, Willy Brandt, became Chancellor and between then and 1980 the SPD held office with the FDP.

The SPD's rival on the left, the KPD, looked like being a major force in West German politics even in 1949. By that time it was rapidly declining but in the first federal elections held in that year it managed to gain 1.3 million votes (5.7 per cent) and 15 seats in the 402-member federal parliament (*Bundestag*). In the second federal elections (1953) it mustered only 608,000 votes (2.2 per cent) and failed to regain entry into the *Bundestag*. It is not difficult to see why this happened. Like other Communist parties during this period, the KPD was totally subservient to the Soviet Union, and the Soviet Union had made itself very unpopular in Germany by its policy of annexing large areas of pre-war eastern Germany, by establishing a 'People's Democracy' in its zone, and by holding large numbers of Germans captive in the USSR long after the other victors had released their prisoners. In addition, many Germans who had seen something of the Soviet Union during the war had been less than impressed by its achievements. It did not seem to have a system from which Germany could usefully learn. Yet, for the German Communists, the Soviet Union remained the most advanced system in the world. This was too much for the average German to swallow. Under Max Reimann the KPD purged those comrades who sought to wed Communism to German conditions. By the time the party was banned as unconstitutional in 1956, it was already dead politically. To some extent the KPD attempted to carry on its work with pacifist- and neutralist-inclined bodies such as the *Bund der Deutschen* (BdP) and the *Deutsche Friedens-Union* (DFU). The DFU received nearly 610,000 votes in 1961, falling to 432,000 in 1965. For the 1969 election the DFU linked up with the DKP, the Moscow-orientated Communist Party permitted to organise in 1968. This *Aktion Demokratischer Fortschritt* polled only about 0.2 per cent of the vote — less than the DFU alone in 1965. In 1972 and 1976 the DKP, standing alone, claimed only 0.3 per cent.

SPD—CDU/CSU Rivalry

Schumacher is often criticised by writers on German politics for being too negative, too doctrinaire, too nationalist and too stubborn. Yet the defeat of Social Democracy in the early years of the Federal Republic cannot, in this writer's view, be blamed primarily on Schumacher's attitudes and policies. No doubt his robust character and sense of mission made him a difficult man to deal with, but was this not equally true of his CDU rival Dr Konrad Adenauer (1876—1967)? Moreover, it is often forgotten that his socialist economic policies were not so very different from those of the CDU, especially in the industrialised British Zone (North Rhine-Westphalia). In any case Schumacher could not afford to appear to be to the right of the KPD in his advocacy of socialist measures. On national questions none of the three major parties — SPD, CDU/CSU, FDP — advocated recognising the *de facto* frontier in the east, the Oder—Neisse line or the German Democratic Republic (DDR). The SPD merely wanted to delay West Germany's Western integration until all possibilities with the USSR had been exhausted. It cannot be said that all these possibilities were exhausted (see below). Perhaps, had West Germany's two major parties been led by others more flexible than Schumacher and Adenauer, it is just possible that a successful grand coalition could have been formed as in Austria. No matter who had led the SPD, the party would have faced a difficult situation.

The SPD was cut off from some of its Weimar strongholds which were in the Soviet Zone. In pre-war Germany roughly one-third of the population was Catholic, in West Germany the figure is nearer 45 per cent. This ensured the mass basis for a party backed by the Catholic Church, and the Catholic Church was far less tolerant then than it subsequently became. Secondly, the distortion of the structure of the population by two world wars helped the Conservative forces. In 1962 11 per cent of the population of West Germany were over 65 as against only 7 per cent in 1939. In the same year, for every 1,000 men in the population, there were 1,110 women. Even in 1976 women still made up 54 per cent of West German voters. As in other European states, West German women have shown a marked preference for political Conservatism. This was especially so in the West German elections prior to 1969 and again in 1976. Dr Adenauer, already 73 when he became Chancellor in 1949, got much of his support from women and pensioners. The CDU/CSU has always gained much of its support from the rural areas and small towns, particularly the *Länder* of Schleswig-Holstein, Lower Saxony, Rhineland-Palatinate and Bavaria. It has also been the beneficiary of financial support from the business community, especially after it emerged as the main right of centre party from 1953 onwards. As such, it has had only a limited appeal for the working class who have constituted the main support for the SPD. In terms of the support it has gathered, the CDU/CSU has been the most successful West German party. At only one election, that of 1972, did its percentage of the vote fall below that of the SPD. In 1957 it achieved a record, as yet unbeaten, in German parliamentary elections, of winning an absolute majority (50.2 per cent) of the votes cast.

This victory was, of course, in part a tribute to the remarkable change in West German fortunes under Dr Adenauer. Internally West Germany was already experiencing the benefits of the 'economic miracle' and externally it was recognised by virtually the whole of the non-Communist world as the sole representative of the German people. Western confidence in the new Republic was shown when it was allowed to join NATO and rearm in 1955. Further, the Saar, which had been separated from Germany in 1945, became part of the Federal Republic in January 1957. It must also be stressed that the Cold War played a role in the CDU/CSU victories of 1953 and 1957. Christian

Democratic propagandists unfairly associated the SPD with the Communists by reference to their common Marxist past. The SPD's apparently unclear position on defence led some voters to fear that the Republic's security would be threatened under a Social Democratic administration. The public remembered the crushing of the East German rising (June 1953) and the Hungarian Revolution (October 1956) by the Soviet Army. The failure of the Christian Democrats to repeat the unique victory of 1957 can, to a considerable extent, be explained in terms of the changes which have been taking place in German society. The imbalance between the sexes has to some extent improved, the churches have lost some of their influence, agriculture has declined and the process of urbanisation has continued. As in other advanced economies, there has also been a growth of the sectors giving employment to technicians and other white-collar workers.

The Free Democrats

The expansion of the professional and white-collar strata among the West German electorate helps to explain the continued existence of the FDP as a significant force in the politics of the Federal Republic. The Free Democrats are proud of the fact that there are more graduates among their voters than among those of the SPD and the CDU/CSU. The FDP is also proud of its record of office. From 1949, when the Federal Republic was established, to 1956, and from 1961 to 1966, the FDP was in partnership with the Christian Democrats in the federal government. Between 1969 and 1980 it has held office as junior partner to the SPD. Two of the Federal Republic's five Presidents, Theodor Heuss and Walter Scheel, have been FDP members. The party is usually in coalition in several of the eleven regional or *Länder* governments. Yet in terms of electoral support the Free Democratic Party's record has been less impressive. In the first federal election of 1949 the FDP gained 12 per cent. It then lost support in the two subsequent elections, reached a record 13 per cent in 1961, fell back again in 1965 and 1969, and remained about 8 per cent in 1972 and 1976. The fact is that, unable to get an absolute majority themselves, each of the other two parties needs a coalition partner if it is to participate in government. Between 1966 and 1969 there was a grand coalition of the two major parties, but this is something they seek to avoid, preferring the small FDP to its main rival. As for the FDP, its change of ally in 1969 was the result of changes within the Free Democratic Party itself.

Traditionally, the German Liberals were divided between those who put nationalism first and the more left-wing, who gave their principles of democracy and individual liberty first priority. In both the Kaiser's Germany and the Weimar Republic they had gone their separate ways in separate parties. After the war the FDP united both factions, but the party leaned more towards nationalism than towards democracy. In economic affairs the FDP of the 1940s and 1950s was more to the right than the CDU. Its reward was financial assistance from industry. In 1956, however, a split occurred in the FDP. The majority, led by Thomas Dehler (Chairman, 1954–57), broke with the CDU. The majority included the more liberal elements and those who believed that Adenauer's foreign and defence policies ran counter to the aim of German reunification. The minority, among them four FDP ministers, decided to remain in coalition with Adenauer and formed their own party, the *Freie Volkspartei* (FVP). This party soon disappeared, most of its members finding sanctuary in the CDU. With the CDU having proved itself the main bourgeois party and the FDP split, its industrial backers declined. Under Reinhold Maier (1957–60) it became more attractive to some liberals among the professional middle class and the students at a time when the SPD appeared to be searching for respectability at almost any price. In 1961 the FDP was the main recipient of voters disenchanted with the ruling CDU/CSU, its domestic scandals and its lack of activity in the cause of German reunification – the election followed within a month of the Berlin Wall crisis. Nevertheless, Erich Mende (Chairman, 1960–68) managed, in spite of electoral promises to the contrary, to renew his party's coalition with Adenauer's CDU/CSU. The FDP was able to force Franz Josef Strauss, the Bavarian CSU leader, out of office in 1962 because of his involvement in the *Spiegel* Affair. It remained in coalition with the Christian Democrats after Erhard replaced Adenauer in October 1963. The coalition partners fell out in 1966 over taxation and the FDP went again into opposition. The election of Walter Scheel to the leadership of the FDP in 1968 represented a turn to the left and the Free Democrats then indicated their wooing of the SPD by voting for the successful Social Democratic candidate for the Presidency of the Republic, Gustav Heinemann, in 1969. Later in the same year the two parties formed the coalition headed by the first post-war SPD Chancellor, Willy Brandt. The FDP had already paid a certain price for this by losing some of its right-wing voters in the 1969 elections. Like the CDU, the FDP has suffered from the decline in the rural vote, but it has gained from the expansion of white-collar voters.

In 1974 Walter Scheel was elected Federal President and Hans-Dietrich Genscher then became leader of the Free Democrats. After the SPD's loss of support in the election of 1976, the FDP once again started to look to the right for a new coalition partner. Despite the FDP's successful search for coalition partners in the past, its future cannot be regarded as secure. Just as its turn to the left in 1969 lost it support, so could any sharp turn to the right in the future. Because of West Germany's electoral law such loss of support could cost the FDP its entire parliamentary representation.

The Electoral System

West German politicians thought and argued a good deal before they finally settled on their present electoral system. In its present form it was only agreed in 1957. It represents a compromise between those who wanted to continue with proportional representation, as in the Weimar Republic, and those who wanted a system similar to that of Britain, with single-member constituencies, the successful candidate being 'first past the post'. Broadly speaking, the FDP wanted proportional representation, the CDU/CSU favoured a 'British' system, and the SPD was in between. There was also consideration of the fact that the Weimar system encouraged small parties and thus made the formation of stable government more difficult. The system adopted incorporates these different elements. Under it the Federal Republic is divided into 248 *Wahlkreise* (constituencies). At the elections, which are normally held every four years, the elector has two votes. The first goes to the candidate of his choice in the particular constituency. The candidate gaining a simple relative majority is elected. In this way half the members of the *Bundestag* are elected. The elector's second vote goes to a party list, each party having a separate list in each of the *Länder*. The other 248 members of the *Bundestag* are elected from these lists in proportion to the number of second votes gained by each party. Since 1961 all the FDP's *Bundestag* deputies have been elected from the party lists. However, the FDP faces the danger of parliamentary extinction because, in order to gain any representation at all, a party must win at least 5 per cent of the vote throughout the Federal Republic. In 1969 it managed only 5.8 per cent. Other parties have been eliminated in this way.

One of those defeated by the 5-per-cent hurdle was the Refugee Party (GB/BHE). Founded in 1950, the party seemed likely to find fertile soil in which to grow among the millions of refugees in West Germany. Official statistics showed that, in 1960, 9.9 million West Germans, 17.7 per cent of the population, were refugees from the 'lost territories' or from other parts of Eastern Europe. A further 3.6 million, 6.5 per cent, had quit the Soviet Zone/DDR. In Schleswig-Holstein and Lower Saxony the percentages were considerably higher and in these *Länder* the Refugee Party did better than elsewhere. In the Federal Republic, as a whole, the party polled nearly 6 per cent in the 1953 elections. Thus it gained 27 seats in the *Bundestag*. Adenauer included it in his coalition but in 1955 internal disagreements resulted in the virtual break-up of the GB/BHE. The leaders, notably Waldemar Kraft and Theodor Oberländer, joined the CDU. Much was being done by the government for the refugees and the other war victims, and this, together with the split, played its part in the party's failure in the 1957 elections, when it gained only 4.5 per cent of the vote. The remnants merged with the right-wing German Party (DP) in 1961, another former coalition partner of the CDU/CSU, to form the All-German Party (GDP). In the federal elections of 1961 it achieved a vote of around 2.8 per cent.

The NPD

Perhaps of far greater significance was the failure of the NPD to breach the 5-per-cent barrier in 1969. The National Democratic Party (NPD) entered the political arena in 1964. It was an attempt to unite the disparate elements of the far right around a nucleus from the neo-Nazi *Deutsche Reichs-Partei* (DRP). The other big contributor to its membership was the GDP. Between November 1966 and September 1968 it achieved successes in local and *Länder* elections which were reminiscent of those of the Nazi party after 1928. It gained representation in the majority of the *Länder* parliaments during this period. In Baden-Württemberg in April 1968 its vote reached nearly 10 per cent, compared with 2.2 per cent for the NPD in that region in the federal elections of 1965. Had the NPD broken into the *Bundestag* in 1969 there would have been no SPD/FDP coalition. There could well have been a major political crisis in the Federal Republic with serious consequences for West Germany's foreign relations. As it was, the NPD won 4.3 per cent (1.4 million votes) and failed to get *Bundestag* representation. After 1969 the NPD virtually disappeared from the political landscape.

How do we explain the sudden rise and fall of the NPD? Firstly, the Republic had difficulty in finding a worthy successor to magnetic Konrad Adenauer. Professor Ludwig Erhard, who replaced him as Chancellor in 1963 and who in the public mind was 'Mr Economic Miracle', failed to carry conviction as the head of government or CDU/CSU leader. Some right-wing voters who had previously supported the Christian Democrats because of Adenauer started to look for a new political home. The NPD was also helped by a recession which badly hit mining and agriculture and some members of these communities turned to the National Democrats. The failure of the orthodox politicians to make any headway on the problem of German reunification also influenced some people towards the NPD at a time when 'Gaullism' had gained some currency from France. As the FDP turned a little pink in the 1960s, so it became less attractive to its more right-wing clientele who found in the NPD an alternative. Another factor in the NPD's favour was the setting up of the Grand Coalition at the end of 1966. Some right-wing CDU voters felt their leaders had sold the pass to the 'Reds'. Other, less political, voters believed the new government of CDU/CSU–SPD proved that the politicians had ganged together against the 'man in the street' who now had only the NPD to champion his cause against the political bosses and bureaucrats. For its part, the NPD played on the prejudices of the 'silent majority' against the trade unions, the foreign workers, the students and intellectuals, 'permissiveness', lack of discipline in schools and so on. The NPD picked up votes from previous supporters of all three main parties, but probably hit the FDP more than the other two. It achieved its greatest successes in the small towns and villages, in garrison towns and agricultural communities. It made less impact among Catholics than among Protestants, and was predominantly a party of men of the Nazi generation, especially of men in lower-middle-class occupations. Though their programme bore striking resemblances to that of the Nazi party, the National Democrats stressed that they accepted the West German Basic Law. If challenged about the many former Nazis in their leadership, they referred to the fact that Dr Kurt Georg Kiesinger, Erhard's successor as Chancellor, had also been a member of Hitler's party. Undoubtedly, the widespread concern among West Germany's neighbours helped to create a climate of opinion unfavourable to it. The success of the Kiesinger–Brandt coalition was important in checking its growth. With the Christian Democrats appearing more right-wing in opposition, after 1969, than they had in government, wavering right-wing voters opted once again for Christian Democracy.

The Parties, the Law and Finance

As Professor Sontheimer reminds us, 'The Federal Republic of Germany is one of the few democratic nations in which the position, organisational principles and functions of the political parties are governed by the Constitution and by a special party law.' Article 21 of the Basic Law lays down that the internal organisation of political parties must conform to democratic principles and that they must give a public account about the origins of their funds. The same article also states that parties which, through their aims or by the behaviour of their followers, seek to impair or destroy democracy or endanger the existence of the Federal Republic are unconstitutional. The Federal Constitutional Court decides the question of unconstitutionality. The interest of the fathers of the constitution in political parties was not, of course, purely academic. It was the result of their experiences in the Weimar Republic. Little use has been made of the constitutional duty to ban anti-democratic parties. As we have seen, the KPD was prohibited in 1956 but many other extreme left-wing splinter groups have not suffered in the same way. In fact, the only other party to be banned was the neo-Nazi *Sozialistische Reichspartei* (SRP) in 1952 and that happened under pressure from the Allies, especially Britain. The SRP had most of its following in the former British Zone, in the *Länder*, Lower Saxony and Schleswig-Holstein, and in Bremen (former US Zone). In 1951 it had won 11 per cent of the vote in the *Land* election in Lower Saxony and 7.7 per cent in Bremen. Its best-known leader was Otto Ernst Remer who had played a prominent part in putting down the July plot against Hitler. After the banning of the SRP there was a succession of ultra-right-wing parties but no attempt was made to outlaw them.

The position of political parties inthe Federal Republic was further codified by the Party Law (*Parteiengesetz*) of 1967. This spelt out in greater detail the principles enshrined in Article 21 of the Basic Law. In practice, the Law's most important section was that dealing with the financing of parties. West German parties first received subsidies from public funds in 1959. This system of public subsidies was gradually recognised as a permanent and necessary feature of political life when it was incorporated in the *Parteiengesetz*. It was essential for the FDP, and very desirable for the other two big parties. The only embarrassment was caused by the use of public funds to finance dubious organisations such as the NPD. The subsidy was based on the number of votes gained by each party at the previous election. In 1969 any party which achieved over 0.5 per cent of the total vote was entitled to financial aid in proportion to its share of the vote. *Länder* elections also attract a subsidy. In 1976 150 million DM were paid out from federal funds to the parties contesting the election of that year. This represented over US $60 million or about £37.5 million. Such aid goes a long way to explain the lavish, American-style, campaigns which are mounted by the major parties in the Federal Republic. The Christian Democrats also received assistance from business undertakings, and the trade unions gave subdued backing to the SPD.

The Christian Democrats are more dependent than the SPD on outside help to mount their election campaigns. The reason for this is the weaker organisation of the Christian Democrats. The Social Democrats pioneered the modern political party. Even in their classical period, before 1914, they strove, with considerable success, to become a highly organised mass membership party. The SPD was a central part of its members' lives. The SPD renewed this tradition after 1945. In December 1947 SPD membership reached 875,479, of whom 161,187 were women. The membership of all parties declined somewhat in the affluent society of the 1950s. In the case of the SPD it had fallen to just under 650,000 in 1951, but in the 1960s there was a turn for the better. In 1962 the SPD claimed 646,584 members. Ten years later membership was given as 934,394. In 1976 the Social Democrats had well over one million members. This mass membership stands in marked contrast to the falling individual membership of the British Labour Party. It also compares favourably with that of the CDU. The CDU has always attracted fewer members than the SPD. Unlike the SPD, it has been a loosely organised body, weak at the centre. Though there was much talk over the years about the need for reform of the party structure, it was only in opposition, after 1969, that the Christian Democrats attempted to imitate the SPD in recruiting a mass membership. In 1976 the CDU alone reported 611,175 members. This compared with only 300,000 in 1969. The CSU had nearly 123,000 in 1975.

The difference in membership brought differences in financing, as is shown in Table 1.1. There is a considerable difference in the amounts the two parties received from members; this reflects the SPD's larger membership and the fact that the CDU was not as serious about obtaining relatively high dues from its members. Even more significant were the different sums the two parties received in gifts. The large contributions to the CDU were channelled through a variety of front organisations such as the *Staatpolitische Vereinigung Schleswig-Holstein*

Table 1.1: Income of Two Main Parties in 1974 (in millions DM)[1]

	Membership dues	Contributions from parliamentarians	Gifts	Subsidies from public funds	Total
SPD	44,147	8,743	7,448	28,754	95,740
CDU	25,808	8,245	26,380	22,380	88,615

Note: Certain less important sources, such as rents from properties, sales of literature, etc., are not included.

e. V and the *Gesellschaft zur Förderung der Wirtschaft Baden– Württemberg e. V.* Behind these and other facades lurk various business and other interests. Despite Article 21 and the *Parteiengesetz*, the West German parties still disguise the sources of an important part of their funds.

Elections

Like elections everywhere, West German elections have changed considerably since 1949. One obvious change has been the rise of television as the main vehicle of election debate and information. Another has been the style of the campaigning. It was the CDU/CSU in 1957 which first turned to market research and public relations for advice on its campaign. The SPD relied on its good traditional organisation, its principles and its instinct — and lost! The Social Democrats dramatically altered their style in the following years, becoming very public relations conscious. In the 1950s the SPD stressed its policies and its team; in the 1960s, with Brandt leading it, the emphasis was much more on the leader. This followed Adenauer's presidential-style, highly successful campaign in 1957. By 1961, these four-yearly contests had become duels between the Chancellor and the opposition candidate for the Chancellorship. The election of 1969 gave both leading parties some difficulties, as they were still in government together throughout the campaign. In this case the CDU/CSU made their Chancellor, Dr Kiesinger, the focal point of their effort, while the SPD stressed their team of competent and, by that time, well-known ministers. In 1972 it was the SPD's turn to emphasise the Chancellor, Willy Brandt, while the CDU/CSU publicised their leader, Rainer Barzel, more as the chairman of a competent team. In 1976 both parties put their main thrust behind their respective leaders, Helmut Schmidt and Helmut Kohl.

The early elections in the Federal Republic were fought on strongly ideological lines, with the CDU/CSU claiming that the choice was Marxism or Christianity (1953), socialism or the successful free market economy (1957). Key policy issues such as rearmament came to the fore (1957). The elections of 1961, 1965 and 1969 were much less ideological and policy orientated because the SPD had accepted much of the CDU/CSU's platform. The election of 1972 was once again fought on vital policy issues — the SPD/FDP government's *Ostpolitik* (see below) and extended co-determination in industry (see below). Finally, in 1976, the Christian Democrats campaigned, without too much conviction, on the issue of *Freiheit statt Sozialismus.* The Social Democratic–Liberal Government was content to be judged on its record. Concern over West Germany's modest level of inflation, and about unemployment, lost the government some support.

Like British general elections, West German federal elections have come to resemble presidential elections rather than old-fashioned parliamentary contests. Unlike Britain, West German elections have moved closer to US campaigns in another sense: the flood of trinkets available to voters. In 1976 the SPD and CDU vied with each other to distribute car stickers, lapel buttons, key rings and even T-shirts and bikinis. The CDU gave away a well-produced tourist map of Germany with holiday tips, a distance chart, menus and, quite naturally, a message from Helmut Kohl. Both sides produced attractive, expensive literature with the emphasis on modern print and layout, with plenty of colour and plenty of colourful illustrations. Unlike earlier campaigns, there was little to remind the electors of war, revolution, sudden death, starvation, slums, loneliness or anything else unpleasant. One feature of the 1976 campaign which has been a feature of all West German elections was the frequent use of the word *Sicherheit* (security). As in earlier elections, all the parties promised the electors every kind of security. They seemed to be appealing to a deep need for reassurance among the West German electorate. Another striking feature of all West German elections is the very high turnout which is similar to that in neighbouring Austria, but much higher than that in the United States, and considerably higher than that in Britain. The reason for this happy state of affairs is not entirely clear. It is more remarkable in view of the fact that the effective choice has been greatly reduced over the years. with most parties having no chance of getting into the *Bundestag.* Perhaps it has something to do with the Catholic Church's appeal to its members to vote, the SPD's high membership and efficient organisation, and the German's traditional sense of civic duty.

Table 1.2: Federal Election Results (excluding West Berlin)

	1949	1953	1957	1961	1965	1969	1972	1976
Turnout % of votes cast	78.5	85.8	87.7	87.7	86.8	86.7	91	91
CDU/CSU	31	45.2	50.2	45.3	47.6	46.1	44.9	48.6
SPD	29.2	28.8	31.8	36.2	39.3	42.7	45.8	42.6
FDP	11.9	9.5	7.7	12.8	9.5	5.8	8.4	7.9
Others	27.9	16.6	10.3	5.7	3.6	5.4	1.0	0.9

Though lower than at federal elections, voter participation in *Länder* and local elections is high. The elections to the parliaments of the ten *Länder* and West Berlin are as highly political as those to the *Bundestag*. They are held at various times during the life of a federal government and are usually interpreted as a test of the government's popularity. Sometimes these elections have important political consequences. The poor showing of the CDU in *Länder* elections after 1961 was a factor in Adenauer's resignation. In the same way, the defeat of the CDU in the election in North Rhine-Westphalia led to the fall of Chancellor Erhard in 1966. Weakening support for the SPD in regional elections was also a consideration when Willy Brandt resigned in 1974.

The election of 1980 will decide whether or not eleven years of SPD/FDP government will be brought to an end. The result could be complicated by candidates from the ecology movement often referred to as 'The Greens'. They draw much of their support from the young and better educated. In a number of *Länder* elections 'The Greens' did surprisingly well, breaking through the 5-per-cent barrier to gain seats in regional parliaments.

The West German party system has at least four achievements to its credit. Firstly, it has created over thirty years of stability in government. Secondly, it has checked the growth of political extremism. Thirdly, it has commanded the loyalty — as indicated by very high turnouts at elections — of the bulk of the FRG's citizens. Finally, it has demonstrated its ability to change from the government of one major party to the government of another without crisis or convulsions. It has not yet been tested in conditions of prolonged economic recession.

Further Reading

Bandholz, Emil. *Wo steht die SPD?* (Hamburg, 1971)

Burkett, Tony. *Parties and Elections in West Germany* (London, 1975)

Chalmers, D. A. *The Social and Democratic Party of Germany* (New Haven, 1964)

Childs, David. *From Schumacher to Brandt* (Oxford, 1966)

Conradt, David P. *The German Polity* (New York, 1978)

Flechtheim, O. K. *Die Parteien der Bundesrepublik Deutschland* (Hamburg, 1973)

Graf, William D. *The German Left Since 1945* (Cambridge, 1976)

Heidenheimer, A. J. *Adenauer and the CDU* (Den Haag, 1960)

Hennis, Wilhelm. *Organisierter Sozialismus* (Stuttgart, 1977)

Kühnl, Reinhard (*et al.*). *Die NPD* (Frankfurt/M, 1969)

Miller, Susanne. *Die SPD vor und nach Godesberg* (Bonn, 1978)

Mintzel, Alf. *Geschichte der CSU* (Wiesbaden, 1977)

Olzog, Günter. *Die politischen Parteien* (Munich, 1968)

Preece, R. J. C. *Land Elections in the German Federal Republic* (London, 1968)

Pridham, Geoffrey. *Christian Democracy in Western Germany* (London, 1977)

History

Balfour, M. *West Germany* (London, 1968, 1980)

Childs, D. *Germany Since 1918* (London, 1971, 1980)

Grosser, A. *Germany in our Time* (London, 1971)

Note

1. These figures are adapted from the *Bundesanzeiger* of 28 November 1975 as given in Jürgen Weber, *Die Interessengruppen im politischem System der Bundesrepublik Deutschland* (Stuttgart, 1977), p. 309.

2 THE *GRUNDGESETZ* AND THE FEDERAL SYSTEM

Particularism and centralism have both left their mark on German history and can still be detected in various modified forms in Western Germany today. The particularism which persisted into the nineteenth century retarded the political and economic development of the German states and principalities; the centralism of the Prussian state promoted economic growth but deprived the majority of citizens of any active participation in politics and, in some respects, prepared the way for the National Socialist regime which was to destroy Germany. The only democratic order ever introduced into Germany before 1949 was the Weimar Republic which was declared after the First World War, and for most Germans it came to symbolise defeat, weak government, the polarisation of political opinion, and economic chaos. It was natural therefore that both the Western Allies and the Germans themselves, mindful of this grim legacy, should after 1945 look for a system of government which would protect the nation against the errors of the past. The most promising answer, and one strongly advocated by the Americans, seemed to lie in the creation of a federal state which would not only ensure a division of powers between legislature, executive and judiciary, but also incorporate safeguards against the kind of political abuses which developed under the Weimar Republic.

In the immediate post-war years West Germany had special problems in restructuring political, social and economic life, and it was felt that federalism was the best way of overcoming these and at the same time of promoting democratic participation at central and regional levels by a population emerging from twelve years of totalitarian dictatorship. To be sure, different West German politicians had different conceptions about how much power the central government should have *vis-à-vis* the regions or *Länder*. The South German Christian Democrats wanted a loose federation. The Social Democrats, on the other hand, favoured a strong central authority. The Basic Law which emerged from the deliberations of the Parliamentary Council — a body made up of the representatives of the *Länder* parliaments — was a compromise between these two points of view.

West German federalism, which was also influenced politically and administratively by the Allied division of Germany, has taken on its

Table 2.1: The *Länder*

Land	Population (millions)	Catholic	Protestant	Capital	Government[a]
Baden-Württemberg	9.2	47.4	45.8	Stuttgart	CDU
Bayern	10.8[b]	70.0	25.7	Munich	CSU
Berlin	2.0	11.4	72.1	Berlin	SPD–FDP
Bremen	0.7	10.1	82.3	Bremen	SPD
Hamburg	1.7[c]	8.1	73.6	Hamburg	SPD–FDP
Hessen	5.5	32.8	60.5	Wiesbaden	SPD–FDP
Niedersachsen	7.3	19.5	74.6	Hannover	CDU–FDP
Nordrhein-Westfalen	17.2	52.5	41.8	Düsseldorf	SPD–FDP
Rheinland-Pfalz	3.7[d]	55.7	40.6	Mainz	CDU
Saarland	1.1	73.8	24.1	Saarbrüken	CDU–FDP
Schleswig-Holstein	2.5	6.0	86.0	Kiel	CDU

Notes:

a. January 1978.
b. This compares with Ohio's 10.6 million in 1970.
c. This compares with S. Dakota's 666,257 in 1970 and West Yorkshire's 744,500.
d. This compares with New York's 18.2 million in 1970.

own particular forms and characteristics during the three decades since its inception. There can be no doubt that it has functioned at least as well as its authors could have hoped. Although there is a tendency for the federation to attract an increasing authority to itself, which is perhaps inevitable, the constituent states are by no means passive. Regional interests have been preserved and, while it is not possible to speak of deep-seated regional enthusiasms in Western Germany outside Bavaria, a certain historical continuity has been maintained. Table 2.1 lists the eleven constituent states, or *Länder*, with population and administrative capital.

The Basic Law

The West German constitution is known as the *Grundgesetz*, or Basic Law, since it was felt in 1949 that a definitive constitution ought to be postponed until such time as the two Germanies were reunited. Moreover, it is stated explicitly in Article 146 of the constitution: 'This Basic Law shall cease to be in force on the day on which a constitution adopted by a free decision of the German people comes into force.' Since it seems extremely unlikely that the FRG and the GDR could ever create mutually acceptable conditions for such a 'free decision of the German people', the original concept of the *Grundgesetz* as a provisional document is gradually receding and it has become to all intents and purposes a fully fledged constitution of an entirely independent sovereign state.

The Basic Law is divided into eleven main sections which are quoted here to indicate its scope:

    I *Grundrechte* (Basic Rights)
    II *Der Bund und die Länder* (The Federation and the Constituent States)
    III *Der Bundestag* (The Federal Parliament)
    IV *Der Bundesrat* (The Council of Constituent States or Federal Council)
    IVa *Gemeinsamer Ausschuss* (Joint Committee)
    V *Der Bundespräsident* (The Federal President)
    VI *Die Bundesregierung* (The Federal Government)
    VII *Die Gesetzgebung des Bundes* (Legislative Powers of the Federation)
    VIII *Die Ausführung der Bundesgesetze und die Bundesverwaltung*

(The Execution of Federal Laws and the Federal
Administration)
VIIIa *Gemeinschaftsaufgaben* (Community Tasks)
  IX *Die Rechtsprechung* (The Administration of Justice)
   X *Das Finanzwesen* (Finances)
  Xa *Verteidigungsfall* (State of Defence)
  XI *Übergangs- und Schlussbestimmungen* (Transitional and
Concluding Provisions)

As these headings show, it is a comprehensive statement of basic
principles governing the organisation and administration of the state
and its constituent elements, and their mutual relationships within the
structure as a whole. It is also a statement of political and moral values
focusing on the German concept of the *Rechtsstaat*. Although the Basic
Law does not use this term explicitly, an understanding of it is essential
when approaching many aspects of the West German state. The term
Rechtsstaat, which lacks an equivalent in English, conveys the idea of a
state the existence and actions of which are related to and limited by a
transcendent law. It is both a 'state of law' and a 'state in law', and
provides the ultimate framework and point of allegiance for legislature,
executive and judiciary alike. The Basic Law also introduces another
important concept in Article 20, where it states: 'The Federal Republic
of Germany is a democratic and social federal state.' The implication of
the word 'social' in this context is that the state accepts the duty of
ensuring that all sections of the community are protected against
political and economic hardship, but it will be appreciated that the
practical application of such a broadly stated principle can lead to
conflicting opinions as to how far the state can go in protecting the
economic interests of one section of society without endangering the
rights — especially the rights of ownership — of another section. The
Basic Law offers no help in this problem since it expressly guarantees
the right to own property (Article 14: 'Property and the right of
inheritance are guaranteed.'), while at the same time permitting
expropriation under certain circumstances (Article 15: 'Expropriation
shall be permitted only in the public weal.'). To solve the problems and
disputes arising from this and other constitutional principles, the
federal system requires a permanent and independent adjudication
body. In the FRG this body is the *Bundesverfassungsgericht*, or
constitutional court, with its seat in Karlsruhe.

Constitutional Court

The *Bundesverfassungsgericht*, which is independent of all other constitutional organs, comprises two senates, each with eight judges. For each senate, four of the judges are elected by the federal parliament and four by the federal council. Their period of tenure is twelve years, after which time they may not be re-elected. The judges may not belong to the federal parliament or to the federal council, nor to any corresponding body in the *Länder*. In order to isolate their deliberations physically from any popular pressure through demonstrations and mass rallies, the area immediately surrounding the constitutional court is out-of-bounds for public meetings and processions.

The disputes which the *Bundesverfassungsgericht* is called to decide are mainly of three kinds: firstly, decisions on the rights and duties of federal authorities; secondly, disputes arising from alleged infringements of the Basic Law by federal or *Land* legislation; and thirdly, disputes arising between the *Bund* and one or more *Länder* in matters of legislation. It should be noted that the *Bundesverfassungsgericht* does not deal with purely theoretical disputes, but only with practical cases where the interests of a body, group or individual appear to be threatened by an alleged infringement of the Basic Law.

Although the task of the constitutional court is clearly to ensure a consistent interpretation of the Basic Law and thus reinforce the internal constituency of the principles on which the *Rechsstaat* is based, the question must arise as to whether its decisions can, in effect, avoid the political dimension. The possibility is recognised that the constitutional court could pass politically biased judgements and, as mentioned above, strict safeguards are operated to ensure that the judges are not involved in political office. Nevertheless, the danger is acute when disputes arousing wide popular interest come before the court, as for example in 1979, when the employers' associations were in dispute with the trade union federation over the number of worker directors to sit on the boards of management in firms. In this case, where the political lines were clearly drawn between organised labour and employers, the constitutional court pronounced a cautious compromise in which both sides had to make some concessions.[1] Another interesting example of the way in which political considerations can be involved in disputes coming before the court is the complaint laid by the CSU *Land* government of Bavaria that the treaty signed by the SPD/FDP coalition with the GDR in 1972 constituted an infringement of the Basic Law. The CSU had opposed the federal government's *Ostpolitik* from the start, so that party political interests were quite clearly involved. In July 1973 the constitutional court ruled that the treaty did not infringe the Basic Law.

While much of the work of the constitutional court is of a less fundamentally political nature, it is obvious that some of its decisions are highly delicate and could have far-reaching consequences. This places an onus on intending litigants to ensure that the disputes they might lay before the court are such as can usefully be settled by the processes of judicial argument, and to avoid those which are substantially political in content.

Subject to certain constitutional safeguards, the Basic Law can be amended and supplemented. An important example of such supplementary legislation is provided by sections Xa (State of Defence) and IVa (Joint Committee), which were introduced in 1968 after a decade of intermittent public debate. It had been pointed out as early as the mid-fifties that the Basic Law contained no provisions which might enable the FRG to meet a state of emergency which could arise as a result of a major catastrophe or could be precipitated through an external military threat. This lack of provision contrasted sharply with the Weimar constitution which had allotted wide powers of intervention to the President of the Republic. Since it was widely held in the immediate post-war years that these very provisions in the Weimar constitution had been abused under Hindenburg to enable the National Socialists to tighten their grip on power, the lawyers who drafted the Basic Law were careful to limit the power of the President in the new Republic, but in so doing they omitted to provide an alternative means of continuing a constitutional form of government in times of disruption or emergency. The *Notstandsverfassung*, or 'emergency constitution', which was passed with the necessary two-thirds majority by the federal parliament and the federal council in May 1968, provoked considerable public opposition since it was felt that it laid the way open for serious infringements of basic human rights and that it could facilitate a political or military *coup* during a time of national emergency. In essence the *Notstandsverfassung* provides for 'internal emergencies', e.g. widespread flooding, devastation arising from serious industrial accidents, serious rioting (but not strikes), and 'external emergencies', e.g. on actual or threatened military attack on the FRG. In the case of internal emergencies the police, the federal frontier protection force (*Bundesgrenzschutz*) and the army can be deployed — the two latter forces only if the *Land* government is either unable or unwilling to deal with the emergency through its own police arrangements. In addition, special legislation can be passed at federal level limiting individual freedom of movement. In external emergencies which are formally declared by the federal parliament a State of Defence comes into force, and the government of the country can be taken over by the *Gemeinsamer Ausschuss*, or joint committee, comprising 22 members of the federal parliament and 11 members of the federal council. No special powers devolve on the President at such times. In practical terms, a state of external emergency means that the federal citizen would lose his freedom of movement and would have to make himself available either for conscription into the armed forces or for deployment on other tasks. Personal surveillance could be operated for security reasons, both by 'tapping' telephone lines and by opening mail. Expropriations could take place without any immediate compensation being made, and elections suspended until six months after the external emergency was officially declared ended by the federal parliament.

The Office of the President

Because of the disastrous experiences of electing a president by popular vote under the Weimar Republic, the Federal President is elected indirectly by the federal convention (*Bundesversammlung*) which comprises all the members of the federal parliament together with an equal number of delegates from the parliaments of the *Länder* – in all, 1,038 votes. A simple majority is required. The period of office is five years, but a candidate can be re-elected for one further term of five years. The Basic Law stresses that the President is a non-political figure whose main task is to preserve national unity by balancing and reconciling conflicting interests. Apart from officially representing the FRG in international relations, the very limited powers of the President include the appointment of federal judges and federal civil servants, the granting of official pardons on behalf of the federation and the appointment of government ministers at the proposal of the Federal Chancellor. In all these matters the President's official actions require the counter-signature of the Chancellor or of the appropriate government minister. The President can exercise real power only in the appointment of federal judges and civil servants, where he might withhold his signature in order to block an appointment. The authority commanded by the office of Federal President and the impact which the holder can make on public affairs depend largely upon his personality. The first President of the Republic was Theodor Heuss who held the office in the years 1949–59 and enjoyed the general respect of his countrymen. His successor, Heinrich Lübke, who held the office for the following decade, came under attack in the late sixties after being unable to refute revelations about his involvement in certain activities of the National Socialist regime. This left his successor, Gustav Heinemann, with the difficult task of restoring the public dignity of the office – a task which he successfully accomplished during his years of tenure, 1969–74. For the following five years the office was held by Walter Scheel, who was prominent in the negotiations leading up to the treaty signed between the FRG and the GDR in 1972. The present Federal President is Karl Karstens, a member of the CDU who has held ministerial posts in defence and in the diplomatic service.

Bund and *Länder*

Article 20 of the Basic Law declares that the Federal Republic of Germany is a *Bundesstaat*, or federal state. By definition, therefore, it is made up of member states, each of which has its own constitution and government which must correspond to the general principles laid down in the Basic Law. The *Länder* are not simply administrative units carrying out instructions from the *Bund*, or federation; they are equal members of the *Bund* which voluntarily surrender certain powers to the *Bund* in their common interest. This arrangement inevitably involves mutual constraints on the power of both *Bund* and *Länder*, in particular to ensure that the authority and status of the individual *Länder* are not undermined by any tendency towards greater centralisation of power. The fate of the *Länder* in the Weimar Republic, where they lost almost all their real power to the central government, is a constant warning in this respect.

The general principle governing the relations between *Bund* and *Länder* is expressed in Article 30 of the Basic Law: 'The exercise of governmental powers and the discharge of governmental functions shall be incumbent on the *Länder* in so far as this Basic Law does not otherwise prescribe.' Thus, the *Bund* can exercise authority only in those areas expressly prescribed by the Basic Law, and the fact is emphasised that it is the *Länder* which are the autonomous units from which the political authority of the *Bund* is derived. The specific application of these general principles is elaborated in Articles 70 (legislation), 83 (administration) and 96 (jurisdiction), which are discussed below.

The pendant to Article 30 is succinctly stated in Article 31: 'Federal law shall override *Land* law.' This does not mean that federal law automatically takes precedence over *Land* law, but simply that it takes precedence in those cases where the *Bund* is expressly entitled in the Basic Law to enact legislation. As with several other Articles in the Basic Law, Article 31 has its origins in German history. In medieval times under the Holy Roman Empire, the legal situation was reversed: local law took precedence over imperial law, which naturally reinforced diversity and political disunity in Germany. The first German parliament (1848) in the Paulskirche in Frankfurt changed this practice, and it is reinforced expressly in the Basic Law. The idea of unity and disunity can thus be seen to play an important part in German political thinking, going back well before the division imposed on Germany in 1945.

In considering the way in which relations between *Bund* and *Länder* are regulated in the Basic Law, two further points need to be emphasised. As might be expected, the *Bund* has exclusive authority in foreign relations, since it would clearly be impractical for the *Länder* to conduct an independent foreign policy. In cases where the interests of a particular *Land* are affected by any proposed arrangement between the *Bund* and a foreign power, the *Land* affected must be consulted beforehand. Likewise, any internal measures by the *Bund* affecting the territorial, economic or environmental interests of the *Länder* must be subjected to full consultation. Such consultations have acquired a special political significance in recent years as a result of the federal government's search for locally acceptable sites for nuclear plant and waste storage facilities. If a *Land* refuses to carry out its constitutional duties to the *Bund*, the latter can take certain measures to enforce compliance, providing that the federal council agrees to this. If, for example, a *Land* refused to collect federal taxes, the *Bund* could enforce constitutional law by applying financial pressure, using the police, or even removing the offending *Land* government from office.

Bundesrat

The key organ in adjusting and regulating relations between the *Bund* and the *Länder*, and at the same time one of the distinctive mechanisms in the West German federal structure, is the *Bundesrat*, or federal council. Article 50 of the Basic Law states simply: 'The *Länder* shall participate through the *Bundesrat* in the legislation and administration

of the Federation.' It must be stressed from the outset that the
Bundesrat is an organ of the *Bund* in which the governments of the
Länder are represented. It is not a simple second chamber. As is shown
below, the *Bundesrat* has clearly defined constitutional rights and can
effectively exert pressure on federal politics and policies. It is important
to note that the *Bundesrat* is completely independent of the federal
government.

The governments of the *Länder* appoint their representatives to the
Bundesrat and instruct them on policy. The number of representatives
which each *Land* can send to the *Bundesrat* depends upon the size of
its population: *Länder* with over six million inhabitants have five seats,
with over two million four seats, and with less than two million three
seats. As reference to Table 2.1 shows, this works out as shown in
Table 2.2.

Table 2.2: *Länder* Representation in the *Bundesrat*

Baden-Württemberg, Bayern, Nordrhein-Westfalen and Niedersachsen hold five seats each	= 20
Hessen, Rheinland-Pfalz and Schleswig-Holstein hold four seats each	= 12
Bremen, Hamburg and the Saarland hold three seats each	= 9
Plus four non-voting members from West Berlin	= 4
	Total 45

The votes relating to these seats must be cast *en bloc*, as members are
never allowed to vote individually. Decisions taken by the *Bundesrat*
need an absolute majority, except where a constitutional amendment is
under consideration, in which case a two-thirds majority is required.
The presidency of the *Bundesrat* changes annually according to a fixed
rota.

The constitution requires the *Bundestag* to submit without delay all
its proposed legislation to the *Bundesrat* for consideration. The powers
of the *Bundesrat* then depend on the type of legislation involved. Apart
from constitutional amendments, which are seldom proposed, there are
two main types of laws: those which constitutionally require *Bundesrat*
approval, and those which do not. With regard to constitutional
amendments and laws requiring approval, the *Bundesrat* is empowered
to exercise a veto. In the case of laws which do not require its approval,
the *Bundesrat* can raise objections which must be debated in the
Bundestag, but the objections can then be overruled by a simple
majority at that stage. Over the years the amount of legislation which

requires the approval of the *Bundesrat* has increased from approximately 10 per cent in 1949 to between 60 per cent and 70 per cent in the late seventies — a trend which clearly enhances the significance of the *Bundesrat* in the federal system. As the demand for *Bundesrat* approval grows, so does the influence of the *Länder* in shaping federal policy.

Within fourteen days of receiving a bill for consideration from the *Bundestag*, the *Bundesrat* can request that a mediation committee, or *Vermittlungsausschuss*, be convened. This committee is a further interesting characteristic of West German federalism, since its effect is to eliminate untidy public debate in favour of an efficiently achieved consensus. The *Vermittlungsausschuss*, made up of an equal number of *Bundestag* and *Bundesrat* delegates, holds its sessions in strict confidence and almost always reaches a compromise agreement. In practice, the *Bundestag* has usually been prepared to accept these compromises rather than press ahead and risk a *Bundesrat* veto. It might thus be said that the power of the *Bundesrat* lies mainly in the use which it makes of the mediation committee.

The *Bundesrat* also has other strengths which help it to maintain its legislative position as almost the equal partner of the *Bundestag*. In the first place, its membership is more stable than that of the *Bundestag* since it is only affected by *Land* elections when these result in a change of government, whereas federal elections usually bring considerable changes in the personal composition of the *Bundestag*. Secondly, the *Bundesrat* members, who are themselves usually of ministerial rank in their respective *Land* governments, can draw on their own administrative apparatus for information on the legislation coming before them. Consequently they tend to have a better grasp of detailed technicalities than the *Bundestag* delegates. On the other hand, the question is sometimes raised as to whether the administrative bureaucracies of the *Länder* do not in this way obtain an undue influence on the deliberations of the *Bundesrat* and thus devalue its political contribution. While it cannot be denied that there is a danger of administrative interests taking priority over political debate, it must also be pointed out that politicians at all levels, including those in the *Bundestag*, depend on their civil servants for technical information, and there is as yet little evidence to indicate that the *Bundesrat* is being abused by the *Länder*. Nor is there any evidence to indicate that the members of the *Bundesrat* are significantly influenced by the organised interests of the trade and commercial associations (*Verbände*).[2] The fact that they are delegated to the *Bundesrat* by their respective *Land* governments and not popularly elected brings them a certain immunity from direct pressure of this kind and is of considerable importance as a counterbalance to the *Bundestag*, amongst the members of which the *Verbände* are inevitably influential. In general it is true to say that the *Bundesrat* has functioned well. Its increasing importance reflects a responsible political attitude on the part of the *Länder*. Naturally it receives its share of criticism from federal politicians whose legislation it might delay (especially their attempts to extend the authority of the *Bund* in financial affairs), but this can also be regarded as a measure of its efficiency. Perhaps because of its technical approach to the matters laid before it, the *Bundesrat* attracts little public interest in the FRG.

Following on from the principle established in Article 30 of the Basic Law, which places state authority firmly in the hands of the *Länder*, Article 70 confers on the *Länder* the right to legislate – under one important condition: 'The *Länder* shall have the right to legislate in so far as this Basic Law does not confer legislative power on the federation.' The legislation conferred on the federation by the Basic Law is divided into three categories, as follows:

1. exclusive legislation (Article 71);
2. concurrent legislation (Article 72);
3. framework legislation (Article 75).

The practical significance of these categories can best be understood by examining the areas they cover. Thus, exclusive legislation covers foreign affairs, defence, questions of citizenship, passports and immigration, currency, customs, trade and payments, roads, railways, air transport, post and telecommunications. In all these matters legislation is exclusively for the *Bund* since any other arrangement would be practically impossible. These are key areas requiring central co-ordination. The areas covered by concurrent legislation, which permits the *Länder* to legislate in so far as the *Bund* provides no legislation, are more technical and limited in scope. They include the organisation of the civil and criminal law and the legal profession, registration of births, marriages and deaths, refugees and expellees from former German territories in Eastern Europe, trade and commerce, shipping and inland waterways, road traffic and motorways. As these examples show, the *Länder* are able to legislate on most of their internal affairs to suit their own requirements. Framework legislation limits the *Bund* to providing an outline which is filled in by detailed legislation at *Land* level. This category covers the public services and other corporate bodies under public law, the environment, land use and regional planning. A recent example of framework legislation is the *Hochschulrahmengesetz* of 1976, covering the development of universities and higher education.[3] Although the terms of framework legislation are sometimes treated very broadly, it should be noted that it can only be used where there is a definable need for federal legislation, e.g. when a matter cannot be effectively dealt with by *Land* legislation because of its repercussions throughout the federal system. Thus, it would have created serious problems if each *Land* had separately reformed its higher education sector according to divergent principles.

While the most important legislation is, in practice, largely reserved for the *Bund*, it is still true to say that the administration of the law is almost entirely in the hands of the *Länder*. Power is thus separated between the *Bund* as legislator and the *Länder* as executive. The constitutional basis for this arrangement is contained in Article 83 of the Basic Law: 'The *Länder* shall execute federal laws as matters of their own concern in so far as this Basic Law does not otherwise provide or permit.' The Basic Law distinguishes between three types of administration:

1. a small area of administration exclusive to the *Bund*;
2. administration carried out by the *Länder* on behalf of the *Bund*;
3. administration exclusive to the *Länder*.

Regarding the first category, the administrative authority of the *Bund* corresponds in part to its exclusive legislative competence and includes the diplomatic service, the treasury, railways, post and telecommunications, inland waterways and shipping, air traffic, defence and frontier protection. In each case the *Bund* maintains its own administrative apparatus at all levels. Regarding category two, administration by the *Länder* on behalf of the *Bund* is limited to a small number of important areas such as motorway and highway construction and maintenance. The federal government leaves the practical arrangements to the individual *Länder* but is empowered to issue general regulations to the *Land* administration. The third category of administration, which is exclusive to the *Länder*, is related directly to the laws enacted by the *Land* itself, as well as the autonomous administration of federal law.

Although this complex system allows for a good measure of controlled integration between *Bund* and *Länder*, it will be appreciated that a strict division and allocation of responsibilities cannot be maintained consistently in all areas of practical administration. Over a long period *ad hoc* agreements have been made between the federal government and the *Länder*. These are known as *Bund-Länder-Abkommen* and are intended to meet specific needs as they arise, e.g. the *Wissenschaftsrat* was based on such an agreement.[4] Voluntary co-operation of this kind is essentially pragmatic and not adequate to deal with the long-term problems of development and planning. In 1969 this was constitutionally recognised and a new section on *Gemeinschaftsaufgaben* (community tasks) was included in the Basic Law, providing for cost sharing and joint planning between *Bund* and *Länder*. Results of the work on community tasks can be seen in the law on providing university buildings and facilities (*Hochschulbauförderungsgesetz*) of 1969 which stipulates cost sharing on a 50—50 basis, as well as in the laws on improving agricultural and regional economic structure, in which the *Bund* accepted between 60 per cent and 70 per cent of the costs. As described below in Chapter 6, the *Bund* is also involved in matters of educational planning and research.

While statutory provisions governing the relations between *Bund* and *Länder* are of considerable importance, it will be acknowledged that the crucial factor in obtaining the desired balance of power is the control and allocation of funds. Whatever provisions are made by the constitution, real power will always lie with those authorities which control the purse strings. The key question in assessing the practical reality of West German federalism is therefore: How are tax revenues apportioned (a) between the *Bund* and the *Länder*, and (b) between the *Länder* themselves?

Finance

The apportionment of financial revenue is known as the *Finanzausgleich,* or balancing the finances. The primary apportionment between *Bund* and *Länder* is the *vertikaler Finanzausgleich*, while the apportionment among the *Länder* themselves is the *horizontaler Finanzausgleich.* The aim of the latter is to alleviate the differences between the industrialised *Länder*, which are populous and financially powerful, and the relatively sparsely populated agricultural *Länder*, which are at a disadvantage with tax revenues.

During the 1950s the financial provisions of the Basic Law proved in practice to be inadequate for the complex relationships which developed. A number of small-scale reforms were introduced, culminating several years later in the financial reform of 1969. Although there is plenty of criticism to be heard, it is generally agreed that the 1969

reform has improved the efficiency and fairness of the system of
financial allocation and distribution.

Financial arrangements are dealt with in a separate section of the
Basic Law, thus emphasising the importance attached to them. The
fundamental principle governing expenditure is expressed in Article
104: 'The *Bund* and the *Länder* are separately responsible for the
expenditure arising from the discharge of their tasks in so far as no
other arrangements are stipulated by this Basic Law.'[5] Thus each is
called upon to bear the costs of its duties and responsibilities
separately. The statement is then qualified: if the *Länder* are acting on
behalf of the *Bund* (see p. 45 above), then the *Bund* has to meet the
resulting expenditure. In principle, therefore, responsibility for
meeting expenditure rests with the executive − not legislative −
authority. Article 104 goes on to state that the *Bund* can grant financial
aid to the *Länder* for important investment projects.

Tax legislation is dealt with in Article 105 which confers comprehensive powers on to the *Bund*. It has exclusive legislative authority
over customs duties and monopolies (spirits and matches), and
concurrent legislative authority over all other important taxes. In
practice the *Bund* makes wide use of its concurrent legislative authority
so that the *Länder* are limited in the main to purely local taxation.

The Basic Law provides for two methods of distributing tax revenue
to *Bund* and *Länder*. Firstly, the yields from a large number of less
important taxes are allotted separately; e.g. the *Bund* receives certain
consumer taxes and road transport tax, together with taxes on capital,
insurance and bills of exchange, while the *Länder* receive the revenue
from wealth tax, estate duty and motor vehicle tax. Secondly, the
revenue from the most productive taxes, i.e. on income, corporations
and turnover, is allotted jointly to *Bund* and *Länder*. Both receive
50 per cent each of income and corporation tax, while their
respective allocation of turnover tax is reviewed annually, and is
usually in the region of 70 per cent to the *Bund* and the remainder to
the *Länder*. This system functions reasonably well, though, as might
be expected, constant friction occurs both between the *Bund* and the
Länder and among the *Länder* themselves over the relative importance
of their claims to a larger slice of the financial cake.

What are the long-term prospects for the special kind of 'co-operative
federalism' which has developed over the last three decades in Western
Germany? As noted above, it is difficult for the federal state to resist
the external pressures from industry, commerce and society in general
towards greater centralisation, and in the FRG it finds its expression in

a range of administrative agreements between the *Länder*, known as *Ländervereinigungen*, as well as in such bodies as the *Konferenz der Kultusminister der Länder*.[6] The pressure has been intensified in recent years by the EEC, in which only the *Bund* is represented. It seems inevitable that the influence of the *Länder* in such traditionally local areas as agricultural policy will be progressively reduced and placed within the constraints of federal requirements and inter-*Land* agreements. For this reason it is sometimes maintained that West German federalism is essentially administrative rather than political, and that this tendency will continue, with a corresponding loss in the active practice of democracy at the local level. Taking a longer view of German history, however, it cannot be denied that the present federal system has provided a framework for a genuinely democratic form of government the institutions of which have acquired self-confidence and flexibility while remaining within the provisions of the Basic Law, and that the level of democracy and practical interest in local politics is as high as it has ever been in Germany. On balance, therefore, it might be said that the federal system in the FRG has successfully reconciled the interests of both *Bund* and *Länder* while preserving the interests of the individual citizen, and there is at present no serious reason to suppose that the system will be unable to achieve this even more successfully in the future.

Further Reading

Ellwein, Thomas. *Das Regierungssystem de Bundesrepublik Deutschland* (Opladen, 1973)

Goldman, Guido. *The German Political System* (New York, 1974)

Plischke, Elmer. *Contemporary Government of Germany* (London, 1964)

Rühring, Hans-Helmut and Sontheimer, Kurt. *Handbuch des deutschen Parliamentarismus* (Munich, 1970)

Sontheimer, Kurt. *The Government and Politics of West Germany* (London, 1972)

Notes

1. Cf. pp. 72–74 below.
2. Cf. pp. 67–68 below.
3. Cf. pp. 127ff below.

4. Cf. p. 113 below.
5. Author's translation.
6. Cf. p. 112 below.

3 GOVERNMENT AND *BUNDESTAG*

The *Bundestag* Deputies

The *Bundestag*, which is roughly the equivalent of the British House of Commons or the US House of Representatives, is elected for four years. Unlike their British counterparts the German deputies (*Abgeordneten*) are fairly certain they will not have to fight another election before the four years are up. The Federal Chancellor, unlike the British Prime Minister, does not have the right to dissolve the legislature and decide the date of the election. Only once since 1949, in 1972, has there been an unscheduled election.

Like the other members of Western democratic legislatures, the *Bundestag* deputies do not form a representative cross-section of the voters who elected them. Although more than half the electorate are women, only 38 of the 518[1] deputies in the eighth *Bundestag* (1976–80) were women. By way of comparison, 19 women were elected to the 635-member British House of Commons in 1979 – fewer than at any election since 1951. In 1979 there were only 16 women members of the 435-strong US House of Representatives. One difference between the lady politicians of West Germany and Britain is that in the German case they are more likely to be Conservative. Traditionally, Social Democratic and Labour parties have given more opportunities to women to climb the political ladder. However, in recent years the CDU/CSU has attempted to field more women candidates, and the result is that in the 1976–80 *Bundestag* there were 19 Christian Democratic women as against 15 Social Democratic and 4 FDP. The respective strengths of the three parties were: CDU/CSU, 254; SPD, 224; and FDP, 40. In Britain, throughout the post-war period, the Labour Party has sent more women to the Commons than have the Conservatives. In 1949, 38 women were elected to the 421-member *Bundestag.* The highest number of women elected was in 1957 when there were 48 women among the 519 *Abgeordneten.* Clearly, the West German political system, like those of Britain and the USA, has not been able to do justice to the changing position of women in society.

As one would expect, the members of the *Bundestag* are better educated than the average voter. On the CDU/CSU benches in 1976 were 187 members with a university education. Among the Social Democrats there were 105 deputies who had been at universities.

Another 27 Social Democrats had received other forms of higher education, as had 12 Christian Democrats. The FDP remained faithful to its image as the best-educated German party — 33 of its 40 deputies had received some form of higher education. The women legislators were better educated than their male colleagues; 32 of them had taken higher education courses. Both the major parties have, since 1949, increased the numbers of their deputies with academic qualifications, but this trend has been more marked in the SPD than in the CDU/CSU. In recent years there has been a tendency to recruit candidates who are experts in particular fields such as taxation, insurance, economics or military affairs. Surprisingly, British MPs have a higher level of formal education than their German colleagues, a higher percentage of them having completed some form of higher education.

In terms of their previous occupations West Germany's federal politicians are highly unrepresentative of the electorate. There has been an increasing number of public employees entering the *Bundestag*. According to Professor Ulrich Lohmar,[2] himself a former *Abgeordneter*, 44 per cent of those elected in 1972 belonged to this category. Roughly another 25 per cent were officials of interest groups (*Verbände*). Unlike most British trade unions, those in the FRG are not affiliated to any political party. Nevertheless, about 21 per cent of the SPD members of the *Bundestag*, in 1972, were officials of the DGB, the trade union federation. In addition, several SPD deputies were officials of other employee organisations. Among the Christian Democrats were 5 DGB officials and 27 closely associated with similar bodies (in many cases Catholic employee groups). Employers' organisations were represented by 21 CDU/CSU members, 3 SPD deputies and 5 from the FDP. There were no fewer than 25 deputies representing agricultural interest groups — thus agriculture was over-represented relative to its importance in the economy. One group which was, by this time, surprisingly weak consisted of the refugees. There were only 6 officials of refugee organisations in the *Bundestag*, all of them Christian Democrats. Apart from officials, Lohmar found that only 2 per cent of those elected to the *Bundestag* in 1972 were workers and 3 per cent were farmers.

Jürgen Weber[3] estimated that, in all, 48.5 per cent of the federal deputies were officials of interest groups. Both he and Professor Lohmar accepted that in a pluralist society various interest groups would seek entry into parliament. However, Lohmar believed the extent of the influence of interest group officialdom and that of the public employees to be detrimental to the functioning of the *Bundestag*. For him this growing influence has meant a strengthening of the 'bureaucratic mentality' in the political ruling stratum leading to the bureaucratisation of the parliamentary groups. He was also concerned about the expanding influence of the interest groups on legislation.

The large number of public employees in the federal parliament, in contrast to the situation in the British House of Commons, is to a considerable extent explained by the security conferred upon such employees in the FRG. They can stand for elected office without losing their positions and can return after membership of the *Bundestag* to the public body from which they took leave.

As we have seen in Chapter 1, religion is a factor in West German politics. Consequently, most deputies give information about their religious affiliations. In the 1976–80 *Bundestag* 163 CDU or CSU members were Catholic, 88 were Protestant and 3 gave no information. Only 25 SPD deputies listed themselves as Catholic, 67 as Protestant and 132 gave no data. The majority of the FDP (24) gave no indication of church membership, 5 were listed as Catholic and 11 as Protestant. The Catholic community is clearly strongly over-represented in the CDU/CSU and under-represented in the SPD. Since the SPD has been projecting itself as a *Volkspartei* there has been a greater tendency among its parliamentarians to give details of church membership.

In terms of their ages the FRG's politicians did not, in 1979, have as many over-60s as the British House of Commons. However, 52 German deputies were over 61 – 29 CDU/CSU, 20 SPD and three FDP. At the other end, only 5 belonged to the post-war generation. In the 1979 Commons 86 MPs were over 61 – 38 Conservatives, 43 Labour, 2 Liberals and 3 others. The poorer pension provision for British politicians probably contributed to this situation. Perhaps the relative youth of the *Bundestag* as an institution, having been first established in 1949, has also been a minor contributory factor. Usually between 25 and 30 per cent of the deputies of the *Bundestag* are replaced at each federal election. In 1976 there were 118 new members, 134 starting their second term, 119 their third, 70 had been returned for a fourth time, 34 were beginning their fifth term and 10 their seventh. Finally, there were 11 survivors of the first *Bundestag* (1949–53) who were facing the challenge of an eighth term.

About 22 per cent of the deputies elected in 1976 were either born in, or had strong connections with, Berlin, the GDR or the 'lost territories'. Thus, quite naturally, there remains a strong interest in Germany East of the Elbe. Several other deputies were born in Eastern Europe, Germany's former colonies, or other places beyond the frontiers of the pre-war Reich.

The members of the *Bundestag* have always been better paid and have enjoyed better conditions of service than have their British colleagues. They have also enjoyed better secretarial and research assistance. In the 1970s there were around 1,600 staff — from porters to technical assistants — employed by the *Bundestag* administration. In addition, there were 120 assistants employed by the party organisations in the *Bundeshaus*, and a further 700 aides working for the *Abgeordneten*. The library of the federal parliament claims to be the third largest parliamentary library in the world, smaller only than those of the US Congress and the Japanese parliament. All in all, the *Bundeshaus* is more likely to remind the visitor of the American Congress or one of the more modern US state legislatures than it is of the Palace of Westminster. Nevertheless, one hears grumbling in the Bonn parliament building about pay and conditions, and it is true that many West Germans in the better-paid professions or in the higher reaches of industry do not find their legislators' remuneration, life-style and prestige particularly attractive.

Bundestag Procedure

The independent is unknown in the *Bundestag*. All members are grouped within the parties — CDU, CSU, SPD and FDP. Since 1961 these have been the only parties represented. The members of each party join together to form a *Fraktion* or caucus. In the case of the Christian Democrats the Bavarian CSU joins with the CDU to form one *Fraktion*, but the independently-minded Bavarians still maintian their own sub-organisation within the joint caucus. Their numbers, organisation and the political skill of their leader, Franz Josef Strauss, have won for them a disproportionate amount of political influence. Discipline appears to be tougher in the *Bundestag* than among the parties of the House of Commons and the SPD in particular has a long tradition of strict discipline going back to the nineteenth century. The Free Democrats have the most relaxed discipline. The caucuses are officially recognised bodies and receive public funds to enable them to carry on their work. Each *Fraktion* elects its executive, usually for one year. On the executive are the chairman, several deputy chairmen, several *Geschäftsführer* and a number of ordinary members. The *Geschäftsführer* are responsible for liaison with the other caucuses and the *Bundestag* administration, and for mobilising their colleagues on appropriate occasions. The chairman is usually a respected and powerful figure. Between 1969 and 1980 the SPD had one chairman, Herbert Wehner, who has been probably the single most influential politician of post-war German Social Democracy. Herr Wehner entered the *Bundestag* in 1949 and was the Minister for All-German Affairs in the Grand Coalition (1966–69) which he did so much to bring about. He preferred chairmanship of the SPD *Fraktion* to ministerial office after 1969.

The Council of Elders (*Ältestenrat*) is responsible for organising the work of the *Bundestag* and its daily agenda. The council is made up of 23 members drawn from the different parties according to their strength in parliament. The President of the *Bundestag* is, by convention, drawn from the largest party. Apart from the years 1972–76, this has been the CDU/CSU. The President leads the Council of Elders, receives all legislation before it is put before the *Bundestag*, is responsible for order in parliament, and in terms of formal status is second only to the Federal President. Karl Karstens of the CDU held the presidency from 1967 to 1980, Annemarie Renger (SPD) was President between 1972 and 1976. So far she is the only woman to hold this post.

The *Bundestag* has a well-developed system of committees which are more important than those of the British House of Commons, yet less important than those of the US Congress. The number of committees has varied over the years. It grew in the early years of the Republic, reaching 26 in the third *Bundestag* (1957–61). It was reduced to 23 in 1965. Between 1972 and 1980 it was 19. The reason for the decline in the number of committees is that the principle has been adopted that each ministry should have a corresponding committee attached to it. Another reason is the decline in importance of some problems. Compared with the earlier period, there have been no committees on refugees, war damage or federal property. Post Office affairs have, in the 1970s, been dealt with by the Committee on Research, Technology, Post Office and Telecommunications rather than by a separate committee. One new committee, established in 1972, is that on sport. This reflects the greater rivalry with the GDR in this field as well as greater interest in leisure-time activities. The chairmanships and composition of the *Bundestag* committees are based on party strengths in the federal parliament. The largest committees are those dealing with the budget, economic, employment and social affairs. There are three of them with 37 members each. Next in size are those dealing with foreign affairs and food, agriculture and forestry with 33 members. Most of the other 14 have 25 members each. The committees are mainly concerned with amending proposed legislation and operate very largely on strict party lines. They do not have the ancillary staffs available to their American counterparts.

Chancellor and Government

Between the setting up of the Federal Republic in 1949 and its development in 1980 there have been only five Chancellors. This compares with ten Prime Ministers in Britain during the same period and seven Presidents in the United States. As an expression of political stability it compares very favourably with Weimar Germany and with the situation in post-war Italy and, to a lesser extent, with that in France. The Federal Chancellors have been as follows:

Konrad Adenauer (CDU), 1949–63
Ludwig Erhard (CDU), 1963–66
Kurt Georg Kiesinger (CDU), 1966–69
Willy Brandt (SPD), 1969–74
Helmut Schmidt (SPD), 1974–

The strength of the Chancellor rests on his constitutional position and the strength of his party in the *Bundestag*, as well as on his own personal qualities. As was explained in Chapter 2, Weimar Germany's experience with the autocratic President Hindenburg led the fathers of the Bonn *Grundgesetz* to limit the office of President and strengthen the Chancellor. According to Article 63, the Chancellor is elected by the *Bundestag* on the proposal of the President. However, if the President's candidate fails, the *Bundestag* can, within fourteen days, elect its own nominee providing he can muster more than half of the deputies. If a third attempt is necessary, only a majority of the votes cast is required. So far the President's nominee has been elected. This is not because of the strength of the President as a kingmaker but rather because of the previous negotiations and the election results. The Christian Democrats had voted at the federal meeting for Heuss to be President because he had already agreed to back Adenauer for the Chancellorship. Adenauer was subsequently elected with a majority of one. It was the Christian Democrat Heinrich Lübke who, as President, proposed both Erhard and Kiesinger for the Chancellorship. In both cases the negotiations to secure majorities for these candidates had already taken place. By voting for Gustav Heinemann to be President, the FDP indicated their readiness, in 1969, to enter into a coalition with the SPD and therefore to vote for a Social Democrat as Chancellor. Heinemann then proposed Brandt, whose party had fewer seats than the CDU/CSU, and he was duly elected with the combined votes of the SPD and the FDP. In 1974 Schmidt was also assured of the votes of the Free Democrats when he was proposed by the President. With the presidency going to Karl Karstens (CDU) in 1979 the incumbent was for the first time not drawn from one of the government parties.

To strengthen the position of the Chancellor the Basic Law lays down that he cannot be removed by a simple vote of no confidence. What is required to bring down a Chancellor is a 'constructive' vote of no confidence. This means that those seeking to dismiss the Chancellor must have an alternative candidate who can command a majority of the *Bundestag*. In such a case the President would be required to appoint the successful candidate. This has not yet happened. In 1972 Chancellor Brandt, having lost his slender parliamentary majority due to defections, was faced with a CDU/CSU attempt to replace him. The attempt failed by just two votes and the FRG's first unscheduled election followed, leading to an SPD victory.

The Chancellor is often compared to the British Prime Minister, but in one respect he is usually weaker. Only Adenauer, and then only between 1956 and 1961, had an absolute majority in the *Bundestag*. Only in the period 1974–79 have post-war British Prime Ministers been without a Commons majority. The Chancellor, unlike the Prime Minister, must accept the need for coalitions and be adept at handling his coalition partners. This was certainly one of Adenauer's qualities. In 1949 he looked like a caretaker. His own party had only 139 seats out of 402 (excluding West Berlin) in the *Bundestag*. His main opponents, the Social Democrats, held 131 seats. His Cabinet was a coalition of the CDU/CSU, FDP and DP. Adenauer's second coalition in 1953 included the new BHE refugee party as well as his previous partners. Looking back it is easy to gloss over the difficulties which Adenauer encountered and forget the times when his position looked precarious. There were often rumours about splits in the Christian Democratic Union, with talk of the left-wing, Catholic working class from North Rhine-Westphalia, opting for a coalition with the SPD. Adenauer usually gave enough to prevent this happening, as with co-determination in industry in the early 1950s. In 1950 there was, of course, a rupture in the government. Dr Gustav Heinemann, Minister of Interior, resigned because he objected to Adenauer's authoritarian attitude towards his colleagues, especially over the issue of a West German defence contribution. Heinemann subsequently established his own neutralist party but it had very little success and Heinemann and most of his followers later joined the SPD. Worse was to come for Adenauer. By 1956 his second coalition was in disarray. The Free Democrats wanted him to make greater efforts to bring about the reunification of Germany. When the party rank and file in the *Bundestag* and in the *Länder* decided to break with the CDU/CSU their ministers opted to remain in the government, setting up their own party. Similar trouble had already developed in the refugee party. Adenauer also faced considerable strikes in the metal industry in 1956. Up until the summer of that year he looked anything but a winner. The Hungarian Revolution, increasing prosperity, the return of the Saar, and a highly successful media-orientated election campaign secured an absolute majority for the old Chancellor in 1957. Obviously external factors greatly influence internal politics and therefore the prestige of the head of government and his standing with his colleagues. West Germany's generally good economic performance must have added to the Chancellor's position just as Britain's ailing economy diminished the credibility of the Prime Minister. Compared with Adenauer and Erhard, Brandt and Schmidt had fewer difficulties with their government partners between 1969 and 1980, though they too suffered potentially damaging resignations — Alex Möller (SPD, 1971), Karl Schiller (SPD, 1972), Georg Leber (SPD, 1978), Dr Hans Friderichs (FDP, 1977) and Werner Maihofer (FDP, 1978).

The Chancellor has great prestige due to his projection by the media and his regular, publicised, encounters with the other powerful world leaders. Several Chancellors certainly brought something close to charisma to the office. These include in their quite different ways Adenauer, Brandt and Schmidt. Of these three, Adenauer was in certain respects the most remarkable, if only because he was the least prepared. His advanced age could not have been an advantage — except perhaps that some of his rivals in the early days underestimated him because of it! He also lacked experience in national politics and had not held any high offices of state. His political experience before 1945 had been mainly as Lord Mayor of Cologne in the Weimar Republic. Brandt, too, had experience of this kind, as Lord Mayor of West Berlin, 1957—66. But in Brandt's case his office had brought him into regular contact with world figures. Between 1966 and 1969 he was Deputy-Chancellor and Foreign Minister of the FRG. Herr Schmidt, too, took with him to Bonn experience of *Land* administration. He served for four years as Senator (Minister) for Interior in the Hamburg administration. He was chairman of the SPD *Fraktion* in the *Bundestag* (1967—69) before holding office as Minister of Defence (1969–72). He then served as Minister of Finance (and part of the period, Economics) until he became Chancellor in 1974. One of the weaknesses of Ludwig Erhard was that his entire political career before becoming Chancellor in 1963 was spent as Minister of Economics. Kurt Georg Kiesinger had gained useful experience as Prime Minister of Baden-Würtemberg (1958–66). He had also been chairman for four years of the *Bundestag* Foreign Affairs Committee. He had not, however, held any ministerial appointments in Bonn. The West German route to the office of head of government is clearly more flexible than the British. Unlike their British counterparts, West German Chancellors do not need to have spent years making their way in the national parliament. *Land* politics offers a suitable alternative.

Like their British counterparts, the West German Chancellors face the difficult task, on taking office, of finding suitable posts for all their powerful party colleagues. In both cases they seek to strike a balance between the various wings of their parties. The German Chancellor has to be careful, too, to ensure that there is a confessional balance, especially when the Christian Democrats are in office, and that regional aspirations are satisfied. Once again, the Chancellor has less room for manoeuvre as head of a coalition. The junior partner(s) expects to get enough senior posts to maintain its dignity. In the SPD–FDP coalitions the Free Democrats have been awarded the prestigious Ministries of Foreign Affairs and Interior. Their nominee became Federal President. Adenauer seems to have increased his Cabinet to placate his coalition partners. His first ministry had a mere 16 members, his last 22. The Erhard government also had 22. The Grand Coalition ran to only 20. Brandt had a small Cabinet of 15, of whom three were from the FDP and one was non-party. Under Helmut Schmidt the number of ministers rose to 18.

The Ministries

Up to 1980, West German Cabinets have been smaller than those of Britain. Comparing Callaghan's (1976) Cabinet with that of Schmidt we find he had 22 members to Schmidt's 18. British governments also include a large number of ministers outside the Cabinet. This is unknown in the Federal Republic. However, since 1966 there have been a number of Parliamentary State Secretaries (*Parlamentarische Staatssekretäre*) – between seven and 17 – who are not officially

ministers. These secretaries often act for their ministers in the
Bundestag and in the Cabinet. They are politicians, not civil servants.
Callaghan's Cabinet included such ministries as Energy, Industry, Prices
and Consumer Protection, as well as Scotland, Wales and Northern
Ireland. The FRG's Cabinet has a special Ministry for Inter German
Relations (formerly the Ministry for All-German Questions). Another
German ministry unknown in Britain is the Ministry for Youth, Family
and Health. Like British ministries since the war, those of West Germany
have been reorganised and amalgamated but the basic ones inherited
from the nineteenth century have survived largely intact — Foreign
Affairs (from 1951), Defence (from 1955), Interior, Justice and
Finance. The 'traditional' post-war ministries include Economics, Food,
Agriculture and Forestry, Labour, Transport, Education and Science,
Economic Co-operation (formerly Economic Aid), Posts and Telegraphs,
Environment, Building and Town Planning (formerly Housing). Since
1955 most governments have included a minister responsible for either
Atomic Energy or Research and Technology. Among the three
ministries which have disappeared are Reconstruction (1949—53),
which was transformed into Housing, Refugees (1949—69), and the
Ministry for the *Bundesrat* and the Affairs of the *Länder* (1949—69).
The Ministries of Economics and Finance have been in keen competition over the years, partly as a result of coalition politics, personal
rivalries and the changing conceptions of the management of the
economy. Between 1961—69 and 1972—80 these two ministries were
headed by politicians from different parties. In 1972 they were briefly
united with Helmut Schmidt as minister. In theory, the Chancellor, as
head of government, plots the path along which he expects the
government to go, whilst respecting the authority of individual
ministers in their respective fields. The practice has been more complex.
The Chancellor usually takes a keen and close interest in foreign affairs
and this was very much the case under Adenauer and Brandt. Adenauer
was his own Foreign Minister between 1951 and 1955 and Heinrich von
Brentano, who held this post from 1955 to 1961, was regarded as little
more than a spokesman and messenger of and for the Chancellor.
Kiesinger, who had some limited experience in this area, was restricted
by the presence of Brandt, his chief SPD rival and Vice-Chancellor, as
Minister for Foreign Affairs, Schmidt has been more interested in
defence, though he too has made important trips abroad which were
as much concerned with economics as with defence. Compared with
Britain, little use has been made of Cabinet committees which, in
Adenauer's case probably meant the strengthening of the Chancellor

vis-à-vis individual ministers. The activities of the Federal Chancellor's Office (*Bundeskanzleramt*) worked in the same direction. The term *Kanzlerdemokratie*, which suggests a presidential type of regime, was popular at the time of Adenauer, and the *Bundeskanzleramt* strengthened this suggestion. In fact, led by Hans Globke, it was widely believed to have too much influence. The *Amt* then lost some of its influence under Erhard and Kiesinger, but it became once again a powerhouse under Chancellor Brandt. Brandt placed a politician, Horst Ehmke, at its head with the rank of minister, and it has remained powerful under Helmut Schmidt. Officially, its most important tasks are to keep the Chancellor informed on current political questions and on the work of the federal ministries, as well as advising the Chancellor on the carrying out of his general policy line. It is a supervisory body and a co-ordinating body, co-ordinating the work of the ministries and of the intelligence services. It is also responsible for preparing Cabinet meetings as well as those of Cabinet committees. The *Amt* is divided into six departments (*Abteilungen*). These are: Law and Administration; Foreign and Inter German Relations and External Security; Internal Affairs; Economics, Finance and Social Policy; Planning; Federal Intelligence Service (*Bundesnachrichtendienst*), Co-ordination of the Intelligence Services of the Federation, Protection of (State) Secrets. Both the Permanent Representation of the FRG in the German Democratic Republic and the *Bundesnachrichtendienst* are under the control of the *Bundeskanzleramt.* Chancellor Schmidt appointed a permanent civil servant as the head of the *Amt.* However, a substantial SPD figure, Hans-Jürgen Wischnewski, was appointed minister with special responsibility for overseeing the work of the *Bundeskanzleramt.* Wischnewski held this office between December 1976 and September 1979. Though it is difficult to be precise, one gains the impression that the Federal Chancellor's Office is a more coherently organised body than the British Cabinet Office.

Even with such a powerful body to aid him, and with a disciplined body of party colleagues as his ministers, the Chancellor must face the realities of coalition government. The hard bargaining that goes with this is likely to mean that many ministers have a fair degree of freedom in their departments. Another factor making for the same end is the long service of politicians in the ministries to which they are appointed. Ministers in the FRG normally remain at their posts — unless their government falls — between one election and the next. There are not the frequent 'reshuffles' which are a regular feature of the British political scene. One reason for this is the concept of the minister as an expert in his own field. Another lies in the exigencies of coalition politics. This factor undoubtedly played an important part in Hans-Christoph Seebohm remaining Minister of Transport from 1949 to 1966, and Theodor Oberländer remaining Minister for Refugees from 1953 to 1960. Seebohm was one of the leaders of the small *Deutsche Partei* until he transferred to the CDU in 1960. Oberländer had made his way through the refugee party before climbing aboard the CDU bandwagon. Adenauer felt he needed both but in ministries of lesser importance. Among the other notable examples of long-serving ministers in the Adenauer era were Ludwig Erhard, Minister of Economics (1949–63), Gerhard Schröder, Interior (1953–61), Franz Josef Strauss, Defence (1956–63) and Franz-Josef Wuermeling, Family and Youth (1953–62). In the eleven years of the SPD–FDP governments up to 1980, only two politicians came within the range of the Seebohm record — Josef Ertl (FDP) was Minister of Food, Agriculture and Forestry, and Egon Franke (SPD) held the politically sensitive Ministry of Inter German Relations throughout the period. This was a shorter timespan with less political stability than before 1969, yet there was the same tendency, as in the Christian-Democratic-led governments, for those appointed to office to serve in one ministry for relatively long stints.

Ministers need not be politicians but in practice only in exceptional cases are they not. Up to 1980 only Brandt's Minister of Education and Science, Professor Hans Leussink, was not a party man. This was in part to allay the fears of the teaching profession about possible reforms in education at a time when the government had only a slender majority. Professor Siegfried Balke, Minister for Post (1953–56) and Atomic Energy (1956–62), though a member of the CSU, was more of a scientist than a politician. Women appear to be tolerated rather than welcomed in West German Cabinets. The first woman to be appointed to office was Elizabeth Schwarzhaupt (CDU) as Minister of Health in 1961. She retained that post until 1966 when it was taken over by Käte Strobel (SPD). In 1969 Frau Strobel added family and youth affairs to her responsibility and this combined ministry has remained in tender female care ever since (Katharina Focke, 1972–76, and Antje Huber, 1976–80). Indeed, it seems that lady politicians in Bonn find it is very difficult to break out of health and welfare. Up to 1980 the only woman to hold any other ministry was Marie Schlei (SPD) who was Minister for Economic Co-operation from December 1976 to February 1978.

Under each minister, and where appropriate his political junior

Parlamentarischer Staatssekretär, is the permanent head of the ministry, the *Staatssekretär*. He is one of the civil servants (*Beamte*) in the higher service (*im höheren Dienst*) — that is, the pinnacle of the profession. Besides those in the higher service there are three other grades of *Beamte*: those in the lower service, those in the middle service (*im mittleren Dienst*) and those in the executive service (*im gehobenen Dienst*). All *Beamte*, whether railway guards, university professors or ambassadors, are placed in one of these grades. The 16 per cent or so in the top category are likely to hold a doctorate in law and be from middle- or upper-middle-class families. After the war the Western allies failed in their attempts to reform the old *Beamtenschaft*. Article 131 of the Basic Law required that a law be introduced to reinstate or care for persons who had been in the public service in 1945, and who as refugees or expellees had lost their jobs. On 1 April 1953 an appropriate law became operative. This played an important part in restoring the old hierarchical civil service. In the top echelons many *Beamte* are the sons of civil servants, thus maintaining the links with the past, with the old attitudes and ways of doing things. Officially non-political, the West German public service permits its members to seek elective office. Over the years membership of one or other of the ruling parties had become more widespread.

As much of the implementation of government decisions is delegated to the *Länder*, the great majority of the *Beamte* are in fact employed by the regional authorities rather than by the ministries in Bonn.

Further Reading

Conradt, David P. *The German Polity* (New York, 1978)

Dyson, Kenneth H. F. *Party, State and Bureaucracy in Western Germany* (Beverly Hills, 1977)

End, Heinrich. *Erneuerung der Diplomatie* (Neuwied, 1969)

Johnson, Nevil. *Government in the Federal Republic of Germany* (Oxford, 1973)

Kürschners. *Deutscher Bundestag 8 Wahlperiode* (Rheinbreitbach, 1977)

Loewenberg, Gerhard. *Parliament In the German Political System* (New York, 1967)

Lohmar, Ulrich. *Das Hohe Haus* (Stuttgart, 1975)

Trossmann, Hans. *Der Deutsche Bundestag* (Darmstadt, 1971)

Weber, Jürgen. *Die Interessengruppen im politischen System der Bundesrepublik Deutschland* (Stuttgart, 1977)

Notes

1. This figure includes 22 members from West Berlin who are elected by the West Berlin legislature and do not vote in the *Bundestag*.

2. Ulrich Lohmar, *Das Hohe Haus* (Stuttgart, 1975), p. 180.

3. Jürgen Weber, *Die Interessengruppen im politischen System der Bundesrepublik Deutschland* (Stuttgart, 1977), p. 282.

4 THE ECONOMY AND INDUSTRIAL RELATIONS

The Social Market Economy

The West German economy is based on the principle of the 'social market economy' (*soziale Marktwirtschaft*). This system, which is an attempt to steer a middle course between the abuses of unrestrained capitalism and the regimentation of the planned economy, tries to grant the maximum scope for personal initiative in business and industry while ensuring by statutory means that harmful developments, e.g. monopolies and price fixing, are curbed. The energetic and inventive *Unternehmer*, or entrepreneur, is encouraged by the profit motive to offer his products in free competition with others, the consumer is free to choose how he will spend his money, and the employee is free to decide where and, within the limits of his qualifications and training, in what capacity he will work. The role of the state is to maintain an overall supervision and to apply correctives only where necessary. No economic theory is ever fully realised in practice, and the theory of the social market economy is no exception to this. Some critics maintain that the system is weighted in favour of the *Unternehmer* who, it is claimed, enjoyed excessively high profits and tax relief on investments throughout the 1950s whilst paying only modest wages to their employees. Others point out that the freedoms accorded to the employee are of a more theoretical nature than the tangible benefits and incentives enjoyed by the employer. By contrast, other critics see the high wage levels currently enjoyed by German workers as a danger to the export trade. The majority of observers agree on one point, however — namely, that the success of the West German market economy has exceeded all the hopes that were placed in it when it was introduced by Ludwig Erhard in 1949–50.

In terms of total foreign trade turnover the FRG is the world's second largest trading nation after the United States. Between 1950 and 1977 the value of West German imports and exports increased approximately twentyfold and thirty-two-fold respectively, resulting in a steadily increasing positive balance of payments which has made the DM the strongest currency in Europe, and, in recent years, in the world. An increasing amount of this wealth has found its way into the wages and salaries of the workforce. The gross wages of the German industrial worker are almost twice those of the British worker for a slightly

shorter working week, while consumer prices in West Germany have
risen at only half the rate of British price increases since 1950. During
the period 1960–75 West German consumer spending increased at
twice the British rate.

Faced with these indications of considerable economic success and
individual prosperity, the observer may well wonder how such
achievements can be explained. Can it all be attributed to excellent
labour relations and high productivity? Is the organisation of German
industry and commerce more efficient than that of its EEC partners?
Do German workers work consistently harder than those of other
nations? Has the West German economy any weak points? Can its
success be expected to last? The present chapter will try to answer
these and other questions. At this stage suffice it to say that the
German economy can be compared to a beautifully maintained high-
powered car which functions perfectly in reasonable weather on the
motorway; its performance in winter on poor roads is as yet unknown.

The main pillars in the structure of the West German economy are
the state, the employers or *Unternehmer*, the employees and, in an
ancillary capacity, the chambers of industry and trade.

In the Basic Law the state is implicitly charged with the duty of
applying such economic, financial and social measures as are necessary
to protect the economy and the interests of all parties involved in it.
Successive federal governments have shown considerable reluctance to
interfere in industry or in the relations between the various sectors,
yet periodically certain government measures have been taken. During
the 1950s, for example, the government supported the ailing Ruhr coal
industry and the textile industry. The federal ministers most closely
involved in the management of the economy are the *Bundesministerium
für Wirtschaft* (economics) and the *Bundesministerium der Finanzen*
(finance).

Banking

The chief agents of government intervention into the running of the
economy are the German Federal Bank, or *Deutsche Bundesbank*, in
Frankfurt and the Federal Cartel Office in Berlin. The *Deutsche
Bundesbank* has two duties: firstly, to manage monetary policy in such
a way that the currency is protected and the economic policies of the
government in power are strengthened; secondly, to supervise the
German banking system as a whole. In co-operation with the

government it fixes interest and discount rates and minimum reserve ratios, and lays down the principles of government credit and open-market operations. It also controls foreign trade payments, and is consulted by the government on any restrictions that might be placed on the movement of capital out of the Federal Republic or on transactions in foreign securities and gold. Its duty to supervise the commercial banking system, which is particularly important in view of the powerful role played by the banks in the West German economy, is primarily concerned with large-scale loans. In recent years the German Federal Bank has been preoccupied mainly with anti-inflationary measures. It has implemented a relatively uncompromising policy in this respect, which has meant allowing unemployment to rise from 1.1 per cent in 1972 to 4.5 per cent in 1977 in order to achieve the lowest inflation rate in Western Europe. Such measures are more acceptable in the FRG than in neighbouring countries because of the ingrained fear of inflation inherited from the 1920s and 1930s.

The main features of the West German banking system can usefully be noted at this point since they are closely connected with the functioning of industry. Unlike the British system which favours specialist banks, the German system is increasingly made up of 'universal banks' offering the full range of banking services under one roof, the leading banks of this type being the *Deutsche Bank*, the *Dresdner Bank* and the *Commerzbank*. The system of universal banking obviously has advantages for the business customer, who can save time and money by having all his transactions carried out by one branch of the same bank, and for the bank itself, which can spread its risk over a wider field of activities. On the other hand, the system brings two very serious disadvantages for a social market economy based on free competition and the plurality of interests: firstly, the universal banks represent an increasing concentration of financial power; secondly, the level of free competition is reduced. This has a serious effect on industry since it means that the banks, which have enormous industrial holdings, are in ultimate control of industrial policy. The freedom and flexibility of industry is restricted, since only those policies can be adopted which meet with the banks' approval (i.e. those which provide sound collateral) even though such policies may not be in the firm's long-term interests. There is no doubt that the powerful influence of the banks on industry is one of the factors contributing to the emphasis on the manufacturing sector, with its solid capital assets in the form of industrial plant, machinery, etc., and the corresponding neglect of the service industries the assets of which tend to be in a less tangible form and therefore less attractive to the cautious banker.

The apparent threat to competition in the financial world posed by the universal banks constitutes the kind of development noted and sometimes investigated by the Federal Cartel Office, which is empowered to investigate any branch or sector of industry and commerce in order to prevent the formation of monopolies. During the latter part of the nineteenth century German industry and banks tended strongly towards the formation of cartels, often with government encouragement. This tradition continued into the twentieth century when some of the most powerful of these groups supported Germany's military ambitions in 1914 and again in the late thirties. The founders of the Federal Republic therefore invested the Cartel Office with considerable statutory powers which it has used to the full since its inception. This has involved it in bitter and costly legal battles with firms under investigation, a fact which makes its activities unpopular with German industry in general. The tendency towards even larger industrial and commercial groupings has made the task of the Cartel Office more difficult — and more necessary — but has done little to add to its popularity.

Employers and Trade Unions

West German employers are organised into employers' associations (*Arbeitgeberverbände*) to represent their interests, particularly in negotiating with the trade unions and the government. Each association is made up of several specialised associations from different branches of industry or business. The most prominent *Arbeitgeberverbände* are the following:

Zentralverband des Deutschen Handwerks (handicrafts and trades)
Verband Deutscher Reeder (shipowners)
Zentralverband der Deutschen Seehafenbetriebe (port operators)
Bundesverband Deutscher Banken (banks)
Deutscher Sparkassen- und Giroverband (savings banks and giros)
Deutscher Hotel- und Gaststättenverband (hotels and catering)
Bundesverband des Deutschen Gross- und Aussenhandels (wholesale and export trade)
Hauptgemeinschaft des Deutschen Einzelhandels (retail trade)
Bundesverband der Deutschen Binnenschiffahrt (inland waterways transport)

Bundesverband des privaten Bankgewerbes (private banks)
Centralverband Deutscher Handelsvertreter- und Handelsmakler
   -verbände (agents and brokers)
Gesamtverband der Versicherungswirtschaft (insurance)
Zentralarbeitsgemeinschaft des Strassenverkehrsgwerbes (road
   transport).

Each of these *Verbände* is represented in the work of the two central
organisations, the *Bundesvereinigung der Deutschen Arbeitgeberverbände*,[1] which is particularly concerned with social questions affecting
the employers, e.g. the operation of industrial co-management, social
benefits, education, etc., and the *Bundesverband der Deutschen
Industrie*, which deals with economic questions and presents industry's
views to the government when new economic measures are under
consideration.

It will be readily appreciated that such a highly developed and well-
organised network of *Verbände* can exert severe pressure in political
circles since their leaders normally occupy influential positions or are in
frequent contact with members of government policy-making
committees. The *Verbände* are a conservative force in economic debates.
They argue that West Germany owes its present prosperity in large part
to the entrepreneurial energy of a relatively small group of men, the
Unternehmer, whose interests must be protected against untried
economic experiments. Consequently they see the extension of trade
union influence from the boardroom into economic policy making as a
threat to the initiative, independence and flexibility that has characterised West German industry for the last thirty years. On the other
hand, they see clear advantages in the present system of industrial
relations, providing it does not impede management's freedom to take
decisions.

The employees (*Arbeitnehmer*) are organised into trade unions
(*Gewerkschaften*). Collectively, the trade unions and the employers'
associations are often referred to as *die Sozialpartner*, i.e. partners
working towards the joint goal of economic prosperity within a social
and economic order which both accept. This concept fits well into the
theory of *soziale Marktwirtschaft*, though serious practical differences
of interpretation sometimes occur between the two partners, as for
example over the question of social security provisions. Here, the
employers regard the unions as trying to undermine the foundations of
a system which relies on rewarding success, while unions accuse
the employers of trying to adapt the system to their selfish interests by

minimising social provisions. The unions are organised according to industrial groupings, unlike the British unions which are based on trades and occupations. This organisational principle, which is summed up in the slogan *ein Betrieb − eine Gewerkschaft* (one factory − one union), has a clear advantage in that it makes for a simpler form of negotiations between the *Sozialpartner*. The fragmentation of industrial disputes which has bedevilled British industry since the Second World War is not a problem in West Germany. Nevertheless, the strong emphasis on majority interests has been criticised by German and foreign observers as a 'typically German' device to avoid open conflict between sectional interests. At its best this system offers a highly efficient and nationally advantageous system of industrial relations; at its worst, it could mean the suppression of the interests of smaller groups in favour of the majority, with enormous power vested in the hands of leading trade union functionaries who themselves are closely allied with state authority. Approximately 40 per cent of the West German workforce belongs to a trade union, compared to 50 per cent in the UK and only 22 per cent in France. Apart from the absence of any 'closed shop' agreements, there is a further fundamental difference between British and West German trade unions which throws some light on the way in which each regards itself and its place in society, namely that the West German union movement is not affiliated to any political party. It considers that the function of the unions is to fight independently for the rights and interests of the members, and fears that this independence would be weakened by any party political affiliations. Thus, while most British trade union members pay an automatic contribution to the Labour Party funds, there are no formal links whatsoever between the SPD and the West German unions.

The umbrella organisation for the trade unions is the *Deutscher Gewerkschaftsbund* (DGB), comprising the following 17 member unions with between them a total of approximately 7.5 million members out of a workforce of some 25 million:

Industriegewerkschaft (IG) Bau-Steine-Erden (building industry)
IG Bergbau und Energie (mining and energy)
IG Chemie-Papier-Keramik (chemicals, paper and ceramics)
IG Druck und Papier (printing and paper)
Gewerkschaft der Eisenbahner Deutschlands (railways)
Gewerkschaft Erziehung und Wissenschaft (education and science)
Gewerkschaft Gartenbau, Land- und Forstwirtschaft (horticulture, agriculture and forestry)

Gewerkschaft Handel, Banken und Versicherungen (commerce, banking and insurance)

Gewerkschaft Holz und Kunststoff (timber and synthetic materials)

Gewerkschaft Kunst (fine arts)

Gewerkschaft Leder (leather)

IG Metall (metal-working trades)

Gewerkschaft Nahrung-Genuss-Gaststätten (food, entertainment and catering)

Gewerkschaft Öffentliche Dienste, Transport und Verkehr (public services, transport and traffic)

Gewerkschaft der Polizei

Deutsche Postgewerkschaft (postal workers)

Gewerkschaft Textil-Bekleidung (textiles and clothing).

The structure of the DGB corresponds to the administrative structure of the federal state with three organisational levels, *Bund, Land* and the smaller subdivisions *Kreis*. The federal congress meets every three years to pass resolutions on matters of general policy. The *Land* districts, which are almost identical in their area with the federal *Länder*, also meet every three years and deal specifically with the economic and social policies of the respective *Land* as these affect their members. They also have a more practical role in co-ordinating the day-to-day work of the *Kreise*. The most powerful members of the DGB are those with the largest numbers of members and biggest contribution towards DGB funds, i.e. *IG Metall* and *Gewerkschaft Öffentliche Dienste, Transport und Verkehr*. The contribution made in this way amounts to 12 per cent of members' subscriptions. The DGB sees its main task as working for the social improvement of its members and the reduction of living costs, ensuring that wage levels keep up with prices, improving productivity and further extending worker participation in economic and industrial decision making. It also represents members' interests in holiday and educational provision and in housing projects. In fact, many well-known and widely advertised commercial undertakings in West Germany are run by the DGB. These include an insurance company (*Volksfürsorge*), a travel firm (*Gut-Reisen*) and three firms involved in the book trade and publishing (*Büchergilde Gutenberg, Bund Verlag* and *Europäische Verlagsanstalt*). There could be no clearer evidence of the DGB's acceptance of the mixed economy as the framework for its activities. Member unions of the DGB enjoy autonomy in negotiating with the employers in their industry, although they take DGB policy into account.

Alongside the DGB there are two other important union

organisations: the 'white-collar' *Deutsche Angestellten Gewerkschaft* (DAG) and the civil service union, *Deutscher Beamtenbund* (DBB). As a practical consequence of the policy of having a single union representing all the workers in each branch of industry, regardless of individual status, the membership of these three organisations has become increasingly mixed. Many *Angestellte*[2] belong to the DGB, while the DBB counts a significant number of both *Angestellte* and *Arbeiter* among its members.

Between the employers' associations and the trade unions stand the chambers of industry and commerce which exercise functions affecting both sides. Unlike the British chambers, the 69 West German chambers are corporations in public law and membership is compulsory for all the firms and businesses in their respective areas. They act in an advisory capacity towards government committees, the courts and other public institutions. When expert assessors are needed in legal, commercial or technical matters, the chambers provide them. One of their main functions is to supervise apprentice training and organise the trade examinations for journeymen and master craftsmen. Their influence in this area is so great that the trade unions have repeatedly tried to obtain representation in the relevant education committees but so far without success.

The chief subject of negotiation between the *Sozialpartner* is, of course, wages. This is covered by a special law, the *Tarifvertragsgesetz* (TVG) or wages contract law, which provides a framework for the *Tarifvertrag* or wages contract, worked out by unions and employers' associations, sometimes in conjunction with large individual employers. This document contains a statement of minimum standards, primarily in wages, but also in working conditions, holidays, gratuities, etc. In practice these minimum levels are exceeded, sometimes by a considerable margin — e.g. in recent years employers have tried to attract qualified staff to specialised positions by offering high salaries with a month's extra salary payable both at Christmas and for the summer holiday. Thus the continued success of West German industry, together with a long period of labour shortage, have made the unions' task in wage negotiation considerably easier than in other EEC countries. The negotiating parties usually stipulate that the *Tarifvertrag* shall be valid for a specified period, after which it is re-negotiated. The *Manteltarifvertrag* (blanket contract) is a long-term contract covering general arrangements, salary and wage classifications, incremental scales, piece-work, bonuses, etc., while the *Lohntarifvertrag* (wages contract) is restricted to wage rates over a short period, usually twelve months.

Co-determination in Industry

Since its formation in October 1949 the DGB has been keen to acquire
for its members a greater say in determining policies at all levels in the
social, political and economic fields. The importance the unions attach
to broad 'co-determination', or *Mitbestimmung*, sprang from the bitter
experience of the 1933—45 National Socialist period, when all the
unions were compulsorily integrated into the *Deutsche Arbeitsfront*, a
political tool manipulated by the ruling clique. By 1951—52 legislation
had been passed providing for the introduction of co-management in all
joint stock companies in the coal and steel industries with over 1,000
employees. This was known as the *Montanmitbestimmungsgesetz*. Since
1952 the *Montan* model of co-management has been modified and
supplemented in several respects. By 4 May 1976, after a decade of
intensive public discussion, a new co-management law had been passed
covering all joint stock companies with over 2,000 employees. In
practice, between 600 and 650 firms come within the scope of the law.
Building on the original model, this law requires all companies to form
a supervisory board (*Aufsichtsrat*) consisting of 12, 16 or 20 elected
members, depending on the size of the company. These boards are made
up of an equal number of employees' and shareholders' representatives.
The employees' representatives are further subdivided into members
who are directly employed by the company and members representing
the trade union. Thus, where six employees' representatives are present,
four will be employed by the company and two will be union
representatives; with eight employees' representatives the proportion is
6—2, and with ten it is 7—3. A chairman is elected who can use his
casting vote to decide issues on which no agreement can otherwise be
reached.

The board of management (*Vorstand*) is also included in the
provisions of the co-management legislation. This board consists of a
commercial director (*kaufmännischer Direktor*) and a technical director
(*technischer Direktor*) appointed directly by the company, together
with a labour director (*Arbeitsdirektor*), whose appointment has to be
approved by the employees' representatives on the supervisory board.
The labour director has special responsibility for protecting workers'
interests at management level.

The trade unions are not completely satisfied with the present state
of legislation, which they regard as a compromise. They point out that
the employers can still in practice appoint the chairman of the
Aufsichtsrat who will always use his casting vote in their favour. (If the

election for chairman does not achieve the required majority for any candidate, the employers appoint the chairman and the employees appoint the deputy chairman.) They also object to the compulsory appointment of a member of the senior management staff (*leitender Angestellter*) to one of the employees' seats on the *Aufsichtsrat*. The legislators maintain that this is the best possible arrangement: firstly, since emphasis must be on reaching agreement, not on confrontation; and secondly, since the *Arbeitsdirektor* has a powerful additional voice in decision making on behalf of the employees. Regarding the representatives from senior management, the legislators point out that such a member can contribute much to the efficiency of the *Aufsichtsrat* through his proven organisational and technical skill and, furthermore, that as an employee of the company he shares the same interests as other sections of the staff. The employers' associations for their part tend to dismiss this union objection as rooted in the class warfare attitudes of a bygone age which have no place in the social market economy based on partnership within a mutually acceptable industrial framework.

Relations between the management and the unions within the individual companies are governed by the *Betriebsverfassungsgesetz*, or works' constitution law, abbreviated *BetrVG*. The principle on which this legislation rests is that since economic decisions taken by the management have a profound effect on the lives of the employees, it is essential for the latter, through their representatives, to participate in the decision-making process. *Mitbestimmung* is exercised in each firm through the *Betriebsrat* (works' council) which is elected for a period of three years by the employees and supported in its work by the relevant trade union. The number of representatives on the *Betriebsrat* is fixed in proportion to the number of workers in the firm. The employers and the *Betriebsrat* meet once a month to settle their differences. Both sides regard it as their primary objective to maintain industrial harmony, so that many of the trivial local disputes which could otherwise interrupt production are settled on the spot. The *Betriebsrat* has to be consulted in matters affecting the employment of new staff, transfer and dismissal of personnel, and factory closures. It participates in decisions affecting working hours, breaks, holiday arrangements, social amenities, entitlement to company housing, and working regulations. In firms with over 100 employees an 'economic committee' is formed with the task of keeping the *Betriebsrat* informed about relevant economic matters. Where agreement cannot be reached, there is provision for the dispute to be heard by an industrial court.[3] Members of the *Betriebsrat* are legally entitled to release from their duties in order to attend courses which will enable them to carry out their function more efficiently.

The most important protective legislation for the employee is contained in three laws:

1. *die Arbeitszeitordnung* (regulation of working hours);
2. *das Kündigungsschutzgesetz* (law on protection against dismissal);
3. *das Bundesurlaubsgesetz* (federal law regulating holidays).

Working hours are based on the eight-hour day, five-day week, with special provisions for certain occupations, e.g. bakers, nurses and drivers. Because of the five-day week in industry, the schools have come under pressure from parents to change over to a five-day system — a good example of school reform brought about by non-educational factors.[4] 'Flexitime' (*gleitende Arbeitszeit*) is widely accepted in West German offices and, within practical limits, in industry. Where a dismissal is being considered for any reason, the management must inform the *Betriebsrat* and take note of its views; it does not, however, require the agreement of that body to the dismissal. Periods of notice vary according to status and length of service. Apart from instant dismissal, which can only be imposed for the most serious reasons, periods of notice vary from a minimum of two weeks for unskilled workers with less than five years' service, to six months for senior managers with twelve or more years' service. Regarding holiday entitlements, the law provides for a minimum of 18 working days per year, though there are few employees in West Germany who do not receive considerably more than this. Like other industrial nations the FRG has been suffering from increased unemployment in recent years. In 1975 unemployment reached over one million for the first time in 17 years. In 1978 it totalled 864,243 of whom 22,420 were university graduates, including several thousand engineers. In the same year there were over 1.8 million foreigners employed in the FRG.

Foreign Trade

Almost half of Germany's economic wealth is produced by its manufacturing industry. The gross national product is made up as shown in Table 4.1.[5] The structure of the manufacturing industry is revealed by a comparison of the most important exports and imports as shown in Table 4.2.

Table 4.1: Contributions of Different Sectors to GNP in 1977

	%
Commodity-producing industries	47.8
Services (including banking)	21.4
Trade and transport	14.9
The state	13.2
Agriculture and forestry	2.7

Table 4.2: Main Commodities in Foreign Trade of FRG 1978

	Exports	Imports
1	Machinery	Oil
2	Vehicles	Agricultural produce
3	Chemicals	Chemicals
4	Electrical goods	Food products
5	Iron and steel	Electrical goods
6	Food products	Vehicles

Source: *Die Zeit*, 27 April 1979.

Among the highest export earners are mechanical engineering and the machine tool industry. Surprisingly for a country which has been forced to introduce a vigorous policy of rationalisation as a result of increasing labour costs, the West German mechanical engineering industry is still based on relatively small firms, many only family businesses, which can specialise in purpose-built products and react quickly to market demands. This branch of the export industry is energy-intensive and its overheads have been drastically increased by rising fuel costs. Between 1972 and 1974 payments for oil imports trebled as a result of the oil crisis which clearly demonstrated Germany's vulnerability to this kind of pressure from OPEC countries. Its depencence on overseas supplies is aggravated by the fact that it has few North Sea oil reserves worth developing, while it imports large quantities of natural gas from the Soviet Union and Algeria. The capacity of the coal industry was reduced during the years when oil was cheaply available and would consequently need massive investment if it were to be revived on a large scale. The obvious answer to the energy problem seems to be the development of nuclear power stations. The leading manufacturer of nuclear plant, *Kraftwerk Union*, has had considerable success in its programme of research and development, and has even managed to secure large and often politically controversial overseas orders for its products. The building of nuclear power stations in West Germany has, however, been powerfully opposed by environmental groups which have turned an apparently seductive economic solution into a major political controversy. In 1977 3.1 per cent of the FRG's energy was provided by nuclear power. This compared with 4 per cent in the UK, 3.7 per cent in the USA, 2.7 per cent in France and 1.9 per cent in Japan.

The dependence on external sources of energy is matched by an almost total reliance on the export industry coupled with a relative neglect of the service sector. Admittedly, the West German export industry has been remarkably successful, not only in selling goods to North America and to its EEC partners, which took 7.9 and 49.1 per cent respectively of the FRG's exports in 1978, but also to the Comecon countries and, under especially favourable credit arrangements, to the GDR. France is the FRG's best customer, followed by Holland and Benelux. Since 1974 the same energy has been devoted to an export campaign in the Middle East, with excellent results. Nevertheless, this increasingly heavy reliance on exports is viewed with some disquiet by German economists and accounts for their interest in the economic and industrial health of EEC customers, to the extent of providing generous credits to support their industries.

The service industries cannot meet the demands placed on them by a population with the highest purchasing power in Europe, if not in the world, and a relatively short working week. A large proportion of the staff of the hotel and entertainment industries is made up of foreign workers, while holidays in Germany are expensive for Germans and foreign tourists alike. This imbalance affects not only German industry, but also that of the customer nations who are encouraged by German spending habits to specialise in services and luxury goods for the lucrative German market while neglecting their own technical development.

Traditionally German industry has shown little enthusiasm for investing in manufacturing plant abroad. The reasons for this may well lie in recent history; German overseas investments were confiscated after the First and Second World Wars. They may also lie in a distrust of the standards and industrial practices of other countries. Rising labour and fuel costs together with severe competition in certain industries have, however, forced some firms to examine the prospects for shifting production to overseas bases, thereby reducing labour costs and transport overheads to customer countries. This tendency is particularly marked in the chemical industry which has keenly felt the rise in labour costs and has greatly increased its investment in the USA. The electrical concern Siemens, the FRG's biggest private employer (the biggest employer is the state itself through the Post Office and federal railways), now employs approximately 98,000 of its staff abroad, out of a total staff of 319,000. Volkswagen, with a total workforce of 192,000, employs approximately 59,000 abroad. The chemical concerns Bayer and Hoechst, which between them employ approximately 351,000 workers, have 150,000 of them overseas. On the whole this policy has worked well for such giant concerns, but for some smaller specialist firms the results have been less encouraging; for example, the well-known camera manufacturer Rollei set up an assembly plant in Singapore in the early seventies in an attempt to meet over-whelming Japanese competition but has achieved only moderate results. The main beneficiaries of West German investments in 1977 were, in order: USA, Benelux, France, Switzerland, Brazil, Canada and Holland.

While Japanese exports have not made the same devastating inroads into traditional West German markets which they have inflicted on the British, there are certain branches of West German industry which have been hard pressed by Japanese pricing policy and the improving quality of Japanese precision engineering products. Apart from the photographic industry, the most seriously affected have been shipbuilding and, as a direct result, the steel industry. Realising that they could not match the Japanese on low wage costs, the West German shipbuilders did not compete with them for orders for supertankers during the supertanker boom of the sixties, but concentrated instead on special-purpose vessels, e.g. roll-on ferries to meet the needs of the expanding inter-national road haulage industry. Unfortunately, the general recession in shipbuilding has inflicted the same problems on German shipyards as on all other West European yards, and the German shipbuilding industry is now one of the weakest sectors of the industrial economy. Faced with the possibility of rising unemployment among skilled engineering and metal workers, some politicians seem to favour a more liberal policy towards arms sales, thus allowing for some expansion in other sectors of the engineering industry and to some extent counteracting shipyard redundancies. There is no doubt that West Germany could increase its arms sales enormously if it were to relax its declared policy of selling only to NATO partners. German arms are in big demand, but since it is likely that the most interested customers would include some of the world's less reputable governments, and also because of the historical associations of the German arms industry, the federal government has so far preferred to avoid the inevitable political complications.

One particularly interesting and controversial aspect of West German foreign trade in which politics and economics are inextricably intertwined is its heavy involvement in trading with Comecon in general and the GDR in particular. Inter-German trade is based on the so-called 'Swing credit' system which permits the GDR to overdraw its import credit account with the FRG at a favourable rate of interest. As a result West Germany has become the GDR's second biggest trading partner after the Soviet Union, and the GDR's foreign trade turnover with West Germany exceeds its total turnover with all other Western industrial nations combined. In the decade 1967–77 inter-German trade turnover increased by 300 per cent, with West German exports consistently exceeding imports from the GDR. Since the GDR, being chronically short of convertible currency, prefers to import advanced technology in return for raw materials or low-grade manufactured goods by way of 'compensation deals', many conservative politicians, disquieted by what they regard as a wholesale transfer of modern technology from West to East, have strongly objected to this inter-German trade as a suicidal policy of providing the enemy with the tools to undermine West German industrial capacity. On the other hand, there are certain political reasons which make inter-German trade interesting to the federal government: firstly, the existence of the special trading arrangements is an admission in fact by the GDR that a special relationship exists between the two German states, however much it may formally insist that it regards the FRG as a foreign country; secondly, the reliance by East German industry on West German technological products is a valuable means of exerting pressure if this should ever become necessary; thirdly, the GDR has provided a constant flow of welcome orders for West German industry during the prolonged recession following the oil crisis.

The FRG has been able to exploit the high reputation of German engineering in Eastern Europe, which was built up early in the century, to become the world's leading East–West trader. The value of the FRG's exports to the Soviet Union amounts to about one-third of the value of those to the USA, while the total value of its exports to the Soviet Union, Poland, Czechoslovakia and Hungary approximates to five-sixths of the value of exports to the USA, and almost equals the value of exports to the UK. This evidence of growing reliance on Comecon for the kind of large-scale industrial orders which keep the engineering sector working at full capacity is regarded with caution by many German politicians. Apart from the self-destructive nature of such a policy, they suspect that Moscow's keenness to buy West German industrial plant is part of a long-term strategy to exert more influence on the prize it covets — West German industrial and technological capacity. Supporters of East—West trade, and particularly of inter-German trade arrangements, regard these fears as exaggerated. They maintain that trading with the GDR is the most effective way of keeping alive the dialogue with the ruling SED party and therefore of obtaining a greater degree of freedom for the population of the GDR. They also point out that the West's technological lead in the industrial sector is so great, partly for historical reasons, but mainly because of the clumsy and inflexible Comecon planning and management systems, that West Germany has nothing to fear from its heavy participation in trade with the Communist bloc.

The 'Economic Miracle'

Whatever reservations may be expressed about the West German economy, particularly by nervous German economists and industrialists who, in the view of their neighbours, tend to exaggerate the mildest symptom of malfunctioning into a grave economic malady, it must be admitted that West Germany has had a remarkably successful economic development. Until the recession of 1966—67 and the first oil crisis some six years later, it was relatively easy to list the factors which were generally acknowledged to have played a part in the country's economic ascent. These included the following:

1. The generous terms of the Marshall Aid programme which was operated by the US government after the Second World War enabled West Germany to get off to a good start by building new factories and equipping them with modern machinery. In this respect the Allied bombing raids during the war, which razed whole areas in the industrial cities, simplified the work of creating new industry.

2. The wretched physical and material conditions in which the Germans found themselves in 1945 sparked off a general will to work for improvements as soon as possible. Work was the only immediate distraction from the surrounding misery and offered the only long-term prospect for a better life in the future. In spite of the heavy losses

inflicted on the German population during the war, there was still a considerable reserve of skilled manpower which was augmented throughout the fifties by refugees from East Germany and expellees from the German territories east of the Oder–Neisse frontier.

3. The system of *soziale Marktwirtschaft* gave full scope to the businessman or craftsman who was willing to work hard and take risks for the sake of high profits. Furthermore, its early success quickly gathered momentum and the majority of West Germans identified themselves with its values.

4. The system of industrial relations was efficiently geared up to the needs of a rapidly expanding economy which needed to invest a large proportion of its profits. The trade unions very rarely resorted to militant tactics and wage demands were low throughout the fifties. This is partly attributable to the workforce's acceptance of the government's economic strategy, partly to the historic fear of inflation in Germany and, to some extent, to the fact that most Germans who had lived through the National Socialist period were not used to the idea of pressing demands on those in authority over them, whether employers, trade union leaders or the government itself. Moreover, after the vicissitudes of the twenties and thirties and the horrors of the Second World War, the pace of improvement seemed so rapid that they felt that further demands were simply excessive. It is probably untrue to suppose, as many do, that the German worker exerts himself more than his foreign counterparts to achieve his high productivity levels. Any such assertion must account for the fact that the VW assembly lines in Wolfsburg are manned largely by Italian workers who, according to popular notions, have a very different attitude to work from the average German. The explanation probably lies in relatively recent historical factors, e.g. in the national pride in quality products and the readiness to identify with the firm and its interests, in the well-established and well-regulated system of vocational training which offers status and incentive to the skilled tradesman, and chiefly in the indisputable German talent for organisation. The British observer will note with interest that labour demarcation disputes and restrictive practices do not exist in West German industry, thanks to the principle of having only one union representing the workforce in each factory.

5. During the late nineteenth and early twentieth centuries Germany had developed an efficient export trade supported by a proper

professional training for staff engaged in the export sales and forward-
ing business. This tradition was resumed with great success, chiefly on
the basis of high quality and reliability, prompt deliveries and keen
prices, but also indirectly assisted by the dilatoriness of West Germany's
competitors in booming world markets. In the early post-war years the
keenness to export was also probably influenced by West Germany's
desire to be accepted as a partner by the other Western nations, though
this political consideration was certainly not the chief incentive for the
entrepreneurs and export salesmen who were actively engaged in selling
goods abroad.

6. Although the FRG had to pay considerable occupation costs for US,
British and French forces within her territory, it was not burdened with
overseas defence expenditure which has weakened the dollar and the
pound. In addition, it gained from the considerable amount of military
expenditure made directly or indirectly in the FRG by foreign
governments which was not charged to the occupation costs. Between
1955 and 1964 the FRG's cumulative net balance on government
invisibles (mostly military) was favourable to the extent of £2,600
million.[6] Finally, right up to the 1980s, West Germany has spent less
of its gross domestic product on defence than has either Britain or the
USA.

These, then, are some of the traditional explanations offered to
account for West Germany's economic success until the late sixties.
Since that time the success has remained undiminished but, as a result
of internal and external political and economic changes, West Germany
has had to come to terms with a new set of factors, in particular rising
labour costs at home, the increasing value of the DM which has added
to the cost of exports, and the consequences of the oil crisis. Over the
last decade the unions have tended to press for higher wage increases
than they did previously, in addition to which expenditure on social
services has more than doubled since 1970 under the SPD government.
This was accompanied by an inexorable rise in the value of the DM
which some German commentators tended to regard less as the price of
success than as the fault of the weaker currencies, an argument which
seemed to ignore the connection between the flourishing German
export trade and the failing currencies of the competitors. Nevertheless,
the fact that German exports have continued to rise shows that a good
deal of effort has been put into finding ways of overcoming these new
problems. Ironically, the disadvantage of high export costs has been

turned into an advantage in that it forced German manufacturers to concentrate on the kind of technical excellence for which customers are willing to pay high prices, rather than merely selling on the basis of low prices as did their competitors.

After three successful decades many Germans are asking themselves what the future holds in economic terms. Can the forces which have made such a signal contribution to the present prosperity be expected to continue working in the country's favour, or are there changes in the offing which could radically affect West Germany's economic supremacy? It would be unwise to try to predict the way in which the German economy will develop, but there are a number of areas of concern which can be mentioned briefly here.

As we have seen, the economy is based on a manufacturing industry which grew rapidly during the early fifties. The factories and the heavy machinery and production lines which were installed in those years are now at least twenty years old, and industrialists are beginning to wonder not only whether this will act as a short-term disadvantage, but also whether present profitability, acting as a disincentive to new investment, will retard technological development in the long term. Economic forecasts made by private research institutes in the early seventies indicated that French industry was rapidly catching up with West German industry in most respects – which came as a shock to the majority of Germans – and that in the application of advanced technology it was at least equal to West German standards and could be expected to overtake West Germany as Europe's main industrial manufacturer in the future. Whatever the accuracy and value of such forecasting, it certainly drew attention in West Germany to the problem of industrial obsolescence. The message was reinforced after the oil crisis in 1973 by the example of the mighty North American car industry which was forced by fuel economy measures, actual and threatened, to start rejigging its production lines for the manufacture of smaller cars. The huge investments required in an operation of this kind have brought lucrative orders to the West German machine tool industry, which, though welcome in the short term to individual manufacturers, are indicative of the way in which currently profitable industries can suddenly find themselves obsolete through neglecting to take long-term precautions.

As has already been shown, the West German economy is based on the manufacture and export of industrial goods, while the service sector is relatively undeveloped. The nature of the problem this presents is made clear by an examination of the trade balance and the amounts

Table 4.3: Trade Balance of FRG 1970—77

Visible Trade Balance	1970	1971	1972	1973	1974	1975	1976	1977
	15.7	15.9	20.3	33.0	50.8	37.3	34.5	38.4
Deduct: Services, transfers, supplementary items	12.5	12.8	17.8	21.5	25.7	27.8	26.0	29.7
Current A/c Balance	3.2	3.1	2.5	11.5	25.1	9.5	8.5	8.7

Source: Bundesministerium fur Wirtschaft, *Leistung in Zahien '77* (Bonn, 1978), pp. 71—3. Figures in billions DM.

deducted for services. The rising tendency of payments for services, transfers and supplementary items is a cause for some concern since it increases the pressure on manufacturing industry to export more each year in order to pay for the necessary services. This in turn makes it more difficult to restructure industry in order to restore the balance between manufacturing and services. This restructuring problem is aggravated by the traditional reluctance of the German banks to provide investment capital for industries not producing tangible commodities. In recent years strenuous efforts have been made by AEG, Siemens and several smaller companies to build up the West German computer and micro-electronics industry in an attempt to redress the balance with a view to exporting service products, particularly to the North American market. Apart from specific projects of this type, it is recognised that West Germany will have to concentrate more on selling 'know-how', mainly in the form of licences for the manufacture of its products in other countries, in order to increase its service earnings. This practice, common in British industry because of bad domestic labour relations, has so far been neglected by the Germans who have preferred to import the services of foreign workers. The remittances made by these workers back to their home countries are one of the main debit items in the trade balance and the situation will not be improved until Germany can reduce its foreign labour requirements by limiting the scope of its manufacturing industry at home.

The problem of Germany's long-term energy supplies has already been touched on. In 1979 West Germany had a current account deficit of DM 9 billion (£2.24 billion) compared with a DM 17.6 billion surplus in 1978. The situation in 1980 is likely to be worse. The main reason for this deficit was the large bill for oil and raw materials. The fact that Western Europe's leading industrial nation is also the most vulnerable to energy shortages is worrying not only to the Germans themselves, who would be the first to suffer, but also to Germany's neighbours, who are not happy about the prospect of a Federal Republic excessively dependent on certain OPEC states or on Comecon supplies. The deal between the steel and engineering concern of Krupp and the Shah of Iran, whereby the latter invested heavily in return for technical exports and know-how, was generally regarded as a beneficial arrangement to both sides: subsequent events have amply illustrated the inherent dangers of such arrangements, and it is now generally appreciated that deals of this kind, entered into for the sake of short- and medium-term interests, could seriously threaten West German industrial independence. This vulnerability to shortages of both fuels and raw materials is also one of the influences affecting the FRG's role in foreign affairs, which its neighbours tend to regard as being altogether too mild and ineffective for a country with such economic strength.

West Germany also harbours certain reservations about its neighbours. For example, since it exports half its industrial production to EEC partners, it would be badly affected by the type of protective policies which have occasionally been debated in Britain and other countries at times when vital industries are seen to be floundering under pressure from foreign imports. If France, Italy and Britain were seriously to reduce their imports of West German engineering products, the largest single currency earner, the effects would be felt immediately in the form of unemployment and a drop in the balance of payments. Exporters and importers are thus seen to be mutually dependent, but in the long term the consequences for the highly specialised exporter could be more serious than for his customers. Another potential threat to the West German economy is the Eurocommunist movement in France and Italy. If a major share of power were to fall to either of these parties in a future election, it is feared that their economic policies, e.g. large-scale nationalisation, would at the very least retard the pace of industrial growth and deprive the FRG of a major customer.

Perhaps the most important problem of all, since it affects the very foundations of the West German system, is the uncertainty about the effects which a prolonged period of economic recession would have on a society which has experienced only success and increasing prosperity since its inception. Could democracy in West Germany survive an industrial slump, widespread unemployment, a high rate of inflation? How would the unions react to such a situation? Would they continue to enjoy the support of their members, or would they be rejected in favour of leaders with more radical solutions. Is democracy in West

Germany based solely on affluence, as some would have us believe? An attempt to answer these questions would go well beyond the scope of a chapter on the economy and into the realm of political speculation. However, the mere enumeration of such questions indicates that, in spite of — or perhaps because of — its enormous success, the West German economy has still to prove its resilience in changing circumstances.

Further Reading

Anker-Oring, Aake. *Betriebsdemokratie* (Frankfurt/M, 1971)

Balfour, Michael. *West Germany* (London, 1980)

Cullingford, E. C. M. *Trade Unions in West Germany* (London, 1976)

Hallet, Graham. *The Social Economy of West Germany* (London, 1973)

———. *Housing and Land Policies in West Germany and Britain* (London, 1977)

Schneider, Dieter and Kuda, Rudolf F. *Mitbestimmung Weg zur industriellen Demokratie?* (Munich, 1969)

Spiro, H. J. *The Politics of German Co-determination* (Cambridge, Mass., 1958)

Vogel, Frank. *German Business after the Economic Miracle* (London, 1973)

Wallich, Henry C. *Mainsprings of the German Revival* (New Haven, 1955)

Winkel, Harold. *Die deutsche Wirtschaft seit Kriegsende Entwicklung und Probleme* (Mainz, 1971)

Notes

1. Dr Hanns-Martin Schleyer, the president of this association, was kidnapped by terrorists on 5 September 1977 and later murdered.

2. See pp. 92–93 below.

3. Cf. pp. 163–165 below.

4. Cf. p. 115 below.

5. Bundesministerium für Wirtschaft, *Leistung in Zahlen '77* (Bonn, 1978), p. 46.

6. Michael Balfour, *West Germany* (London, 1968, 1980), p. 176.

5 CLASSES, WEALTH AND SOCIAL SECURITY

Industrialisation and affluence have brought to West Germany the same and similar problems as those experienced throughout the prosperous countries of Western Europe. In a society which frequently requires the individual to move for the sake of promotion and which permits a high measure of social mobility, it is not to be wondered at that family ties have loosened and that the extended family no longer plays any significant part in the lives of most West Germans. This is not to say that contacts are not maintained, but simply that the family is no longer so influential in determining the individual's way of life, standards or ambitions. Births, marriages and deaths are the only occasions which bring families briefly together, while the high divorce rate seems to indicate some impatience with an institution rooted in a set of loyalties which are apparently no longer appropriate in a modern industrial society. Like his British counterpart, the modern German experiencing personal, professional or financial difficulties would be more likely to go for help to a professional counsellor than to a member of his own family, while at the same time the federal government and other organisations see it as an increasingly important part of their task to offer the kind of support which until quite recently was confined to the family.

Another result of industrialisation is the gradual merging of town and country which has brought about the loss of many distinctive features and, in some ways, has blurred regional differences. The strength of regional affinities and local loyalties seems to vary in West Germany according to whether the area is Catholic or Protestant, rural or industrial, and whether certain local specialisms are present, e.g. a seaport or an ancient industry. The material standards enjoyed in country districts are the same in all important aspects as those of the towns and cities, which is a further levelling factor. As factory-based industry has moved into the countryside it has brought the working rhythms of the industrial city with it. Factory workers in the country develop the same attitudes to their work as their urban counterparts, while the villages in which they live gradually lose their separate identities as the village schools are closed and the children are 'bussed' to a *Mittelpunktschule*[1] in the neighbouring town.

As in Britain, church membership and formal religion play a less important role than they used to do, although regional variations are wide. The number of church marriages and baptisms has steadily decreased since the last war, while the number of people formally relinquishing church membership took a very steep rise in the decade 1966–75. Twice during this period the federal government introduced legislation to levy a higher rate of income tax; since a church tax (*Kirchensteuer*) is also levied on all those who have not formally relinquished church membership, it seems probable that many people preferred to retain a higher proportion of their income than to continue as members of the church. This movement was more pronounced in the industrial conurbations than in rural areas, and the Protestant Church lost more members than the Catholic Church. To go through the formal procedure of relinquishing church membership and thus gaining exemption from *Kirchensteuer* was, until relatively recently, regarded as an extreme course of action embarked on mainly for reasons of conscience — and not without the risk of some social stigma. That the movement away from the church could develop so rapidly within a single decade is a remarkable reflection of changing social values within the FRG.

As a country which enjoys a very high standard of living, West Germany has not been spared the kind of social problems generally regarded as the concomitants of affluence. Whether at home in lavishly equipped flats, or on holiday with their complete range of camping gear, West Germans show an increasing tendency to separate themselves from the rest of the community during leisure hours. At the same time there is a gradual rise in the crime rate, particularly among young people of both sexes. Universal education has cut across social barriers and enabled many West Germans to move into positions which would formerly have been closed to them; at the same time, those who fail in the educational system suffer severe disadvantages as there is little room or reward for them in the affluent West German society. It is notable that 80 per cent of young offenders failed to complete their schooling satisfactorily and 55 per cent of adult offenders have no professional training of any kind. Such symptoms as these, and the complaints about the depressing anonymity of life in a modern industrial society as business and industry is organised into ever larger units, are as familiar to West Germans as they are to the British. What, then, are the specifically German features which we should bear in mind when trying to understand current events in the FRG?

Of fundamental importance is Germany's unique and violent

history during the first part of the present century, from the aftermath of which the Federal Republic was created. Although a generation has now grown up in post-war conditions, history still weighs heavily on West German society in many ways. Approximately one-third of the present population spent at least some of its formative years in the National Socialist state, with all its brutal over-simplifications, only to be clumsily 're-educated' by the Allies according to their particular version of democracy. A smaller proportion of the population consists of expellees from the former eastern provinces of the German Reich which were annexed by the Soviet Union and Poland in 1945, and refugees from the GDR who crossed over the frontier during the austerity period of 'socialist reconstruction' in the fifties. Many of these people have lived under Fascism, Communism and capitalism in succession and eagerly accept the high standard of living and the freedom from state interference offered by the FRG. The existing order should not, in their view, be subjected to experimentation, nor should proven leaders be cast aside in favour of the lesser known, however attractive their ideas might sound to the younger generation. Such attitudes have provoked hostility and accusations of political apathy in recent years and have contributed to the peculiarly uneasy relationship between the generations in West Germany.

In this connection it is interesting to note that the proximity of the GDR, and the fact that many West Germans have relatives there, exercises some influence on social attitudes. For many it stands as a grim warning of what could happen in the FRG; for others the comparison between living standards in the two German states is a reason for pride in West German achievement; for a small minority it is a model to be imitated. For all sections of society it provides an instant first-hand comparison of life under Communism and capitalism which is unique in Western Europe, though its effects are difficult to assess fully or accurately.

Another characteristic which distinguishes West Germany from its neighbours is its acute self-criticism in its contacts with outsiders. This is partly the continuation of a tradition of over-willing acceptance of foreign cultural models, partly a result of recent history, and probably also connected with the FRG's contemporary role as a kind of model industrial welfare state. Articles on the foreigner's view of the FRG are regularly published in the serious press, as are readers' letters deploring the extensive use of foreign words, usually English, in advertising. This preoccupation with the external image is accompanied by a quick impatience with relatively minor flaws which may be identified in the institutions or administration of the country. This lack of pragmatic tolerance and of confidence that the system will mature and overcome current problems seems to lend a peculiar brittleness to the more public aspects of West German society.

Social Class

There is little agreement among German sociologists about the class structure of the FRG. Indeed, some would reject from the outset the notion that social divisions in the FRG are based on class at all. In general, however, two main theories predominate: the theory derived from Marx which sets out to prove the existence of two more or less antagonistic classes; and the theory that the FRG is a pluralistic society in which the interests of diverse groups can be tolerated and balanced against each other.

As anyone with a slight acquaintance of the late-nineteenth- and early-twentieth-century German novel will know, German society before the First World War was highly authoritarian. The extreme attitudes portrayed in Fontane's *Effi Briest*, or in Heinrich Mann's *Der Untertan*, now belong firmly to the past; yet, in spite of years of student unrest in the late sixties and early seventies, a strong emphasis on discussion and freedom of expression in education, enthusiasm for anti-authoritarian kindergartens, sex education programmes and feminist movements, West German society still retains certain basically authoritarian attitudes. In public life considerable deference is shown towards the powers of office, however humble the office might be, while at the same time a remarkable degree of contempt is reserved for authority once discredited. The university professor is traditionally a respected figure in Germany, enjoying the highest social prestige among all professional groups and representing state authority in cultural politics; it was logical, therefore, that the most virulent and excessive attacks should have been directed against the whole professorial concept during the period of student unrest. Or again, at about the same time, when public confidence was lost in the Federal President Heinrich Lübke, he became the butt of a continuous and apparently spontaneous stream of 'Lübke-jokes'. However justified this may have been, it must strike the outsider as remarkable to witness a whole nation actively ridiculing its head of state, and tempt him to interpret it as one aspect of established attitudes towards authority.

In recent years the protagonists of the women's movement have conducted a lively debate on the position of women in German society which they regard as having suffered as a result of the traditional authoritarian attitudes being weighted in favour of men. German women are in a very similar situation to French and British women as regards their position before the law, in their professional life and in the opportunities open to them. Approximately one-third of women of working age in these countries are in full-time employment, yet only 4–7 per cent are self-employed, while 25–30 per cent are employed in industry and 60–70 per cent in the service industries. The most spectacular and symbolic act of recent legislation on women's rights was the reform of the hotly disputed Paragraph 218 of the Federal Criminal Code referring to the termination of pregnancy. Since June 1976 abortions for medical reasons have been legal and relatively easy to obtain in view of the broad definitions used in the relevant legislation. A variety of problems remains, as the industrial recession and accompanying unemployment since 1973 have shown. The fact that women are generally not as well qualified as men excludes them from many professions and occupations and hinders their promotion. Their careers are also limited by their husband's work — for example, the need for him to move for promotion — and by their domestic commitments. It is also widely felt that women tend to be politically and socially inactive and unaware of their rights under the social security legislation, and various federal projects are under way with the aim of removing these disadvantages. Whether these constraints are due to ingrained male authoritarianism in West German society, as some of the women's leaders maintain, or to natural and economic exigencies, remains to be seen.

However we interpret the various groupings or classes in West German society, one fact is clear: West Germany has no 'establishment' in the British sense. There is no hereditary class in the FRG which is characterised by its background, accent, school and university, and membership of particular clubs, or which is represented in many leading positions in politics, industry and the professions. Nor is there much evidence of the strong class consciousness which typifies British life and is based on a long and uninterrupted tradition. The class divisions of the pre-1914 era have been destroyed by two world wars and replaced by other more recent divisions based on the FRG's view of itself as a *Leistungsgesellschaft*, a society in which achievement and efficiency are the main determinants. Thus, an individual's social position depends on a variety of factors including his level of education and professional qualification, his function in the organisation to which he belongs, his membership of certain prestigious professions — e.g. university professor, medical consultant — and perhaps chiefly on his success in business, especially if this is reinforced with external signs of wealth. Class antagonisms in the Marxist sense appear to play little if any part in West German public life, nor are they appealed to by any of the main political parties. *Der deutsche Michel*, the traditional symbol of Germany in political cartoons, persists in the West German press as a figure with whom the whole nation can identify regardless of social position. By contrast, John Bull is rarely seen in the British press, perhaps because most readers feel he is an outdated figure who never stood for the majority in any case. It is also important to note in this connection that the West German trade unions regard themselves as the partners of industrial enterprises, not as primarily working-class institutions set up to defend the interests of their members against exploitation. This difference of emphasis is reflected in the fact that it is difficult to distinguish between the appearance and personal characteristics of trade union leaders and the representatives of senior management who sit opposite them at the negotiating table.

Instead of an establishment, West German society seems to have developed a number of separate elites, or relatively small groups of highly qualified individuals, in different areas, who wield power and influence disproportionate to their size. According to this view the key elite is made up of the leading politicians of government and opposition, surrounded by a wide range of groups including economic elites (bankers and chairmen of large industrial undertakings), organisational and administrative elites (chairmen of the various associations in industry and commerce,[2] trade union leaders, senior civil service administrators), legal elites (senior judges, leading government officials, senior police officials), and intellectual and cultural elites (writers, artists and critics whose works dominate public interest). A number of surveys have been carried out in an attempt to define the characteristics of the elite groups and their members and, although many conflicting results have been presented, it is generally agreed that the elites are made up almost entirely of men from a middle-class Protestant background who have reached a high level in academic qualification, usually in law. It is pointed out that the elites are exclusive, both in their membership and in their interests, and that there is little intermingling between them. This presents a direct contrast to the practice of the British establishment, where individual members are often simultaneously represented both in politics and in industry or commerce. The extent to which these elite groups control or influence events is very difficult to assess in precise terms, partly because they are informal groups whose activities are impossible to monitor, and partly because their influence is, in the nature of things, exerted unobtrusively. The obvious exception to this pattern consists of the intellectual and cultural elites whose influence is exercised directly on the public through creative works and critical reaction. A good example of this in recent years was the way in which the writer Heinrich Böll was able to polarise public opinion in the FRG through his writings and public statements on the Springer press.

However influential the elite groups might be, they make up an infinitely small proportion of the population and, since it is practically impossible for the average West German to enter their ranks, they are remote from everyday life. For many West Germans it is a more practical and attainable ambition to aim at a career in the public service, to become a *Beamte*. The prestige of the *Beamte*, of being appointed into the service of the state, is rooted in the hierarchical world of pre-1914 Germany, and the fact that it lingers on is due in part to the fact that the apparatus and traditions of the civil service have maintained a high level of continuity in spite of two world wars and the drastic social changes which ensued. West Germans can, with justification, still regard their civil service as incorporating the Prussian virtues of thoroughness and incorruptibility, and to be a *Beamte* is in itself a recommendation of trustworthiness and good character. The translation of the word into English as 'civil servant' or 'official' may well prevent English speakers from fully appreciating the role of the *Beamte* in West German society; he is generally regarded as a pillar of the existing order and as one who enjoys absolute security together with ideal working conditions, career prospects and related benefits.

The division of society into *Beamte, Angestellte* (white-collar workers) and *Arbeiter* (manual workers), as is regularly done for administrative purposes — e.g. in connection with social security schemes — is ultimately derived from the Prussian view of the state and society. Interestingly enough, the grades within the West German civil service correspond closely to the stages in the unreformed Humboldtian school and university system, thus creating a systematic integration of political, administrative and cultural institutions unknown to the piecemeal approach traditionally adopted in Britain.[3] It is also note-worthy that the *Beamtenlaufbahn*, or civil service career, still runs in families in West Germany as one of the few traditions which has not suffered from the severe criticism to which almost all German institutions were subjected after the Second World War.

The largest group in the working population are the *Angestellte* and *Arbeiter* employed in industry and commerce. As noted above, their status in society depends on a number of objective and tangible factors such as level of qualification and responsibility exercised, and this is usually reflected in their pay and standard of living. Although there is a tendency to base the pay scales for *Angestellte* on the public service model, the wide range of occupations they are employed in produces spectacular differentials — e.g. the chief executive of a large company and the junior accounts clerk are both classified as *Angestellte*. This, together with the noticeable trend in recent years for skilled manual workers to be 'upgraded' into *Angestellte*, not only blurs class distinctions but also reflects a widespread aspiration to move up the social ladder on the basis of educational and professional qualifications.

Gastarbeiter

The lowest category of workers in the FRG is made up by the two million *Gastarbeiter*, or foreign workers, who were recruited mainly from Italy and southern Europe during the boom years of the fifties and sixties. Many of these workers, some of whom brought their families with them in the course of time, live in poor conditions and are isolated from the rest of society, a problem which has attracted more public interest as the rate of economic growth has slowed down. The problem is exacerbated by the fact that the FRG never regarded itself as a country able to accept a significant number of foreign immigrants for permanent settlement. Apart from the fact that it is becoming increasingly difficult to employ all the *Gastarbeiter* — legislation has become introduced to halt further recruitment by firms — there are many grave social problems which the federal government is only just beginning to tackle seriously. Foremost among these is the difficulty of assimilating into a highly industrialised and educated society large groups of poorly educated people from the rural areas of Sicily, Greece, Spain, Portugal, Turkey and Yugoslavia who bring with them the customs and attitudes of their native countries. There is little contact between German workers on the shop floor and the *Gastarbeiter*, or between the various national groups among themselves, and it is pointed out by some German commentators that there is a certain amount of underlying hostility, although there have been very few serious signs of this. The original aim of most *Gastarbeiter* was to spend a number of years working in the FRG in order to save up a lump sum for use on their return home, but this aim tended to become less attractive in view of the very high social benefits paid to all workers in the FRG. A *Gastarbeiter* with five children living in his country of origin can, at present rates (1979), claim child allowance totalling DM 580 per month in addition to his basic wage, which is a considerable inducement for him to remain in West Germany and send for his family to join him. Such a development is viewed with concern by the federal government which fears a worsening of existing social problems. If, on the other hand, the government were to introduce measures which would make eligibility for child allowance dependent on the children being resident in the country of origin, it is feared that this would encourage the *Gastarbeiter* to keep large families at home and thus add to the problems of the poor regions of Europe and Turkey. No solution has yet been found for long-term problems of this kind, and at present the federal government is concentrating on immediate practical measures which include co-operation schemes with the countries of origin to encourage *Gastarbeiter* to return home, and intensive German language courses, vocational training programmes and social welfare activities for the families of those who remain, the ultimate aim being to integrate them as equal members into German society.

Incomes and Expenditure

Each year the Federal Ministry of Labour and Social Affairs (*Bundesministerium für Arbeit und Sozialordnung*) publishes a detailed study of the distribution of income and wealth in the FRG (*Einkommensund Vermögensverteilung*). Because of the extraordinary complexity of the subject matter and the problems of method, the compilers frequently point out that their findings have only limited validity. Nevertheless, since the first publication of the study in 1970, three broad conclusions emerge:

1. wages for all three working categories (*Beamte, Angestellte* and *Arbeiter*) have risen steadily, with a parallel rise in savings;
2. the number of persons living on unearned income such as property or shares has diminished to a very small proportion;
3. the wealthiest group in society are the successful *Unternehmer*, or independent entrepreneurs.

As noted above, the highest salaries are earned mostly by leading

Angestellte in large industrial concerns which are able to adjust salaries according to individual performance. The salary scales for *Beamte*, who enjoy complete security of employment and non-contributory pension schemes, and sometimes occupy flats at a subsidised rent (*Dienstwohnungen*), are progressive over an incremental period with very substantial salaries for senior officials. The earnings of the *Arbeiter*, which depend on a wide range of factors, such as qualification, branch of industry, overtime, bonuses, piece-work, weather conditions, etc., as in all industrialised countries, show considerable differentials between skilled and unskilled workers, though these have shrunk in recent years.

A survey carried out to determine patterns of saving in West Germany in 1975 yielded the results shown in Table 5.1.

Table 5.1: Main Groups with Newly Opened Building Society Savings Accounts

	%
Angestellte	34.9
Arbeiter	28.6
Beamte	12.1
Self-employed	8.4

Source: Bundesministerium für Arbeit und Sozialordnung, *Einkommens--und Vermögensverteilung* (1977), p. 113.

It should be noted that while the *Angestellte* formed the largest group of new accounts with the highest proportion of savings (33.7 per cent), the small group of self-employed accounted for a disproportionately high 11.7 per cent of the total amount saved. The second largest group, the *Arbeiter*, accounted for 23.8 per cent of the amount saved, while the *Beamte* accounted for 14.7 per cent.

The picture is reversed if we compare these figures with the distribution pattern for home ownership. This shows twice as many people in the self-employed category own their own homes as in any other category and is a clear reflection of their relative affluence and their high level of involvement in ownership of all kinds of property. The figure also shows that in relation to their numerical size, the *Arbeiter* have the lowest stake in the country's wealth, despite the fact that the West German industrial working class is probably the most prosperous in Europe.

While successive West German governments have never doubted that

Table 5.2: Main Home Ownership Groups

	%
Self-employed	66
Beamte	39
Arbeiter	37
Angestellte	35

one of the reasons for the FRG's economic success has been the high incentives accruing to initiative and enterprise in business, they have from time to time expressed their uneasiness about the resulting concentration of wealth on a small proportion of the population. The general level of affluence has risen considerably over the years, but the gaps between the wealthy and the rest of the working population have also widened. Various solutions to this problem have been proposed by the trade union federation, usually with the aim of promoting and facilitating saving among the lower paid in order to achieve a gradual redistribution of wealth. The SPD party is particularly concerned to remove what it sees as the danger of social conflict arising from the crass disproportions in wealth and property ownership between the various groups in society. The SPD also is in favour of promoting the idea that savings should be built up systematically against hard times during a possible economic recession, and of counteracting to some extent the prevalent consumer ideology of living for the day. The government has introduced several savings schemes over a period of years, all of them encouraging regular planned savings through a formal savings contract, offering bonus incentives and a preferential rate of interest, with the aim of enabling the lower paid to build up a sum of money which will be worth re-investing.

The most popular government savings scheme is commonly known by the name of the piece of legislation on which it is based, the 624-*Mark-Gesetz*, or *624-Mark-Law*. All employees earning below a specified limit are eligible to join this scheme, provided they save up to DM 624 per annum over a period of six years, at the end of which they receive interest on their savings plus a variety of bonuses from the state. The level of bonus depends on the amount saved and on the saver's family status. Approximately 75 per cent of West German employees save in this way, although there has been a slight decrease in recent years due to the economic recession. The fact that 50 per cent of the money saved under the scheme was re-invested on maturity indicates that the idea of long-term saving and investment has gained wide acceptance among the public. Nevertheless, as critics of the scheme point out, the sums amassed in this way are relatively low and can provide little more than immediate protection against a rainy day, and it is still very difficult for the lower-paid worker to build up a significant stake in the nation's economy.

One of the safest, and most satisfactory ways of investing one's income is to buy a house or flat as owner-occupier. In this respect there are considerable differences between the British and German systems, and in general the lower-paid worker in Britain has a better chance of owning his own home than has his West German counterpart. Apart from the small proportion of homes built or subsidised with public funds, the vast majority of flats and houses are in private ownership or are owned by property companies. By UK levels rents in the FRG are high, but this has traditionally been so over many years. Due to the widespread devastation of residential areas during the Allied bombing campaign in the Second World War, the present housing stock is considerably more modern than in the UK.

The current level of home ownership in the FRG is about 33 per cent, compared to about 51 per cent in Britain, and is slowly on the increase. As part of its savings promotion programme the state encourages people to save for their own homes by offering premiums and tax relief. The operations of the building societies, or *Bausparkassen*, differ considerably from those of the British building societies, however, since the latter are based on a longer history and a different pattern of housing. The *Bausparkassen* are primarily concerned with people saving to build a new house, not to buy a second-hand house as is more often the case in Britain. Also, the prospective home owner in West Germany has to find much more than the 10-per-cent deposit normally required in Britain. The West German saver enters into a formal 'building savings contract' (*Bausparvertrag*) with the *Bausparkasse* for a minimum of eighteen months, but usually considerably longer, during which time he aims to save 40 per cent of the cost of building his new home. At the end of the so-called 'saving phase', i.e. when the savings contract has been fulfilled, the *Bausparkasse* will then advance the balance of 60 per cent of the building costs. The saver must use his savings for the purpose of building a house, otherwise he forfeits his premiums and tax concessions. The 'repayment phase', normally twenty or twenty-five years in the UK, is often ten years or less in the FRG. Since building costs are very high in the FRG it will be appreciated that to become an owner-occupier in this way is a major undertaking, often associated

with considerable sacrifices in other areas of expenditure, and for this
reason it fails to attract many Germans, especially when rented flats
are readily available. In order to recoup some of the outlay and to meet
the repayments to the *Bausparkasse*, a significant number of people
build a house consisting of two separate flats, one for their own
occupation and the other to let.

For those unable to afford the cost of buying their own
Einfamilienhaus, or one-family house, an alternative is offered by
the increasingly popular owner-occupied flats (*Eigentumswohnungen*)
built by property companies and building consortia. While such well-
appointed blocks of flats have undoubted advantages for single people,
or those without children, they are obviously less suitable for families
with children and therefore appeal only to a limited section of the
population. As recent surveys by the press and private research
institutes show, 90 per cent of West Germans are very interested in
principle in owning their own home – preferably an *Einfamilienhaus*.

While expenditure on rent or building repayments claims a high
proportion of the West German citizen's income, his proportional
outgoings on food and clothing have been steadily decreasing since
the late fifties. In 1958 the four-person family spent 46.3 per cent and
12.7 per cent of their total income on food and clothing respectively;
by 1977 these figures had been reduced to 29 per cent and 9.1 per
cent. This decrease, together with the rising wage level, has made
available a larger proportion of income which can be devoted to
consumer spending, the so-called disposable income. There can be no
doubt that consumer spending plays a very important role in the FRG,
and the consumer ideology which is used to justify it might be said
to have certain specifically West German characteristics, especially in
its reflection of the *Leistungsgesellschaft*. Health, youth, energy, high
spirits, sexual vigour and efficiency at work are commonly emphasised
as the characteristics of the federal citizen who is living life to the
full in a demanding but successful consumer society. The successful
West German will wish not only to display signs of his prosperity,
e.g. a new Mercedes car to indicate that he has 'arrived', a swimming
pool or a sauna in his home, but will be constantly out to demonstrate
his discrimination by being acutely critical of the goods and services
on offer. For this type of person, created and encouraged by the
advertising media but also representative of some important aspects
of West German affluence, the expressive term *Konsumheld*, or
consumer hero, has been coined.

Social Insurance

Social insurance was introduced into Germany about a hundred years ago. Since that time it has developed from a scheme which was devised to protect the hierarchical German state from the Social Democratic threat, to one of the most comprehensive and generous schemes ever operated.

Between 1883 and 1889 the German Chancellor Bismarck introduced state insurance schemes against sickness, accident, old age and permanent loss of health. These compulsory schemes were organised and staffed by the state, but contributions were borne entirely by the employees. The normal principles of insurance applied, with benefits adjusted according to the number and level of premiums paid. Unemployment insurance was not introduced until after the First World War, in 1927. Whatever view we might now take of Bismarck's motives in introducing these schemes, there can be no doubt that they were excellent in their own time and they became a model both for subsequent German governments and for foreign governments alike. It should be noted, however, that Bismarck's scheme was based firmly on the notion of the all-powerful state organising and making more secure the lives of its citizens; the concept of self-help by the workers, such as characterises the British institutions of the time, is absent. It is therefore particularly interesting to note that the inspiration for a more comprehensive social security provision in Germany should have been derived from Britain after the Second World War. William Beveridge, the architect of the British social security system, propounded the idea that the state scheme should not merely protect its members from the worst effects of accident, unemployment, etc., but should also be actively involved in removing the causes and improving the conditions from which many of these ills spring. This goes well beyond the original insurance principle of Bismarck's scheme, and provides many benefits as a 'human right', rather than as a return for premiums paid. In the FRG, as in Western Europe generally, the social security system is regarded as far more than an organisation simply for alleviating misfortune. It is one of the main economic and political institutions of the state, contributing in many different ways to the health, prosperity, full employment and social harmony on which modern industrial society depends.

In 1976 the Federal Ministry of Labour and Social Affairs published the first volume of a new code of social legislation, or *Sozialgesetzbuch*. The declared aim of this project is to bring together

and harmonise the scattered and complex legislation on social security
so that the citizen will have available a clear and authoritative
statement of his rights under the system. Apart from this, the project
might be said to reflect the high level of public interest and expectation
in the system, despite the unprecedented level of personal affluence.
Why this should be so is difficult to explain. It may be due to the fact
that the self-employed sector of the working population is dwindling,
so that increasing numbers of people look to the state for protection
where they previously made provision through private arrangements.
Another more tangible reason is the recession since 1973 which has
put approximately one million West Germans out of work and has
encouraged both the government and the individual to regard early
retirement on pension as an attractive way of reducing the unemployment figures.

   The main divisions of the West German social security system
covered in this survey are as follows:

1. *die Rentenversicherung* (pensions insurance);
2. *die Krankenversicherung* (sickness insurance);
3. *die Unfallversicherung* (accident insurance);
4. *die Arbeitslosenversicherung* (unemployment insurance);
5. *die Sozialhilfe* (public assistance).

Pensions

The pensions insurance scheme, particularly for old age pensions, is
the central pillar in the whole social security system. For administrative
purposes it is divided into three main categories, for *Arbeiter,
Angestellte* and employees of the mining industry respectively. This
terminology, which has already been commented on briefly, no longer
implies that there is any significant difference in the basic rights and
benefits which can be claimed by each category of employee. It is
interesting to note, however, that the original class differences lived
on until the late fifties in some of the basic concepts with which the
system operated. Thus, for example, the wife of an *Arbeiter* received
a lower widow's pension under certain circumstances than the wife of
an *Angestellte*, since it was originally assumed that a manual worker's
wife would go out to work, whereas this could not be expected of the
wife of an *Angestellte*. Approximately 50 per cent of the social budget
is devoted to pensions. Unlike the British scheme which grants an old
age pension at a standard level for everyone of pensionable age, the

West German scheme links the level of pension to the number of contribution years. The age of retirement in the two countries is the same: 65 for men and 60 for women. As pointed out above, there has been in recent years a tendency towards earlier retirement, and there is some evidence to show that a majority of German workers would be in favour of a flexible retiring age.

The old age pensions scheme is based on the so-called *Generationenvertrag*, or 'contract between the generations', which means that current contributions are used to pay the pensions of those at present living in retirement. This is intended to ensure that at any given time pensioners will have an income directly related to the state of the economy and the general level of prices and incomes, and will not be at a disadvantage *vis-à-vis* the working population. This system works well so long as there is a favourable balance between the number of workers paying contributions to the state pensions fund and the number of retired persons drawing pensions. Demographic trends in the FRG have meant that this balance has not been maintained; as more people have entered retirement, fewer workers have been left to pay pension fund contributions, which has resulted in a deficit in the pension funds. The effects of this trend are well illustrated in figures issued by the federal government: the retirement of 200,000 full-time employees means a loss in contribution revenue amounting to DM 1,000 million at present rates. Since 1973 the loss of revenue has been made more severe by the lower wage increases which are awarded annually; each percentage increase means approximately DM 1,000 million in contributions to the pension funds. Current forecasts indicate that the deficit which the pension funds incurred in 1976 will continue until at least 1982.

The contributions to the pension funds are paid in equal proportions by the employer and the employee, and are based on the employee's gross earnings. Since the late sixties the contribution rate has increased steadily from 14 per cent in 1967 to 18 per cent in 1978. The level of old age pensions is generous. A pensioner with forty-five contribution years receives a pension amounting to approximately 75 per cent of his average net wage. To take a concrete example based on 1977 wage levels: an industrial worker who retired in that year with an average net monthly wage of DM 1,460 would receive a monthly old age pension of DM 1082.80. Pensions are kept in line with wages and prices by means of a formal legal mechanism which is operated from 1 January each year and known as the *Rentenanpassung* or pension adjustment. The following table shows the substantial adjustments which have taken place since 1970; it is also a good indicator of how living costs have risen in the FRG over the same period.

Table 5.3: Rate of Pension Adjustment since 1970

		%		%
	1970	6.35	1974	11.2
	1971	5.5	1975	11.1
Jan	1972	6.3	1976	11.0
July	1972	9.5	1978	9.9
	1973	11.35		

While old age pensions are the main item in the pension funds, a variety of other kinds of pension are paid to smaller groups in the population, e.g. widows and orphans, breakdown pensions, and pensions to victims of Nazi persecution. Until 1978 pensions were also paid to Germans who, though not directly persecuted by the Nazis, left Germany as a result of the activities of the National Socialist regime. It is now felt that the payment of these pensions can no longer be justified, since the beneficiaries have never contributed to the federal pensions scheme and they have had over thirty years in which to put down roots in their adoptive countries. This measure, introduced primarily as a minor economy at a time of pension fund deficit, can also be regarded as an example of the way in which the passage of time is very gradually removing the burden of the Nazi era from West Germany's central administrative system.

Sickness Insurance

All employees, whether *Beamte, Angestellte* or *Arbeiter,* earning below a certain adjustable income level are compulsorily insured against sickness and the cost of medical treatment. The compulsory insurance also covers the members of the employee's family as well as pensioners and the unemployed. Self-employed persons may elect to pay contributions to the scheme, or they can opt for private insurance. Approximately 90 per cent of West Germans are covered by the state scheme, the remaining 10 per cent being privately insured. The insurance covers the cost of medical treatment, benefits in kind and loss of income. German employees are entitled to receive full pay for the first six weeks of absence due to illness, after which the insurance funds make up the difference between the reduced wages and the normal wage. In addition to paying benefits of this kind, the state sickness insurance scheme is devoting more attention to preventive medicine, thus reflecting the growing tendency in the FRG for the social and welfare service to look at causes as well as effects.

The state sickness insurance system is administered by the *Krankenkassen* or sickness funds. There are approximately 1,800 *Krankenkassen* scattered throughout the FRG, mostly *Ortskranken-kassen* (abbreviated OKK) or local sickness funds, which might be responsible for a town or city, or *Betriebskrankenkassen*, which are based on an industry. Their position in law is that of self-administering corporations, run by a committee of employers and employees elected on a parity basis. The *Kassen* draw their funds in equal contributions from the employers and employees and, within certain limits, are also responsible for setting the level of contributions payable. This arrangement provides an interesting contrast with the British system where a standard contribution is levied by the central department of state. The advantage of the German system is that it permits a certain measure of flexibility so that local conditions can be taken into account — e.g. a rural area in South Germany will probably need a different level and type of preventive medicine from an industrial conurbation in the Ruhr. Each *Krankenkasse* maintains a list of medical practitioners recognised by them — in practice doctors are usually recognised by all the local *Kassen* — and the patient has a completely free choice among the doctors on the list at any time. Unlike the British National Health Service, which requires the patient to be formally registered with a general practitioner of his own choice, the *Krankenkassen* impose no such restrictions. This freedom of choice is highly prized and full use is made of it, as the rising expenditure on medical treatment clearly indicates.

The West German health service is well equipped with highly trained personnel and excellent facilities. As the following comparative table shows, however, it lags considerably behind France and the UK in the provision of nursing staff. This concentration on the highest levels of skill, training and refined medical technology, together with the ever-increasing demand for medical services amidst unprecedented affluence, has led to a veritable explosion of costs since 1970. Between 1970 and 1976 the expenditure incurred by the *Krankenkassen* almost trebled on certain main items — for example, payments to dentists rose by 278 per cent, to hospitals by 219 per cent, to chemists by 127 per cent and to doctors by 118 per cent. During the same period the average cost to the sickness insurance scheme per head of

Table 5.4: Selected Medical Personnel/Facilities

	UK	France	FRG
No. of doctors per 100,000 population	136	154	193
No. of dentists per 100,000 population	28	50	52
No. of nurses per 100,000 population	385	387	259
No. of hospital beds per 100,000 population	9	8	12

membership increased by 143 per cent, while gross wages, from which the contributions to the *Kassen* are deducted, showed an increase of only 74.5 per cent. In spite of the inevitable increases in the rate of contribution (from 8.2 per cent of gross wage in 1970 to 11.3 per cent in 1976) the funds of the *Kassen* are precariously balanced and there is a strong feeling among those who are responsible for their administration that methods must be devised which will maintain the present high level of service while curbing expenditure.

One of the most contentious items of expenditure is the fee payable to doctors and dentists which is sometimes criticised as excessive, arbitrary and unrelated to the time and effort devoted to the patient. The professional associations of doctors and dentists are naturally, like the British Medical Association, in a strong monopoly position and concerned with maintaining the status and income of their members. Their negotiating position with the *Krankenkassen* and the government is strengthened by the fact that the public is generally well satisfied with the lavish medical treatment and services offered and would not wish to see any reduction in standards. Their critics point out that the West German medical system is not without flaws when compared in certain basic respects to those of its neighbours. Thus, surprisingly, both the infant mortality rate and the number of deaths in childbirth are higher than in either France or the UK. The critics are also worried about the tendency for doctors to invest heavily in advanced medical equipment in order to be able to offer their patients the technical services which command high and relatively easily earned fees from the *Krankenkassen.* This has apparently led to the traditional personal consultation between doctor and patient being relegated to a position of secondary importance. As a result of consistent criticism of this kind, new legislation has been introduced which strengthens the negotiating

position of the *Krankenkassen* by linking medical fees more closely
with the general development of wages in other professions. In 1978
a standardised scale of medical fees was introduced which placed the
emphasis on personal rather than on purely technical services, and
measures have been introduced to encourage doctors to make more
use of central technical facilities in hospitals rather than invest in
their own — often under-used — private clinics.

Economy measures have also been introduced to limit the
considerable sums spent by the *Krankenkassen* on medicines and
drugs. As in the UK, prescription fees are charged, though as a matter
of principle these are low and make an insignificant contribution to
the over-all drugs and medicines bill. Doctors have therefore been
provided with lists of comparable drugs and their relative cost as an
aid to economical prescription, the main aim being to reduce
consumption of drugs on a national scale and to counteract the
widespread tendency in West Germany to regard the use of certain
drugs, e.g. valium, as a necessary safeguard against stress diseases.
Many of the items which previously could be supplied on prescription,
e.g. bandages, ointments and antiseptics, now have to be paid for by
the patient, and arrangements have been made to try to improve the
co-ordination between the general practitioner, the specialist consultant
and the hospital. At present there is still a good deal of duplication of
effort and expense because of poor co-ordination and the relative
independence enjoyed by each doctor and each sector of the health
service.

No survey of West German health facilities would be complete
without mentioning the *Kur*, or 'health cure', which is scarcely known
in the UK but goes from strength to strength in the FRG as one of
the most popular methods of medical treatment. Patients can be sent
to stay for a month at a *Kurort*, or spa, specialising in their particular
complaint. There are approximately 250 state-registered *Kurorte* in
the FRG, set in attractive parts of the country and equipped with all
the facilities — social and recreational as well as medical — which their
visitors might require. Thus, apart from its medical advantages, the
Kur appeals to many West Germans as an opportunity to step aside
from the demands of working life for a brief period. If a *Kur* is
prescribed by a doctor the full costs are met jointly by the
Rentenversicherung and the *Krankenkasse*, though doctors are now
required to show that the *Kur* is medically necessary and not merely
desirable. Furthermore, in order to qualify for a free *Kur* the patient
must have been contributing to the *Rentenversicherung* for fifteen

years, instead of the pre-1977 requirement of only five years. This is
intended to prevent certain abuses of the system whereby *Beamte*,
self-employed people and highly paid *Angestellte,* who are not
required to contribute to the state pensions and sickness schemes,
could take a regular *Kur* at public expense on the strength of only
five years' contributions early in their careers.

Accident Insurance

Unlike the pensions and sickness insurance schemes, accident
insurance is financed solely by the employers and is covered by state
legislation. This clearly acts as an incentive to industry to ensure that
factories and workshops are made as safe as possible so as to keep
claims on the insurance funds down to a minimum. The scheme
covers all types of industrial accident and occupational diseases.
Retraining grants are paid where the claimant is unable to follow his
original trade or occupation as a result of impaired health, and the
pensions to widows and orphans are based on the insured person's
average wage and adjusted to the cost of living under the terms of the
Rentenanpassung. It is rarely necessary for the victims of an industrial
accident to have recourse to legal proceedings in order to gain
compensation.

Unemployment Relief

The first German legislation on unemployment insurance was
introduced in 1927 under the Weimar Republic, and with its strong
emphasis on the relief of bitter poverty it reflects the needs of a
different age. It was not until 1969 that the original legislation was
completely replaced by the *Arbeitsförderungsgesetz*, or 'labour
promotion law', a name which clearly indicates that the emphasis is
now on ensuring that work is available for all who are fit to do it. The
new law aims to create a framework for an adaptable labour and
employment policy, by providing a wide range of retraining
opportunities to meet changing technical needs and by alleviating the
hardship that accompanies long-term unemployment.

For the first two decades in the history of the FRG labour was in
such short supply that large numbers of foreign workers had to be
imported into the major centres of production and unemployment
benefits attracted little public interest. Later, between 1973 and 1975,
following the first oil crisis and world recession, unemployment trebled.
Since that time it has remained stable at approximately 4.5 per cent, or
1.03 million unemployed, and at present (1979) it shows little sign of

significant reduction. Unemployment benefits are therefore of urgent practical importance to between 4 and 5 per cent of the West German working population and their families.

Labour and employment policy within the terms of the *Arbeitsför-derungsgesetz* is administered by the *Bundesanstalt für Arbeit* (Federal Labour Office) in Bonn and put into practice by the local *Arbeitsämter* (labour offices) in each town or district. Contributions are levied equally from both employers and employees towards the cost of unemployment insurance and are usually collected by the local *Krankenkasse* along with the contributions to the sickness insurance. In general all workers who are compulsorily insured under the state sickness insurance scheme are also required to pay contributions towards unemployment insurance funds. This excludes *Beamte* who, as noted above, are protected against unemployment by their conditions of service. The levels of unemployment benefit (*Arbeitslosengeld*) are generous and related to the individual's previous earnings and family status. Thus, a married man with two children will receive about 70 per cent of the last wage earned. Full unemployment benefit, which is not payable to workers on strike, can be drawn for a maximum period of 312 days, after which time a claim can be made for the so-called *Arbeitslosenhilfe*, or unemployment relief, at a maximum level of 60 per cent of the last wage earned. This is regarded as a last resort and is not payable until after the applicant has passed a stringent means test which requires him to show that he has not only used up all his own assets, but has also drawn on those of his wife and parents.

The demographic and economic problems facing the social security services in the FRG are not as severe as those encountered in West Berlin, which is not only isolated geographically from the rest of federal territory, but has also an ageing population. Unless more people of working age, especially those with young families, can be persuaded to settle there, the economic consequences could be grave. It has therefore been the policy of the federal government since the early sixties to offer attractive incentives to those willing to move to West Berlin to live and work. These include generous travel allowances, grants towards setting up home in Berlin, an 8-per-cent Berlin allowance on wages and an interest-free loan of DM 5,000 to young couples who marry and set up home in Berlin. Since 1961 approximately a quarter of a million West Germans have moved to Berlin and availed themselves of these benefits.

Public Assistance

For the relatively small group of people whose existences are threatened by circumstances beyond their control, and who have no claim on any other social security department, the *Sozialhilfe* can provide both financial help and benefits in kind. The system is administered by the local authorities, and the help given is intended to ensure that the recipients can retain their human dignity while wherever possible overcoming their circumstances by their own efforts. In general the *Sozialhilfe* is concerned mainly with looking after the helpless who are either very old or very young. Apart from this it provides assistance for handicapped people and the blind, especially in the form of training courses, and for the victims of tuberculosis. Expenditure on *Sozialhilfe* has risen very steeply over the last decade, partly due to changes in legislation, from DM 3,500 million in 1970 to DM 12,000 million in 1979.

The services provided by the *Sozialhilfe* are supplemented by those of the main independent charitable organisations in the FRG, including the German Red Cross, various workers' welfare societies and the Roman Catholic and Lutheran organisations. These maintain hostels, special schools, hospitals and advisory centres for those with all kinds of personal, health or financial problems. One aspect of their work is comparable to that undertaken in the UK by the Citizens' Advice Bureaux, staffed partly by volunteers.

Special arrangements exist for the payment of compensation and pensions to Germans who suffered particular hardship during or in consequence of the Second World War. Many categories are included under this heading, ranging from the victims of Nazi persecution to civilians who had to flee and leave all their property when the Soviet army entered Germany in 1945. Although considerable sums are still disbursed in pensions to groups who suffered in this way, they are naturally decreasing in size and importance with the passage of time. Of more recent interest are the native Germans and their families who have been allowed to leave Poland, Rumania and the USSR to settle in the FRG since the initiatives of *Ostpolitik* during the Brandt—Scheel government. These groups arrive in West Germany carrying all their worldly possessions in suitcases and bringing with them young families who know little German. Apart from granting capital allowances to help them start a new life in the FRG, the federal government provides the financial means for language and vocational training courses. Help is also available for refugees from the GDR, especially for political detainees who are released to the West. It is in areas of this kind that the West German social security system, like many other aspects of the West German state, finds itself becoming directly involved in political questions arising from the East—West confrontation on its borders.

Further Reading

Beyme, Klaus von. *Die Politische Elite in der Bundesrepublik Deutschland* (Munich, 1974)
Chester, Professor (Em.). 'Health care in West Germany and France: A Comparative Analysis', in *The Three Banks Review* (December 1976)
Claessens, Dieter, Klönne, Arno, and Tschoepe, Armin. *Sozial Kunde der Bundesrepublik Deutschland* (Düsseldorf, 1965)
Dahrendorf, Ralf. *Gesellschaft und Demokratie in Deutschland* (Munich, 1968)
Hallett, Graham. *The Social Economy of West Germany* (London, 1973)

Notes

1. See p. 116 below.
2. Cf. pp. 67—68 above.
3. See pp. 115—123 below.

6   THE EDUCATION SYSTEM AND ITS PROBLEMS

Education in West Germany has been undergoing a relatively rapid change since the late sixties. The change has not been uniform throughout the country, nor has it proceeded at the same pace in the different *Länder*. Consequently the situation which now obtains is one in which the old system and the partially developed reformed systems often exist alongside each other and present a confused picture to the outsider. In order to be able to understand the system and the changes it is undergoing, especially when considering it from the perspective of the English educational system, it is necessary to bear in mind the traditional pattern of education in Germany and the framework of educational administration in the FRG.

Länder Responsibilities

Responsibility for the administration and organisation of education in West Germany is settled firmly on the *Länder*. The Basic Law restores the principle of the cultural sovereignty of the *Länder* (*Kulturhoheit der Länder*) which existed before 1919 but which was modified during the Weimar Republic and removed altogether by the National Socialists. The responsibilities of the *Bund* in the educational sphere, exercised by the *Bundesministerium für Bildung und Wissenschaft* (Federal Ministry for Education and Science), are limited to certain prescribed areas which do not impinge on the cultural autonomy of the *Länder*. These responsibilities include long-term planning and research on vocational and non-vocational education, the administration of student grants and some involvement in the financing of university buildings and research in the universities. In all other respects the *Länder* are responsible for secondary, vocational and higher education.

    Occasional disputes over areas of responsibility between *Bund* and *Länder*, which are inevitable in the administration of a complex and overloaded educational system, have in recent years led to demands for an enlargement of the sphere of competence of the *Bund*, especially in higher education. Since a move in that direction could not be made without an amendment to the constitution it is unlikely that such demands will achieve any tangible results in the foreseeable future.

Because of the division of powers between *Bund* and *Länder*, the separate cultural autonomy of each *Land*, and the recent reforms, it can be misleading to speak of one West German educational system. It is more accurate to regard the system as eleven variations on a set of generally accepted ideas.

The administrative pattern in each of the *Länder* is broadly similar. At the central level the *Kultusministerium* (Ministry of Culture) has over-all responsibility. The Minister of Culture is a political appointee who exercises considerable administrative and academic power. For example, his permission must be granted before a textbook can be adopted for use in schools or a professor appointed to a university chair. The ministry is organised into several specialist departments: e.g. legal affairs; arts and science; higher education and teacher training; primary, secondary and vocational schools; examinations; specialist institutions. The *Land* is divided up into several large units (*Regierungsbezirke*) which form the intermediate level in the administrative structure, while at local level the smaller units (*Stadtkreise* and *Landkreise*) administer the schools in their areas through a *Schulamt*, or education office. The chief official at local level is the *Oberschulrat* who directs the activities of a number of *Schulräte* with responsibility for different types of schools. The link between administration and classroom teaching is represented by the head teachers of the grammar schools (*Oberstudiendirektor*) and of the other types of schools (*Schulleiter*). In contrast to the English practice, the authority of the head teacher is limited and individual responsibility is less, as are the salary differentials which separate the headmaster from the classroom teacher.

While this basic administrative structure is common to all the *Länder*, it should be noted that there is a range of influences at work which creates diversity, and the student who undertakes a detailed study of the educational structure of a particular *Land* will perceive many local differences from the simplified outline given here. The political party in power in the *Land* exercises its influence through the *Kultusminister*. The predominant religious denominations can exert pressure on the content of the school curriculum as well as on the organisation of education, particularly in rural areas. The economic pattern of the *Land*, whether it is industrialised or agricultural, is also reflected in educational provision. Some critics regard this diversity as one of the chief reasons for the FRG having lagged behind its neighbours in reforming its education system. Others maintain that diversity is a necessary brake on the hasty rejection of proven ideals.

The *Kultusminister* of the *Länder* consult each other on a voluntary basis through the *Ständige Konferenz der Kultusminister der Länder* (Standing Conference of the Ministers of Culture of the *Länder*, abbreviated KMK), which seeks to co-ordinate the work of the *Länder* by issuing recommendations on important educational and administrative matters. These recommendations are not binding on individual *Länder*, but they do represent a considerable influence on educational policy making. Another important task of the KMK is to draft administrative agreements between the *Länder*, known as *Ländervereinigungen*, on matters not covered by legislation. Agreements of this kind regulate the dates of school holidays, examination standards and grades, recognition of textbooks as suitable for use in schools, and the recognition of foreign qualifications, in particular those acquired by West German citizens who spent the earlier part of their lives in the GDR. In general the practical work of the KMK is important in holding the system together by promoting a common approach to the treatment of basic matters which, if allowed to diverge radically, could result in severe bureaucratic obstacles for families with children moving from one *Land* to another.

In 1970 a further step was taken towards 'co-operative' federalism with the setting up of a permanent forum for educational planning, the *Bund-Länder-Kommission für Bildungsplanung*, abbreviated B-L-K. The commission is composed of seven representatives of the *Bund* and one from each of the *Länder*. The aim of the B-L-K is to promote consultation and co-operation between the federation and the *Länder* in the planning and financing of education, and it was set the specific task of drawing up a plan for the development of education in the FRG. The result of its work is the *Bildungsgesamtplan* (comprehensive plan for education) which was accepted by the federal government in 1973. The plan recommends considerable structural and curricular changes throughout the whole system with a view to achieving a greater degree of uniformity and integration between the different branches of education. The formulation of the plan represents one of the most important stages in educational planning at national level in West Germany, and certain changes it recommends have already been partially effected in some of the *Länder*. These are discussed below in connection with the reformed system.

In elaborating its plan the B-L-K consulted outside bodies with a special interest in education. Foremost among these was the *Deutscher Bildungsrat* (German educational council) which was set up in 1965 to investigate educational resources and future national needs. The

Deutscher Bildungsrat has produced a structural plan (*Strukturplan*) which was used as a basis for the work of the B-L-K. The work of the *Wissenschaftsrat* (council for arts and sciences) which was set up as long ago as 1957 to co-ordinate the *Bund,* the *Länder* and outside institutions, was also consulted with particular reference to higher education.

Kindergarten

Although it has given the word 'kindergarten' to the rest of Europe, Germany never developed pre-school or nursery education within the state system, and it is only very recently that the *Länder* have considered assuming some responsibility for this sector. Traditionally, nursery education has been provided by charitable religious organisations, e.g. the Protestant *Innere Mission* and the Catholic *Deutscher Caritasverband*, as well as by a number of relatively small organisations who base their work on the theories of some of the pioneers of nursery education. The *Grundschulen* (state primary schools) often operate a pre-school class, or *Schulkindergarten*, to cater for the needs of children who have reached school age without having attained the required level of maturation. They attend the *Schulkinder-garten* until they have reached a stage which will enable them to make progress in the first primary school class, at which point they are transferred.

For many years the aims, methods and content of nursery education went unquestioned in Germany. Emphasis was on play, music and art, usually with a strong Christian element in the curriculum. The underlying assumption was that at this early age the child was best allowed to develop at its own pace in a sheltered atmosphere. More recently the kindergartens have come under pressure in two ways: firstly to provide more places, and secondly to adapt their methods to what the critics regard as the needs of members of a modern industrial society.

Regarding the first point it can be said that the response has been relatively swift. The independent organisations have made more places available and, in some *Länder*, e.g. Baden-Württemberg, the state has considerably extended its involvement in the pre-school sector. By 1977 there was an average of 50 per cent provision of kindergarten places throughout West Germany. The demand for more kindergartens was not entirely due to a greater awareness among parents of the value which pre-school education would have for their children; it can be partly explained by the tendency for more women to go out to work and to regard the kindergarten as a convenient child-minding service. The kindergartens are open from very early in the morning to accommodate the children of working mothers, most of whom start work at eight o'clock or earlier, and unlike schools they remain open until the late afternoon. To counteract this attitude and to maintain contact with parents some kindergartens arrange programmes of evening lectures on their work and on topics relating to child health and development.

The demands for changes in the aims and methods of the kindergartens have met with fairly strong resistance from the established organisations, but have nevertheless had some influence on nursery education. These demands reflect the views of educationists who believe that the child can and must be prepared for adult life from a very early age. American theories of nursery education have made a great impact in West Germany, especially the attempts to teach very young children to read and to replace traditional toys by 'structured learning games'. It is pointed out that, in order to compete and achieve in the *Leistungsgesellschaft*, children must be exposed to the reality of life from the earliest possible age. The other end of the scale is represented by the 'anti-authoritarian' kindergartens which base their approach to education loosely on the ideas of A. S. Neill, the founder of Summerhill school in Suffolk, whose works have created some interest in recent years in West Germany, particularly in student circles.

Both types of kindergarten reflect different views about society and the corresponding political beliefs. They also result from initiatives taken by active groups of people whose children might be expected to do well in school in any case. By contrast the children of working-class families, who would stand to benefit most by attending kindergarten, are the very children least likely to have a kindergarten place. Much of the debate on pre-school education is devoted to this particular problem: how to improve kindergarten provision for working-class children. The main demands which have emerged from this energetic debate can be summed up under three headings:

1. an adequate number of kindergartens to provide places for all children from the age of three, though attendance would remain voluntary;

2. a more systematic curriculum;

3. the lowering of the school age to five.

In order to meet the last demand, some *Länder* have set up
experimental classes and pre-school playgroups e.g. in Hesse and Berlin.
The *Bildungsgesamtplan* favours the extension of pre-school education,
while some educationists would like to see the kindergarten
incorporated entirely into the state system.

General and Vocational Schools

The West German education system makes a formal distinction between
allgemeinbildende Schulen (schools offering a general education) and
berufsbildende Schulen (vocational schools). Under the traditional
system the *allgemeinbildende Schulen* begin with the *Grundschule* at
primary level and divide into three branches at secondary level —
Hauptschule, Realschule and *Gymnasium.* Although this arrangement
has been reformed to varying degrees over the last decade, an outline
description of it is necessary for an appreciation of the aims and results
of the educational reforms.

While the majority of West German schools still operates on the
basis of six mornings per week with each morning session divided into
six lessons between 8.0 a.m. and 1.30 p.m., an increasing number of
schools are becoming *Ganztagsschulen* (whole-day schools) with a five-
day week. This change is due to social rather than educational reasons.
With the general introduction of the five-day working week, and
increasing affluence offering greater possibilities for leisure pursuits,
many West German parents came to regard Saturday morning school as
an intrusion into their freedom at weekends. There is also some support
in the teaching profession for the five-day week, though it is in no way
unanimous on the issue.

Schulpflicht, the legal obligation to attend school, begins in a child's
sixth year and ends in his eighteenth. The school year in West Germany
now begins uniformly in autumn. During the first nine years of the
period of *Schulpflicht* the child must attend school full time and at the
end of this period may either leave school to get a job, in which case he
has to attend a vocational school on a part-time basis for three years,
or may continue in certain types of full-time education.

The first step in the school life of all West German school children is
the *Grundschule.* Unlike the English system, which includes a
flourishing preparatory school sector at primary level, the West German
system makes no provision for private education at this stage. About
three months before the beginning of the new school year, the six-year

olds who are due to start school in the autumn are invited for a medical examination and a simple psychological test to determine whether they are *schulreif*, i.e. whether they have reached the appropriate stage of mental and physical development. Compared to English practice, this indicates an important difference in basic attitudes towards primary education. Whereas in England the primary schools have to accept all children at the age of five (unless they have special disabilities) and integrate them into school life, the West German primary school sets an entry requirement. The barrier between school and the outside world is thus apparent from the earliest stage. Some West German educationists criticise this system on social grounds and maintain that it would be more advantageous for the child and for society to lower the school age by extending the *Grundschule* downwards into a more highly developed kindergarten system.

The day on which a child begins its school life is regarded as very important in Germany and is marked by a ceremony on the first day of the autumn term, to which the children and their parents are invited. Parents can claim time off work to attend, and the children are welcomed to the school with a traditional gift of sweets.

The timetable of the *Grundschule* is very light in the first year, comprising two or three lessons per day and a few minutes' homework. From the first half-year onwards the children are issued with reports in a report book and are awarded a *Note*, or mark, on their general performance. The form of marking is the same throughout for all types of schools: a set of *Noten* from 1 to 6, with *Noten* 1 to 4 covering the range 'very good' to 'adequate'. *Note* 5 indicates an inadequate performance which could be remedied with effort, while 6, which is rarely used, denotes a serious failure to reach the standard required in a particular class.

The *Grundschule* consists of four classes for the age groups six to ten. In addition to teaching the children the basic skills they will require at the next stage of their education, the *Grundschule* has in recent years also included in its curriculum subjects such as *Verkehrserziehung* (road safety) and *Sexualerziehung* (sex education) — another indication of the way in which current social preoccupations affected the curriculum from the sixties onwards. In the predominantly Catholic *Länder*, particularly in rural areas, *Grundschulen* are still sometimes separated according to religious denominations, although this pattern is slowly giving way as the single-class village schools are replaced by *Mittelpunktschulen*, or district schools, which take children by bus from groups of surrounding villages. The village schools are generally regarded as disadvantageous for country children.

At the end of the fourth class in the *Grundschule*, when the child is ten, the decision is made regarding the type of secondary school he should attend. The decision used to be made purely on the basis of a single examination, as in England, but more recently the system has been refined and other methods and assessment factors have been introduced. The wishes of the parents are also taken into account. There is at present no standard assessment procedure, but it is often based on a combination of continuous assessment, trial lessons and written tests. Another method is to postpone the final decision until the end of the first two years at secondary school. This period is known as the *Orientierungsstufe*, or orientation stage.

Secondary Schools

The secondary school system comprises three branches: the majority of children go to the *Hauptschule*, while those who are selected as suitable for more demanding courses go either to the *Realschule* or to the *Gymnasium*. In recent years the number of children entering the *Realschule* and *Gymnasium* has increased significantly, while the *Hauptschule* has shown a corresponding decrease. Thus, in 1968, there were approximately 1,270,000 pupils at *Gymnasien*, compared to 1,910,000 in 1976. The figures for the *Realschule* are 761,000 and 1,218,000 respectively.

The *Hauptschule* is the 'main school' in the sense that it provides an education for the majority of children at secondary level. It comprises five co-educational classes covering the age range 10 to 15. Streaming into ability groups is undertaken on a limited basis only. In fact, one of the characteristic features of the whole traditional primary and secondary school system is the principle of class teaching in all subjects. This principle works well for the 'good all-rounders', but is less suitable for pupils whose ability is not so evenly balanced through the range of school subjects.

The curriculum in the *Hauptschule* concentrates on a practical approach to a limited number of subjects, foremost of these being German and mathematics. A foreign language, usually English, is also introduced. Pupils are required to do homework unless the school is open for five full days.

One of the important functions of the *Hauptschule* is to bring the pupils up to the stage where they can make the transition from school to work. This aspect has been given much attention in recent years, with the result that a new subject, *Arbeitslehre* or education for work, has been developed and introduced into the curriculum. This subject is treated in different ways according to local industrial conditions. Generally it comprises a systematic preparation for working life, including an introduction to a variety of trades and instruction on the rights and duties of an employee, together with at least two periods of practical work experience in local firms during the last school year. The aim is to provide the school leaver with a basis from which to choose the kind of work for which he is best fitted. The importance for the national economy of making the most efficient use of the labour force in this way has been emphasised by demographic predictions which forecast that by the year 2000 there will be more old age pensioners in West Germany than persons of working age and that this trend will continue for some years before levelling out, so that a diminishing workforce will have to maintain an increasing number of pensioners.[1] Problems of this kind, as well as the rapid pace of technical development, have prompted the demand that more attention should be devoted to the final year of the *Hauptschule* to the subject *Arbeitslehre*, or that it should be converted into a basic vocational training year during which the pupils would learn the skills required for several trades and occupations. This would enable them to make a better career choice and would also give them flexibility when they had to learn new skills.

When pupils leave the *Hauptschule* they receive a certificate: if they have completed the course successfully, with average or above average *Noten*, they receive an *Abschlusszeugnis*, or completion certificate, which is normally the qualification required in order to take up an apprenticeship for a skilled trade; for those who fail to reach this standard there is the *Abgangszeugnis*, or leaving certificate. Evening courses are run for those who, later in life, wish to convert the *Abgangszeugnis* into an *Abschlusszeugnis* and such courses are usually well attended.

A difficult problem confronting the *Hauptschule* in some industrial areas is the education of large numbers of children of immigrant workers. The schools were entirely unprepared to accommodate children with a different cultural background speaking little or no German, and emergency measures have been taken to train staff and devise suitable methods of teaching, with a view to integrating these groups of children at an early stage into the normal school system.[2]

The *Realschule* is the school which occupies an intermediate place between the *Hauptschule* and *Gymnasium*. Its name, which cannot be adequately translated, indicates that it provides an education concerned with the practical affairs of the present day. It is co-educational and comprises six classes covering the age range 10–16. Like the *Gymnasium*, its history goes back well before 1945, but since that time it has enjoyed a remarkable increase in popularity and esteem. Since 1950 the number of pupils attending *Realschulen* has increased fivefold. What are the reasons for this? Over the last three decades the expanding West German economy has created many employment opportunities for those qualified for technical, commercial and administrative work in both the private and public sectors. Industry has come to regard the *Realschule* qualification as a useful practical basis for professional training, while for the individual it has the additional advantage of offering a flexible choice of careers and further education opportunities. Of the three traditional branches of secondary education, the *Realschule* can be regarded as that which has most successfully bridged the gap between school and the world of work.

The *Realschule* curriculum is taught by specialist subject teachers. A second language, usually French, is introduced, as are specialist technical subjects – e.g. typing – which have vocational importance.

Pupils who successfully complete the *Realschule* are awarded a certificate known as the *mittlere Reife* or *Realschulabschlusszeugnis* (*Realschule* completion certificate). The award of the certificate usually depends on the results of continuous assessment and examination, and an adequate standard must be attained in the main subjects – German, English and mathematics. For the sixteen-year-olds who have an *Abschlusszeugnis* three possibilities exist: most enter a trade or profession, some continue their education at a full-time vocational school, while a very small proportion transfer to the *Gymnasium* or grammar school.

Das Gymnasium

The *Gymnasium* looks back on a long and proud tradition. Like the *Realschule*, it has experienced an increase in pupil members since 1945, but on a smaller scale. It comprises nine classes taught by specialists who have undergone a full university education in two subjects and are known as *Studienräte*, or 'study counsellors'. The *Studienrat* is not permitted to teach in the *Hauptschule* or *Realschule*, just as teachers in these schools are not permitted to teach in the *Gymnasium*. This is one aspect of the sharp distinction between the three branches of traditional secondary education in which the teachers are separated by qualification, length of training and conditions of service. For this and other reasons the *Gymnasium* has been the subject of more educational controversy since the mid-sixties than any other type of school.

The humanistic principle on which the curriculum of the *Gymnasium* is based seeks to impart a general education which will enable the individual to develop all his faculties and gifts in a balanced way. Unlike the other types of secondary school, the *Gymnasium* takes no account of the requirements of commerce and industry but places strong emphasis on the theoretical approach to learning. In contrast to English sixth form practice, a wide range of subjects is taught through to the highest classes and, although the manner in which these subjects is treated has become less rigid, pupils must still achieve the *Klassenziel*, or class standard, every year in all main subjects if they want to be sure of holding their place in the school. Pupils who fail to achieve this have to repeat the class, or leave the school. Since the personal consequences of such a move can hardly ever be made good in later life, pupils are under some pressure to reach the *Klassenziel*, and this has led to the widespread practice of private coaching which is undertaken mostly by teachers after school hours. Many parents are willing to pay out considerable sums to ensure that their children complete the *Gymnasium* successfully. It is obvious that the children of the better-off are at an advantage in a system where this kind of additional help is regarded as normal.

The qualification awarded by the *Gymnasium* is the *Abitur*, based on the results of a written and oral examination in all main subjects and a number of optional subjects. The examination is set and marked by the teachers but externally moderated. The contrast with the English system of early specialisation and external examining bodies is particularly marked at this stage. In theory the *Abitur* confers a legal right to study any subject at a German university; in practice this right has been restricted in recent years by lack of places in higher education for the increasing number of prospective students coming forward. The restriction imposed by the universities on the number of students accepted in a particular subject is known as the *numerus clausus*. It was first introduced in the sixties in medicine and dentistry, which depend on laboratory and clinical places, and later in several other popular subjects. Instead of taking all prospective students with the *Abitur*, as was possible in former days, the universities are taking only those who have attained the best over-all *Note*. This means that the final years at the *Gymnasium* become a kind of 'rat race' for high marks which is having a bad effect on the quality of education imparted at this level.

A pupil who successfully completes the *Gymnasium* can enter the civil service in the *gehobener Dienst*, which approximates to the executive grade in the British civil service, or he can go into industry or commerce. Many well-known West German firms have shown increasing interest in taking entrants with *Abitur* and putting them through their own training schemes, rather than in recruiting university graduates.

The Universities

The traditional German university system was run on the principles of *akademische Freiheit* (academic freedom), *Einheit der Forschung und Lehre* (unity of research and teaching) and *Selbstverwaltung* (autonomous internal administration). It is necessary to comment briefly on these principles since they form the background to the recent legislation on the reform of higher education.

The principle of academic freedom in its purest form means that, just as a professor is free to study and teach those aspects of his subject which appear to him most interesting and useful, without being bound by an internal or external board of studies, so the student is free to choose the subjects he will study and the lectures and seminars he will attend, and to present himself for examination after an unspecified number of semesters beyond a set minimum. Clearly this principle has to be modified for practical purposes — e.g. professors usually accept the necessity of holding courses of lectures in basic subjects, and students are required to write seminar papers on specific aspects of their subjects — but such modifications do not seriously affect the underlying principle. This means that in the absence of tutorial guidance the students themselves are responsible for working out their own course of study. This system differs fundamentally from the undergraduate course at an English university in which the student progresses in a planned fashion through the three years of the course with only a limited number of options available. Under the German system there is always the danger of time being wasted through uncertainty, ignorance or aimlessness, and students have to apply considerable self-discipline if they are to work consistently throughout their period of study.

At the head of the internal administration of the traditional university is the *Rektor*, who is usually a professor of the university elected by the senate. The *Rektoren* of the West German universities have their own organisation, the *Westdeutsche Rektorenkonferenz*, the aim of which is to co-ordinate administrative and academic policy at all West German universities. Like the *Kultusministerkonferenz*, it issues its decisions in the form of recommendations which are not binding on its members. The senate is the university's governing body, made up of representatives of the academic staff and elected to make policy decisions on all academic and administrative matters affecting the university. Below the senate are the faculties, each of which elects a professor as its dean for a fixed period. The traditional faculties are philosophy, theology, medicine, social sciences, mathematics and natural sciences, each made up of a wide range of individual subjects.

The academic staff structure is very different from the pattern at English universities. Each subject or branch of a subject is represented by an *Ordinarius*, or full professor, who must hold the highest doctorate awarded by German universities for original published research, the *Dr. habil.*, and his appointment to the position has to be approved by the *Kultusminister* of the *Land*. The German university professor still enjoys high social prestige. The professorial salary is substantial and can be increased by the university as an inducement for a good professor to remain in post, or as a bargaining counter to attract a distinguished academic from an outside institution to accept a chair. Furthermore, the professor continues to draw full salary after retirement as a mark of the esteem accorded to him by the state.

The professor's personal authority in all academic and staff matters relating to his own department goes largely unchallenged. He appoints his own staff who belong to one of two categories: the professor's *Assistenten* (temporary assistants), on the one hand, and the various established *Dozenten* (lecturers), on the other. The *Assistenten* are employed on a limited contract to teach and administer part time while working under the professor's supervision for a higher degree. They are thus dependent to a large extent on his goodwill. A favourably disposed professor can further their academic career prospects quite considerably, but if he is not so inclined he can make their lives very difficult indeed as they have no redress against unfair treatment.

Most students conclude their studies by taking the *Staatsexamen* (state examination) in two subjects. This examination, which is set and marked by the university acting for the *Kultusministerium* of the *Land*, and is administered by the ministry's *Prüfungsant* (examinations office), is the minimum qualification for entry to the *höherer Dienst*, which is equivalent to the administrative grade of the British civil service, and for several professions such as medicine, law and teaching in the grammar schools. It should be noted that this is not a university degree in the English sense, nor does it qualify the holder for an academic career in higher education. For this he needs the *Dr. phil.*, which is awarded by the university on the basis of a published dissertation and an oral examination. In technological, commercial and certain other faculties the universities now also award a diploma in one subject, e.g. *Diplom Volkswirt*, which approximates to the British BSc. Econ.

Most students nowadays receive a grant to cover the full or partial cost of their studies. This is administered by the *Bund* under legislation known as the *Bundesausbildungsförderungsgesetz*, abbreviated *Bafög* (federal law on educational grants). The current maximum grant is DM 585 per month (1979).[3] Parents are required to contribute to the cost of their children's higher education according to a scale based on income. This financial factor has created a strong tendency for students to study at a local university and if possible to live at home, since most parents who are required to make a contribution to the student grant find it easier and more economical to do this by providing free board and lodgings than by paying out a fixed monthly allowance over a period of at least four years, and perhaps considerably longer.

Whereas the traditional system does not specify an upper limit on the number of semesters a student spends at university, the minimum number for enrolment for the *Staatsexamen* is fixed at eight, although in practice it is usually much longer. Recent figures show that most students study for eleven or twelve semesters before they feel ready to take their examination. The German university system places far more emphasis on oral examinations and on dissertations in all subjects than does the English system. The *Staatsexamen* consists of a combination of *Klausuren* (written papers), orals and a dissertation.

Teacher training in Germany is carried on partly at the *pädagogische Hochschulen* (colleges of education) and partly at the universities. Prospective *Studienräte* study two subjects to *Staatsexamen* level, after which they are accepted into the educational service as trainees for a period of two years ending with a further qualifying examination. *Realschullehrer* study two subjects for a minimum of eight semesters at a *pädagogische Hochschule* or a university before undergoing a similar period of practical training, while *Hauptschullehrer* and *Grundschullehrer* are trained for six semesters at a *pädagogische Hochschule.* The majority of students at colleges of education are women, which seems to indicate that many women students regard the lengthy period of study required for a career as a *Studienrat*, which leaves them unqualified until about the age of twenty-eight, as personally disadvantageous.

SDS Demands

The strongest pressure for reform of the West German educational system came from the various student organisations which were responsible for 'actions' and demonstrations from 1967 onwards and which clashed violently with the university and civil authorities. This pressure had been building up over a number of years. By 1961 the main student organisation, the *Sozialistischer Deutscher Studentenbund* (SDS), was sufficiently infiltrated by Communist elements for the SPD to decide to separate itself formally from the student organisation. This had the effect of isolating the SDS and leaving it open to further infiltration by political extremists, as was to become apparent later in the decade. During the mid-sixties the SDS organised occasional demonstrations at the Free University in Berlin which were modelled on the anti-Vietnam-War campus demonstrations in the United States, but no violent disturbances occurred until 1967 when a demonstration was held in West Berlin protesting against a visit by the Shah of Iran and a student was shot and killed by a policeman. This event marked the beginning of a phase of violent demonstrations in the university and on the streets, and of extreme demands for educational reform. Lectures were boycotted or disturbed, university professors were terrorised in their homes by gangs of extremist students, university premises were damaged and walls were daubed with political slogans. The unrest spread from West Berlin to other West German universities and from there to the upper forms of the *Gymnasium*. The controlling organisation in the schools was the so-called APO (*ausserparlamentarische Opposition*), or opposition outside parliament — a reference to the coalition government of the time. By 1970, however, the protest movement had lost its momentum and the students were splitting up into extremist factions with uncoordinated political programmes.

Many excesses were committed and the SDS and APO lost much sympathy through their wild tactics and crude left-wing propaganda, but some of their demands were basically reasonable. As mentioned above, the traditional education system was inflexible and it bestowed considerable arbitrary power on individual professors and ministerial officials. The SDS and APO demanded a reform of both secondary and higher education. In secondary education they were chiefly concerned with the upper forms of the *Gymnasium* where they wanted to see a more modern curriculum, especially in the arts subjects. In the teaching of German, for example, they called for the rejection of established classics in favour of modern authors or mass circulation literature of all kinds. Methods of teaching should be less authoritarian, new subjects should be introduced – sex education being the favourite – and above all there should be more political discussion. They also demanded more organisational reforms to increase the number of pupils able to take the *Abitur*, and an increase in public spending on education. In higher education an end to the *Ordinarienuniversität* was called for, i.e. the university which appears to be run by and for professors, together with reforms in the curricula and the examinations system, and an abolition of the *numerus clausus*. Both the SPD and the CDU tended initially to condemn the extremist tactics used by the students, but were soon forced to recognise that the demonstrations were not without substance. From their point of view the education system needed improvement in the long-term interests of the national economy; it could not be denied that educational spending in the FRG was the lowest among the industrial nations of Western Europe, nor that the rigid educational structure failed to exploit the nation's reserve of talent.

Children from working-class families were at a severe disadvantage in West German schools compared to their counterparts in the United Kingdom. As late as 1971, only 7.5 per cent of those taking *Abitur* came from working-class homes. (In 1980 the figure is expected to be approximately 25 per cent.) It could also be shown that children from rural areas, girls in general and, to some extent, the children of Catholic families had to suffer handicaps in their education. In particular, the tripartite system worked against the majority of children in two respects: in the first place, the divisions imposed and the standards required were firmly rooted in the middle-class view of society, and it was tacitly assumed that only those families which could afford to pay for their children to go to university had any right to encourage them to stay at school beyond the minimum leaving age; and secondly, the sharp distinction that was drawn between the exclusive education offered by the *Gymnasium* and technical and vocational training meant that the majority of children, however bright they may have subsequently proved to be, were never able to use their vocational qualifications as a route into higher education.

The main positions that emerged from the internal debate within the two parties were that the SPD favoured an integration of the three types of secondary school into one *Gesamtschule* (comprehensive school), while the CDU/CSU preferred to improve the existing system while retaining its main features intact.

1973 Proposals

By 1973 the *Bund-Länder-Kommission* published its comprehensive plan for education, the *Bildungsgesamtplan*, which clearly favours the replacement of the traditional tripartite school system by an integrated comprehensive system which would permit 25 per cent of the pupils of each year group to gain the *Abitur* and proceed to university. The terminology used by the plan indicates the radical nature of the proposed structural reforms and the emphasis on continuity and progress within the system at all levels. The educational process is divided into horizontal stages, replacing the traditional vertical division between the different types of school. The *Primarbereich* or *Primarstufe* corresponds to classes 1−4 of the *Grundschule*. The *Sekundarbereich* is divided into two stages covering classes 5−10 and 11−13 respectively. Higher education is the *Tertiärer Bereich*, while the many forms of adult education and continuing education become the *Quartärer Bereich*.

The plan and the discussion surrounding it are primarily concerned with ensuring equality of opportunity and movement from one branch of education to another without formal obstacles. This is to be achieved through structural and curricular changes. It is recommended that in the *Sekundarbereich I* the *Orientierungsstufe* should be established to ensure that all pupils have the best possible opportunity to follow the courses for which they are naturally fitted. Subjects in the curriculum should be divided into a *Pflichtbereich* (compulsory group) and a *Wahlbereich* (optional group), while assessment and marking systems should be made more objective and standardised throughout the country. Pupils who leave school at the end of the *Sekundarbereich I* should be awarded a qualification to enable them to go straight into further vocational training or education, while the *Sekundarbereich II* should attach equal importance to vocational and academic education. The traditional divisions in the teaching profession, which reinforced the divisions between the schools and the status of their pupils, should be replaced by the concept of the *Stufenlehrer*, i.e. the teacher trained to teach at a particular stage of the educational process, but within the same school. In classes 11 and 12 of the *Sekundarbereich* a new type of school is envisaged, the *Fachoberschule*, which would bridge the gap between vocational and academic education and offer a smooth transition into higher vocational education. The *Abitur* would continue to be taken at the end of class 13 of the *Gesamtschule*.

The reaction of the *Länder* to the concept of the *Gesamtschule* has

been mixed. Hessen was the first to embark on a process of radical reform and in 1972 had already issued a set of guidelines, the *Hessische Rahmenrichtlinien* which caused a national controversy, particularly the proposed changes in the curriculum for the teaching of German. The general reaction has been to introduce different models of the *Gesamtschule* while at the same time retaining a slightly modified form of the tripartite system.

The practical implementation of the reforms, especially where no experimental phase has been possible, has brought many problems and conflicts, and it is as yet too early to assess to what extent the *Gesamtschule* is succeeding in its objectives. In the organisational sphere there is no general agreement on whether the *Gesamtschule* should be 'co-operative', i.e. should permit the various branches of the school to retain something of their own identity within a loose over-all structure, or 'integrated', i.e. should merge the different branches physically into one school. In practical terms the problem is usually solved by the resources available for reorganisation. Not all teachers are happy about the concept of the *Stufenlehrer*, particularly the teachers of the *Gymnasien* who fear that their longer training and higher academic qualifications are being devalued. In the pedagogical sphere it is not yet clear whether the measures to improve equality of opportunity will not have an adverse effect on the education of more academically gifted children, and it is often stated that the new system, by reducing the importance of the class as the basic group, weakens the pupil's sense of identity in the school community. The reorganisation has also meant that certain subjects have suffered a loss in teaching time or have been removed from the curriculum altogether — e.g. the teaching of French in Lower Saxony has been severely curtailed. Teachers complain that curricular changes involve them in excessive administration and committee work which impairs their teaching efficiency. It is also important to note that many of the criticisms brought against the *Gesamtschule* are of a political nature. Many Germans regard it as a product of a specific ideological position which seeks reform for political and social rather than educational reasons. The intrusion of politics into the educational sphere is viewed with caution in West Germany after the experiences of recent history.

Higher Education Law (1976)

In 1976 the *Hochschulrahmengesetz* (framework legislation on higher

education, abbreviated HSR) was accepted and published in its final form. This document, which is based on several years of consultation and deliberation by the *Westdeutsche Rektorenkonferenz*, takes into account the criticisms raised during the previous decade and establishes a framework within which the *Länder* are required to reorganise the universities and institutions of higher education for which they are responsible. The time set for implementing the reorganisations is three years. In seven chapters the HSR deals with many contentious issues. It states clearly that it considers the Humboldtian type of university no longer able to meet the demands placed on it by modern industrial society; it is therefore to be replaced by the *Gesamthochschule*, or comprehensive university. Existing universities, *pädagogische Hochschulen* and other specialist institutions are to be brought together, either as an integrated whole, or to work co-operatively, in the *Gesamthochschule*. The courses of study are to be co-ordinated in order to enable students to change from one course to another without loss of time and waste of effort. In addition, students are to be regularly credited with courses already taken, in contrast to the traditional system which was fairly inflexible in this respect. As well as providing for systematic tutorial guidance for students, the HSR places emphasis on improving the practice of teaching — another point on which the traditional university tended to be weak — and on the design of integrated teaching and research programmes which draw upon the resources of the whole institution. The inefficient use made of university buildings and facilities, which customarily remain empty for almost half the year, had been sharply criticised by some politicians over the years as a glaring example of waste in the increasingly expensive educational sector, and the HSR meets this criticism by making provision for a more intensive use throughout the year. One of the most controversial innovations in the HSR is the provision for a *Regelstudienzeit* (fixed period of study up to final examination) of 3–4 years. Taken out of context and viewed from an English perspective such a provision does not seem to be particularly drastic, but in the West German context it imposes a corset on the process of studying and teaching which severely reduces the freedom permitted by the old system. Lecturers have to co-ordinate the courses they teach and take their turn in teaching subjects of little interest to them personally, while students have to follow a concentrated course which does not allow them to follow up or develop those parts of the curriculum which interest them most, nor to study at their own pace. The university authorities, on the other hand, see certain advantages in the

Regelstudienzeit since it focuses the students' attention on their studies and away from excessive political agitation. The *Regelstudienzeit* has been stubbornly contested by the student organisations which now find themselves accused, with some justification, of wanting to have their cake and eat it: after years of demonstrating for a more vocationally orientated, open and democratic system, they are now protesting in favour of the most characteristic feature of the old system.

The HSR reorganises the faculties of the traditional university into *Fachbereiche*, or subject areas, which become the basic units of internal academic administration. Each *Fachbereich* elects a council representing all the groups employed or present within it, chaired by a professor. This arrangement is intended to introduce more democratic decision-making procedures and to ensure that the interests of the professors do not always take precedence over those of the other groups of academic staff or students, as was often the case in previous years. The universities are not to be directly responsible for the admission of students: this is to be administered through a *Zentralstelle zur Vergabe von Studienplätzen*, or central office for university admissions, which bases its decisions on the average *Note* achieved in the *Abitur*.

The strong emphasis in the HSR on the functions of the university in preparing students for professional life marks a drastic break with tradition. In this respect it is responding not only to the arguments developed during the prolonged debate on higher education but also to the prognostication by government and independent researchers of mass unemployment among traditionally educated graduates in Western industrial societies. It has concluded that the strict division between academic and vocational education is a luxury which the country can no longer afford.

It will be appreciated that the discussion surrounding the HSR and its reformulation in the legislation passed by each of the *Länder* includes a variety of complex issues at many levels, and it will be several years before the initial response is clarified in the light of experience. Some critics regard the HSR as a compromise which has blurred the original demands for reform; others regard it as the ruination of a proven system. Many established institutions which had acquired a high independent reputation over many years resent the loss of their separate identity. Nor is this reaction confined to the older universities. The *Fachhochschulen* (colleges of advanced technology) point out that they stand to lose their essentially practical function by being integrated into an academic structure which will require their involvement in courses of a more theoretical nature. In particular, there are tensions

between the universities and the colleges of education over the question of status and standards. A frequent complaint from university teachers is that the time-consuming committee work which the HSR has generated is affecting not only their teaching but also their research, and this at a time when the FRG needs to intensify technological research in order to maintain its position among the industrial nations of the world. As evidence of the declining efficiency of the universities they point to the increasing volume of scientific research undertaken in private institutes outside the universities. These are only a few of the conflicts and criticisms arising from the implementation of the HSR by the *Länder*. Of course, there are many academics who see the HSR in a more positive light, but it will be some time before either the supporters or the opponents of the reforms will be able to draw any firm conclusions to support their case.

Vocational Schooling

About 80 per cent of West German children still leave school between the ages of 15 and 16, with the aim of going straight into a trade or occupation. Since the *Schulpflicht* extends until the age of 18, the school leavers have to attend some form of state school for a further three years. For most of them this means attendance at a *Berufsschule*, or vocational school, for one day a week in conjunction with their work. There are two other main types of vocational school which can be attended on a full- or part-time basis — the *Berufsfachschule* and the *Berufsaufbauschule*.

Before explaining the functions of these three forms of vocational education, it is important to note that the system of industrial craft training in the FRG differs in certain respects from the British system. Apprenticeships in Germany are shorter, their length depending on the degree of skill involved; in general they last between two and four years. The chambers of industry and trade also participate actively in the supervision and examining of apprentices. On successfully completing his apprenticeship, the apprentice (*Lehrling* or, in more recent parlance, *Auszubildende*) becomes a journeyman (*Geselle*), which entitles him to the full rates of pay for the trade. While most tradesmen do not progress beyond this stage, a proportion continues to become master craftsmen (*Meister*), which involves a further period of study and a practical examination. To some extent, state provision of vocational education can be regarded as complementary to this old established

system. Some large firms run their own internal training schemes comprising both practical and theoretical experience. Although these schemes are sometimes criticised on the grounds that they train their apprentices for specialised work in the firm rather than for the trade as a whole, there is no doubt that some internal apprentice-training schemes enjoy high regard because of the standards they achieve. An outstanding example is the *Stufenausbildung* (training in stages) scheme operated by the firm of Krupp.

The *Berufsschule* is a significant and traditional element in the German educational system, with a long history which reaches back well into the nineteenth century. In its present form it can be regarded as a product of the industrial revolution in Germany. The three aims of the *Berufsschule* are:

1. to provide the simple theoretical background to the trade being learned at work, together with systematic practice in certain technical skills;
2. to provide political and social education relating to the citizen's rights and duties in the FRG and to the position of the worker;
3. to provide general and moral education.

The second and third aims are understood to be a continuation of the work begun in the secondary schools.

While there is a general consensus on the basic aims, there is some disagreement on the emphasis and organisation of the curriculum. The *Berufsschulen* tend to attach some importance to background studies of a general nature, whereas the employers' associations maintain that technical education should be given priority. They also complain that the *Berufsschulen* offer out-of-date instruction which does not take account of latest methods and equipment. It is interesting, however, that the employers' associations have supported the move to raise the school leaving age by one year in order to introduce the *Berufsgrundbildungsjahr* into secondary education. The trade unions favour an extension of state control in vocational education and a reduction of the part played by the chambers of industry and trade. They also point out that there are too many 'dead ends' in the system, so that people are faced with the prospect of never being able to progress beyond a certain level of qualification because of lack of integration between technical and academic education.

The organisation of the *Berufsschulen* reflects the pattern of local industry or agriculture. Small towns with a specialist industry, e.g.

mining, have a *Bergberufsschule* (mining school); agricultural areas have a *landwirtschaftliche Berufsschule* (agricultural school); larger cities have a variety of appropriate specialised schools, e.g. *kaufmännische Berufsschulen* (commercial schools).

By the mid-seventies proposals had been formulated for changes in the structure of vocational education. The reasons for this were connected with the rapid pace of technological development which threatens some trades with obsolescence, and with the demographic predictions mentioned above which make it urgently necessary that the nation's technical manpower resources should be exploited to the full. A reformed system has now been introduced in certain *Länder* and different patterns are emerging.

The new system comprises three stages. Stage I is the *Berufsgrundbildungsjahr*, a one-year full-time vocational course based on the *Hauptschulabschluss*. Its aim is to enable pupils to acquaint themselves with the type of basic skills required in the different broad categories into which trades can be grouped. This first year includes extensive practical experience which is intended to facilitate the choice of a specific career. Stage II is a two-year full-time course spent partly in full-time apprenticeship and partly in vocational education. Successful completion of stage II qualifies the apprentice to practise his trade and is equivalent to the *Geselle* under the traditional system. Many tradesmen, having reached the end of stage II, will not wish to continue training, but for those who do there is stage III, lasting a further two years, which not only leads to an advanced specialist qualification corresponding to *Meister*, but also opens the way to a university-level qualification through the *Gesamthochschule*. This is a radical improvement on the traditional pattern of vocational education from the shop floor, which allowed a worker to qualify to the level of *Meister*, but then placed enormous obstacles in the way of any further qualification at a more theoretical level.

The reforms in vocational education also affect the teachers who staff the *Berufsschulen*. At present the teachers are either practical craftsmen or teachers trained for secondary education. In contrast to the other branches of education in the FRG, there is still a shortage of qualified teachers for the *Berufsschulen* and the fact that over half the staff at these schools are paid by the hour gives some idea of the unsatisfactory nature of much of the teaching. It is planned that all staff teaching at *Berufsschulen* should be academically and professionally trained, though little progress has as yet been made towards this goal.

The arrangements for the *Berufsfachschule* vary according to the *Land*. As a rule, however, it is a full-time school offering courses lasting from one to three years, leading to the qualification of *Fachschulreife*, which is equivalent to the *mittlere Reife* awarded by the *Realschule*. In some occupations the *Fachschulreife* is accepted as equivalent to a practical vocational qualification, in others it has to be supplemented by a period of practical apprenticeship. The holder of the *Fachschulreife* has the advantage of being able to continue his education at a *Fachhochschule* or *Ingenieurschule*, as they are sometimes still designated. Since these latter institutions are to be integrated into the *Gesamthochschulen*, it will be possible for a student to work his way up from the *Berufsfachschule* to a full university education. Although the benefits for the individual offered by the reformed system cannot be disputed, fears have been expressed that the integration of the *Fachhochschulen* and *Ingenieurschulen* into *Gesamthochschulen* will create a vacuum at the intermediate level of technical education between the shop floor craftsmen and the university-trained technologists. This is a serious problem at a time when industry's greatest need is for competent middle-level technologists rather than for tradesmen or university graduates.

The *Berufsaufbauschule* is the smallest branch of the vocational educational sector and the number of students attending has been in steady decline for over a decade. By contrast, the *Berufsfachschule* has been expanding and the *Fachoberschule* has newly appeared on the scene. The *Berufsaufbauschule* offers full- and part-time courses over one and a half to three years. Students may enter if they have achieved a certain standard after the first semester at the *Berufsschule*, and the aim of the course is to provide specialised vocational education leading to the *Fachschulreife*.

The *Fachschule* is also run on a full- and part-time basis. Its usual purpose is to offer training for *Gesellen* who wish to qualify as *Meister*, and for this reason it is still sometimes referred to as the *Meisterschule*. The entry qualifications are *Geselle* status together with substantial trade experience, and the course, which is of a practical nature, lasts from six months to three years.

Whether we consider vocational education, with its plethora of institutions, or any other branch of education in the FRG, the effects of the radical changes initiated during the seventies are clearly apparent. The debates which preceded and accompanied these changes have been protracted and bitter, and it is as yet too early for an objective

judgement to be formed on the success — or failure — of the new system. It will, however, be interesting to see whether the new institutions will be able to match the academic and technical excellence of the traditional system which has contributed so much to German pre-eminence in science and scholarship.

Further Reading

DAAD. *Higher Education in the Federal Republic of Germany* (Bonn, 1965)

Hearnden, Arthur. *Education in the Two Germanies* (Oxford, 1974)
——. *Education, Culture, and Politics in West Germany* (Oxford, 1976)
——. *The British in Germany:Educational Reconstruction after 1945* (London, 1978)

Hundeck, J. and Wolff, I. *Der Lehrer an der hoheren Schule* (Munich, 1968)

Knoll, J. H. *Bildung und Wissenschaft in der Bundesrepublik Deutschland* (Munich, 1976)

Notes

1. See also p. 101 above.
2. See also pp. 93–94 above.
3. Average monthly wage in industry during the same period was DM 2,200, not counting family allowances.

7 THE MASS MEDIA

Origins of the Press

The development of the mass media in Germany followed the same pattern as in the other advanced industrial societies. The development of cities, populated by large numbers of semi-literate, newly enfranchised voters, enjoying a modicum of prosperity, provided ideal targets for would-be press barons. In Britain most town dwellers got the right to vote in 1867; in Germany universal male suffrage was introduced for the Reichstag in 1870. By that time a majority of Britons and over 36 per cent of Germans lived in towns. By the turn of the century over 71 per cent of the UK population were urban dwellers, as were over 54 per cent of the Reich. In both countries the legal framework covering the press became easier in the second half of the nineteenth century, but in Germany there remained more restrictions than in Britain or the United States. The Reich Press Law (*Reichspressegesetz*) of 1874 was in some ways more liberal than the many regional press laws it replaced. Chancellor Bismarck, however, retained powers over the press which some Anglo-Saxon politicians could only envy. In particular, the anti-socialist laws (1878–90) prohibited the publication of socialist ideas.

The most successful of Germany's early mass circulation papers was the *Berliner Lokal-Anzeiger*, established in 1883 by August Scherl. Like Alfred Harmsworth's *Daily Mail*, founded in 1896, and the New York 'penny papers', Scherl's paper was a mix of entertainment, human interest stories, and short, easily digested political articles with a right-wing bias. Advertising as a means of financing these popular newspapers was already an integral part of the press economy. By 1900 the German press world was seeing the emergence of publishing empires associated with Scherl, Rudolf Mosse and Leopold Ullstein.

Germany had produced Europe's first regular newspapers at the beginning of the seventeenth century and there was, therefore, a more traditional type of quality newspaper as well as the popular press. The most distinguished of these old papers was the *Vossische Zeitung* (1704–1934). This paper is often compared to the London *Times* (founded in 1785) and the Swiss *Neue Zürcher Zeitung* (1780). The *Allgemeine Zeitung*, first published in 1797, was also part of this tradition. Three quality papers were established in the second half of the nineteenth century — the *Frankfurter Zeitung* (1856), the *Norddeutsche Allgemeine Zeitung* (1861), which became the *Deutsche Allgemeine Zeitung* in 1919, and the *Berliner Tageblatt*. These papers were independent of party politics, but were broadly nationalist and conservative in sympathy.

In this period there emerged another type of German news publication — the party press. The most successful of these was the Social Democratic press which developed after 1875. The SPD's central organ *Vorwärts* first appeared in 1876 and within a year had 12,000 regular subscribers. This represented a better-than-average circulation at that time. *Vorwärts* was banned during the years of the anti-socialist laws, reappearing on New Year's Day, 1891. Later in the same month a women's magazine, *Die Arbeiterin* (*The Woman Worker*), was brought out by the SPD. This was to become famous as *Die Gleichheit* (*Equality*) from 1892 onwards. The SPD had its own papers in most of the larger towns, such as the *Hamburger Echo*, the *Leipziger Volksblatt* and, in Dresden, the *Sächsisches Wochenblatt*. By 1904 the total circulation of SPD-owned newspapers was just under 600,000. They employed 151 editors and nearly 1,500 other technical personnel. The Catholics also developed a considerable press in the early days of the new Reich. Perhaps their most distinguished paper was the *Germania*, which first appeared in Berlin in 1870.

As in Britain, Weimar Germany (1919–33) experienced the growth of great press empires engaged in circulation wars against their rivals. The most sinister of these in Germany was that of Alfred Hugenberg (1865–1951). Hugenberg was an influential industrialist before he went into the mass media. Together with some others, he took over Scherl's assets in 1913. He built the most powerful press, publishing and communications empire in Europe. This he used for right-wing political purposes. In 1927 he captured the UFA film company which was responsible for three-quarters of German films, including the weekly *Wochenschau* (newsreel). Hugenberg was chairman of the reactionary DNVP and as such played a major part in winning over the industrial and military establishment for Hitler. For a short time in 1933 he was a member of Hitler's government. The Nazis themselves, contrary to popular belief, did not manage to sell many of their publications under free conditions. Their principal paper, the *Völkischer Beobachter*, had a circulation of only about 40,000 in 1930. By comparison, in 1931, the Catholic press sold 2.3 million copies daily. The Catholics owned 448 daily papers at this time out of a total of 4,500 German daily papers

with a circulation of 20 million. In the same year the SPD owned 196
dailies.

Weimar Film Industry

The inter-war period is known as the golden age of the cinema, as the
film became an increasingly popular form of entertainment. As an
advanced nation, Germany made an important contribution to the
development of the film as a means of entertainment, education and
propaganda. German film production in 1921 rivalled that of the
United States. Later in the 1920s it was overtaken by Hollywood but
even in 1925, with 228 feature films, it outstripped both Britain (44
films) and France (74). The film directors and actors of the Weimar
Republic became renowned for their great skills. Among the best-known
directors were Fritz Lang, G. W. Pabst, Richard Oswald and Joseph von
Sternberg. Actors such as Emil Jannings and Marlene Dietrich became
world famous for their parts in *The Blue Angel* which was made in 1930
with an English as well as a German version. Many other German actors
– Peter Lorre, Lotte Lenya, Lilli Palmer and Conrad Veidt among them
– became well-known screen faces in Hollywood films after 1933.
German directors cast a wide net for subject matter, using everything
from contemporary thrillers, adapted from Thea von Harbou's novels,
to science fiction, popular history, the novels of Thomas Mann and
even the plays of Shakespeare. As one would expect in a mass
entertainment industry, most of the production consisted of not very
demanding musicals, thrillers and 'family entertainment'. Indeed, the
first German film to exploit sound was *I Kiss Your Hand Madame*
(1929) which was a musical romance featuring Marlene Dietrich and
Harry Liedtke. Occasionally, directors chose more controversial
subjects, risking empty seats, public disapproval or even prohibitions. A
form of censorship existed under the Reich Film Act of May 1920.
Boards of censors in Berlin and Munich were required to examine films
for public exhibition. They could declare films unsuitable for public
screening. Officially this censorship was aimed at pornography but the
very fact of censorship tended to make directors think twice about
taking an unconventional line. On the other hand, the Act did
encourage directors to attempt to raise the artistic level of their work
by offering entertainment tax reductions for films of special artistic
merit. The Act also encouraged the German movie industry by imposing
a quota on foreign films.

Among the German films which were of more than passing interest were Pabst's film exposing the horrors of war (*Westfront 1918*, 1930) and his film promoting Franco-German understanding (*Kameradschaft*, 1931). Richard Oswald's mockery of Prussian militarism (*Der Hauptmann von Köpenick*, 1931), Leontine Sagan's denunciation of authoritarian boarding schools (*Mädchen in Uniform*, 1931), Piel Jutzi's sympathetic look at Berlin life during the slump (*Berlin-Alexanderplatz*, 1931) and Max Ophüls's attack on the military code (*Liebelei*, 1933). *Kuhle Wampe* (1932) also deserves special mention with its look at life among the unemployed of Berlin. It was directed by the Bulgarian Slatan Dudow.

Weimar Germany's film industry also made an important contribution to the early documentary. The most celebrated German documentary of the 1920s was directed by Carl Mayer, assisted by Karl Freund and Walter Ruttmann. Called *Berlin, Symphony of a Great City*, it attempted to create a 'melody of pictures' out of the life and pulse of the capital.

There was another type of German film at this time which had a purpose other than entertainment. A considerable number of films were made by Gustav Ucicky, Werner Krauss and others which had a strongly nationalistic flavour about them. At the very least, these films strengthened the rising tide of nationalism and it is not an accident that many of them were the products of Hugenberg's UFA.

The Nazis were great believers in propaganda and once they gained power in 1933 Hitler sought rapidly to mould the mass media into one mighty orchestra led by one conductor, Joseph Goebbels, which would pour out its symphonies of praise for the *Führer* and hymns of hate against his enemies. Apart from the few who emigrated, most of those employed in the press, the radio and the cinema were happy to join the orchestra, having passed the audition as 'Aryans'. Perhaps one should not be too hard on most of those in the movie business. After all, most actors and directors the world over regard themselves as 'non-political', and Hollywood's stars of the period were merely clay in the hands of the tycoons they served. Even actors like Emil Jannings prostituted their talents to feature in Nazi propaganda epics like *Ohm Krüger* – a heavy-handed tale, based on fact, about the South African War. Pabst also directed films in the Third Reich, managing, however, to steer clear of political films. Leni Riefenstahl's *Triumph of the Will*, which purported to be a film record of the Nazi party congress of 1934, remains the most impressive of the 'symphonies'. Possibly the most evil film ever made was *Der Ewige Jude* (*The Eternal Jew*) directed by

Franz Hippler. Using documentary techniques it claimed to be a history of the Jews, but was really a vile hymn of hate preparing the Germans psychologically for the genocide policy of their leaders. Goebbels was more sophisticated than his master and realised that most Germans were not very politically minded, and wanted relaxation and escape in the cinema. For the most part, therefore, the film industry in the Third Reich continued with the old diet — comedies, musicals, adventures and women's-magazine-style romances.

Films of 'Anno Zero'

Like every other institution in Germany after the war the motion picture industry was powerless to commence production again without a licence from the appropriate occupying power. In the Soviet Zone the authorities decided early on to keep the industry centralised and placed all its assets in one new company — DEFA. This company had the advantage of excellent studios at Neubabelsberg close to Berlin. It was liberally funded and in its early years had some success with a number of serious films. The best known of them was Wolfgang Staudte's *Die Mörder sind unter uns* (*The Murderers Are Among Us*) which was Germany's first post-war international success. Made in 1946, its story was that of a former officer and war criminal, who managed to conceal his past and to establish himself as a model citizen. He is later exposed by a doctor and a young woman. Thus the film dealt with a theme which has remained relevant even in 1980. One other aspect of the film which is of minor interest is that it launched Hildegard Knef on her movie career. Unfortunately, much of DEFA's opportunity was subsequently wasted due to suffocating political control.

In the Western Zones the industry was broken up into small units which faced severe financial pressures. Nevertheless, a number of intelligent, low-budget films did find their way on to the screens between 1946 and 1948. Studio 45, in the British Zone, produced *Zugvögel* (*Birds of Migration*) which was a fair attempt to deal with the problem of refugees. Helmut Käutner directed the successful *In jenen Tagen* (*In Former Days*, 1947) which was a tale about an old motor-car and the fate of its changing owners during the Nazi years. One of the best films to emerge from the American sphere of influence was Robert Stemmle's *Berliner Ballade* (*Ballad of Berlin*, 1948) which, through its central character, Otto Nobody, expressed the average German's scepticism about the post-war world. A moving film shot in the French

Zone was *Germania Anno Zero* (*Germany Year Zero*, 1947). It was directed by the Italian Roberto Rossellini but made in German with German actors. It is a grim account of a starving German family, of murder and suicide amid the engulfing ruins which was all that was left of many German towns.

As well as political, psychological and financial problems, the post-war German cinema faced another difficulty, which lay in finding enough film theatres to show its products. In Munich, for instance, there were only about ten cinemas open in January 1946 as compared with 80 before the war. Berlin was much better served, partly because of the inter-Allied rivalries. But there too the number of cinemas in operation was well below the pre-war figure.

Films During the 'Economic Miracle'

The 1950s brought a resurgence of the European film industry as it battled against the increasing competition from television and from imported films. The 'new wave' swept through Italy, France and Poland. In West Germany, as in Britain, only the faint ripples of this wave were felt. In the studios of Hamburg and Munich, as well as those of Elstree and Ealing, commercial considerations were usually the decisive factor in deciding what themes should be handled and how they should be handled. The result in the FRG was that the staple fare of the West German filmgoer were slap-stick comedies, cheap thrillers, historical romances and *Heimat* films. The latter could be defined as movies set in picturesque Bavarian villages which were populated by cardboard figures who invariably dressed in traditional costumes, and who invariably got up to a variety of lighthearted pranks in the barns and hostelries of their native land (*Heimat*). The West German directors of this *genre*, just like their British colleagues who directed the 'Carry On' series, would defend them on the grounds that, given the severe foreign competition and lack of capital, they could not afford to take risks, and that, anyway, they were giving the public what it wanted. Certainly there was some truth in these claims. More than half the films available were American, usually dubbed, and there were many others from Britain, Italy and France. There were also a considerable number of co-productions. As in the Weimar Republic, films considered of special merit were granted a tax rebate and subsidies and prizes were introduced for suitable films. As the austere forties gave way to the affluent fifties, audiences sought *Ablenkung* (diversion) and escapism in their local cinema. Many citizens of the *Wirtschaftswunderland* did not want to be forced to examine their part in Germany's recent past nor did producers credit them with the wit to confront the many unsolved problems of the affluent society. Whether a less commercially orientated cinema could have done more in this direction is difficult to say, but Germans did flock to see serious movies from other countries and a handful of German directors did have some success in their struggle to come to terms with reality.

Pabst was one of that handful. His *Der Letzte Akt* (*The Last Act*, 1954) and *Es geschah am 20. Juli* (*It Happened On 20th July*, 1955) dealt respectively with Hitler's last days in Berlin and the Stauffenberg bomb plot against the *Führer*. They did not have the dramatic impact of his 1931 films. Two West German films of the period which did gain international success were Laszlo Benedek's *Kinder, Mütter und ein General* (*Children, Mothers and a General*, 1955) and Bernhard Wicki's *Die Brücke* (*The Bridge*, 1959). Both had similar plots involving the senseless sacrifice of schoolboys taking part in the last ditch defence of the doomed Third Reich. The outstanding West German director of the 1950s was undoubtedly Helmut Käutner. He tried to combine entertainment with exposure of Germany's Nazi and militarist past. *Des Teufels General* (*The Devil's General*, 1955) admitted that the professional soldiers of Germany between 1933 and 1945 worked for the devil. It also paid brief tribute to the working-class anti-Nazi activist. To some degree, however, it glamourised and re-established the professional soldier, for the General (played by the charming Kurt Jürgens) is portrayed as a ladykiller, a flyer with great achievements to his credit, and a gallant gentleman who bravely submits to Gestapo torture and then in an act of self-sacrifice crashes his plane. Käutner also did a remake of the *Captain of Köpenick*. In some respects this was a fairly safe theme as it was a comedy (albeit a serious one) dressed up in the colourful (unreal?) uniforms of the nineteenth century rather than the more familiar ones of the twentieth. On the other hand, it did poke fun at old-fashioned military obedience at a time (1956) when West Germany was debating just what kind of discipline its new armed forces, established in 1955, should have. Käutner's first film of this type, *Die Letzte Brücke* (*The Last Bridge*, 1954) was the best of the three. Shot in Yugoslavia, it was about the conflict of loyalties of a German nurse (Maria Schell), captured by the Yugoslav partisans. In so far as it treated the Yugoslav resistance fighters as courageous, intelligent and honourable combatants it helped to destroy the Nazi stereotype of the Slav. The film was made at a time when West Germany was seeking close diplomatic ties with Yugoslavia and was indeed a co-production.

Whether they were West or East of the Elbe German directors found it easier to examine the realities of the past than those of the present. Very few films were made which questioned the standards of society as it was emerging. Rolf Thiele made some sort of attempt in *Das Mädchen Rosemarie* (*The Girl Rosemarie*, 1958) which, in effect, carried the message that the prostitute (Nadja Tiller) was more 'moral' than the industrialists who were enjoying her favours. Wolfgang Staudte, by this time working permanently in the Federal Republic, also directed films which turned the spotlight on to the dark corners of West German society. In his *Rosen für den Staatsanwalt* (*Roses for the Prosecutor*, 1959) he made the entirely justified point that many West German judges had worked in the same capacity for the Nazis, presenting a legal façade for an inhuman system. In the conservative Adenauer era it required some courage to direct such films.

The Rebirth of the Press

Even more than the cinema, the post-war German press appeared brand new. All publications established before the summer of 1949 had to be licensed by the Allies. Most of the old titles disappeared, not to reappear. The distinction of being the first non-Nazi paper to reappear on German soil goes to the *Aachener Nachrichten*. The Americans allowed a Social Democrat, Heinrich Hollands, to publish the first edition of 24 January 1945 – i.e. three and a half months before the German surrender. In the months after the German capitulation several publications were licensed which were to play a vital role in the rebirth of the West German press and in the political arguments in the Federal Republic. Among these were *Die Zeit, Der Spiegel, Süddeutsche Zeitung*, the *Frankfurter Rundschau* and *Die Welt*. The last named was one of a group of papers owned and operated by the four powers to present their views to the Germans. *Die Welt* was British owned. After the two German states were set up the powers gradually came to the conclusion that these papers had outlived their usefulness. The French, Soviet and US papers disappeared; only *Die Welt* survived, having been sold by the British to Axel Springer in September 1953.

The *Grundgesetz* of the Federal Republic gives formal legal guarantees on freedom of expression in Article 5:

  (i)   Everyone shall have the right freely to express and disseminate his opinion by speech, writing and pictures and freely to inform himself from generally accessible sources. Freedom of the press and freedom of reporting by means of broadcasts and films are guaranteed. There shall be no censorship.

(ii) These rights are limited by the provisions of the general laws, the provisions of law for the protection of youth, and by the right to inviolability of personal honour.

(iii) Art and science, research and teaching, shall be free. Freedom in teaching shall not absolve from loyalty to the constitution.

The closer formulation of laws concerned with the press was held to be a matter for the *Länder* and, gradually, they enacted appropriate legislation. As one would expect, there are formal limitations on this freedom of expression. Article 353c of the Criminal Code prohibits publication of official news supposed to be secret. Under it a journalist may be compelled to reveal his sources. Article 187a of the same code makes it an offence to defame public figures. The reality behind the constitutional provisions for free expression is that West Germany is a state in which a wide variety of opinions are freely expressed in books, plays, the press, on radio and television. If he is interested enough the individual has the materials at hand to inform himself on the great issues of the present or the past. However, all is far from perfect. As far as the press is concerned, there is an unhealthy tendency towards concentration of ownership (something not unknown in Britain), and the right of centre view is far better represented than the left of centre (again, a similar situation exists in the UK).

Press Concentration

In 1975 there were some 375 daily newspapers appearing in the Federal Republic, with a combined circulation of over 22 million — the highest circulation claimed anywhere in Western Europe. This would appear to be a healthy situation; but in reality many of the papers were part of large organisations, differing from other papers merely in their titles and perhaps one page of local news. The number of units with independent editorial staffs has dropped steadily over the years. The biggest publishing organisation, that of Axel Cäsar Springer, is the biggest in

Western Europe. The Springer Concern publishes West Germany's largest daily paper, *Bild Zeitung*, which in 1979 had a circulation of 4.9 million. It is a paper which bears many resemblances to *The Sun* in Britain. The same firm is responsible for the two largest Sunday papers — *Bild am Sonntag* (2.6 million) and *Welt am Sonntag* (340,000) — *Die Welt* (229,000), which is one of West Germany's three 'quality' dailies, and two dailies in Berlin. These are *B.Z.* and *Berliner Morgenpost*, which together account for over 90 per cent of West Berlin's sales of daily newspapers. Axel Springer also controls Hamburg's largest evening paper, the *Hamburger Abendblatt*, and a host of women's magazines, periodicals and the largest weekly radio and television guide, *Hör Zu*. Herr Springer takes an active interest in politics and could be described as a staunch anti-Communist of the national right. Precisely because of his strong political views, the growth of Springer's empire has worried, even frightened, many of the liberally inclined in the Federal Republic. Herr Springer has not hesitated to use the full power of his publications to attack individuals or policies of which he does not approve. Heinrich Böll, West Germany's best-known writer and a Nobel Prize winner, has been pilloried in the pages of Springer's various publications, and his papers were used to campaign vigorously against the *Ostpolitik* of the Brandt government. Using an illiberal and sensationalist approach, Springer's publications have spread fear of dissent and self-criticism. Just how much influence they have wielded it is impossible to say, but the continued growth of their circulation would seem to suggest that they have struck a responsive cord among wide sections of the West German population. Nevertheless, it must be admitted that *Ostpolitik* became reality under Brandt in spite of the opposition from Axel Springer.

Two official commissions have investigated the West German press, the first in 1964, the second in 1967. The second, *Günther Kommission*, reported in 1968 and suggested restriction by law on the proportion of the market that an individual publisher should be permitted to control. The commission believed that a 20-per-cent share of the market in either newspapers or periodicals dominated by one company represented a danger to the freedom of the press, whilst a 40-per-cent share would be positively detrimental to the freedom of the press. In the case of companies publishing both newspapers and periodicals, the thresholds should be correspondingly lower. Thus the commission proposed that a company controlling 40 per cent in one field should be restricted to 15 per cent in any other. Axel Springer subsequently sold five popular magazines though he rejected the commission's view.

In addition to commissions, the Federal Republic has a permanent German Press Council (*Deutscher Presserat*). This was set up in 1956 and comprises 20 members, ten representing the publishers and ten the journalists. The council has four main tasks: protection of the freedom of the press and ensuring unhindered access to sources of information; locating and dealing with defects in the sphere of the press; observing the structural development of the West German press and preventing the formation of business organisations and monopolies which represent a threat to freedom; representing the German press to the government, parliament and the public, especially in the event of proposed laws having a bearing on the existence and responsibilities of the press. Like its British counterpart, the *Deutscher Presserat* has no legal powers to enforce its rulings. It has to rely entirely on moral pressure.

Apart from *Die Welt*, the Federal Republic has three other quality dailies. These are the *Süddeutsche Zeitung*, the *Frankfurter Allgemeine Zeitung* and the *Frankfurter Rundschau*. With a circulation of around 320,000 in 1979, the *Süddeutsche Zeitung* is liberal in tendency and wins most of its readers in southern Germany. The *Frankfurter Allgemeine Zeitung* was founded in 1949, its journalistic team being built around the former staff of the *Frankfurter Zeitung*, the only non-Nazi paper allowed in the Third Reich until its closure in 1943. This paper is conservative in orientation and sets high journalistic standards. Its 300,000 readers (1979) are concentrated largely in the Frankfurt area and in northern Germany. In its format the *Frankfurter Allgemeine Zeitung* makes virtually no concessions to the 1970s. Also based in Frankfurt is the *Frankfurt Rundschau* (circulation 183,000), which for many years was a local paper but in the last decade or so has developed a national readership. It is the only substantial West German paper which could be described as left — meaning here a paper strongly committeed to libertarian, egalitarian ideas, giving nominal, critical support to the Social Democrats.

Decline of the Party Press

The SPD's own organ, *Vorwärts*, appears weekly. Only about 74,000 copies are sold despite the party's large membership. Probably a significant part of the membership finds it too conservative for its taste. The weakness of *Vorwärts* is symptomatic of the decline of the party political press in West Germany. After the war many party newspapers were founded, following the earlier German tradition, and Social

Democratic papers were prominent among them. Most of them disappeared in the 1950s and 1960s. They found it difficult to attract advertising which was becoming ever more important in keeping newspapers viable. Advertisers were reluctant to become associated with a particular political party or cause, especially, in some cases, with the Social Democrats. Secondly, the party papers tended to appear rather dull in an era (the 1950s) when most West Germans were trying to escape the austerity of the 1940s. Because of their declining resources the party papers could not offer their readers the wider coverage, with up-to-the-minute reports from far-flung wars and revolutions, conferences and elections, which their better-off competitors could provide. Finally, their editors had to take a too cautious and non-committal line on many party issues, in an effort to maintain party unity. This did not make for good, informative journalism. In this respect West Germany shared experiences similar to those of the British press — as opposed to Austria and Scandinavia where party newspapers still retain a considerable hold. The only other party publications in the FRG are the (hardly read) German Communist Party's *Unsere Zeit* and the weekly *Bayernkurier* (circulation 175,000), organ of the Bavarian CSU. The West German trade unions maintain a large press for their members which in 1978 had a circulation of around 14 million. These publications are mainly house journals informing members of their own union's activities. However, the DGB itself puts out weekly the *Welt der Arbeit* (186,000) aimed at a wider readership.

West Germany has few Sunday papers but it makes up for this with very impressive weeklies. Of these, *Die Zeit* (circulation 368,000) and *Der Spiegel* (1.1 million) are undoubtedly the Federal Republic's best journalistic ambassadors. In fact, *Die Zeit* has editions printed in Toronto and Buenos Aires. Both these weeklies are published in West Germany's 'press capital', Hamburg. Both are fairly liberal in outlook, but *Die Zeit* is more clearly orientated towards the capitalist economic system. *Der Spiegel*, which was one of the British occupation's success stories, has a format similar to that of *Time Magazine*. *Die Zeit* looks more like a bigger edition of the *Observer*, complete with colour supplement which it introduced in 1970. It is equally good on politics, economic affairs, travel and modern living, books and the arts. *Der Spiegel* made its name through probing series and investigative journalism. It was also at the centre of West Germany's most celebrated controversy concerning the freedom of the press. This controversy started on 10 October 1962 when *Der Spiegel* published details of the NATO autumn manoeuvres, 'Fallex 61', showing that the West German armed forces were in some respects not up to standard. Conrad Ahlers, the author of the offending piece, was arrested on holiday in Spain, and the publisher, Rudolf Augstein, was arrested in Hamburg together with some of the magazine's staff. *Der Spiegel's* offices were occupied by the police. After a national and international outcry over the issue, the federal constitutional court ruled in May 1965 that the main case against Augstein and Ahlers should not be brought. The court later rejected some of the magazine's countercharges. Franz Josef Strauss, the Defence Minister who initiated the moves against Ahlers and Augstein, was forced out of office. *Der Spiegel* went from strength to strength and the law was amended, somewhat restricting the definition of material concerned with state security. Ahlers himself was elected to the *Bundestag* on the SPD list, becoming a government press official under Brandt.

Like France, Italy and Spain, West Germany supports a number of illustrated weekly magazines more in the tradition of *Paris Match.* The best of them is *Der Stern*, which is a clever combination of everything from serious political analysis and contemporary history series, to crime, sport, gossip, motoring and fashion. *Der Stern* (circulation 1.1 million) prides itself on its photo journalism and has published some outstanding pictures during the 30-odd years of its existence. Politically, *Der Stern* is somewhere left of centre. Like *Die Zeit* and *Der Speigel,* it has not been afraid of reminding the German people of what was done in their name between 1933 and 1945. One other interesting aspect of this weekly's operation is that it has a constitution, agreed in 1969 between publisher and staff, which gives the staff a considerable say in its running.

Another weekly which is not bashful about discussing what happened in the Third Reich is the *Deutsche Nationale Zeitung* (circulation 136,000). Unlike the editor of *Der Stern*, however, the editor of this paper does not believe that anything really unpleasant happened in the Nazi concentration camps. On the contrary, reading the *Deutsche Nationale Zeitung,* one cannot escape the conclusion that its editor thinks that the Allies were the real war criminals and that Hitler had much to his credit.

Radio under Occupation

After the Nazi regime capitulated it was in the interests of the four occupying powers to restore the radio service as soon as possible. It was

the easiest way for them to reach most of the population, thus giving
their prohibitions, directives, orders and advice the widest possible
currency. Luckily for the Allies, there was a relatively high density of
radios in Germany, higher than in other continental countries. Within
a matter of days after the end of hostilities the German population
could listen once again to broadcasts from stations on German soil. The
British were first off the mark with Radio Hamburg on·4 May 1945.
The four powers introduced radio organisations similar to those of
their respective states. The British and French followed their own
traditions with centralised systems. In the British Zone the *Nordwest-
deutscher Rundfunk* (NWDR) was established for the whole zone. It
had stations in Cologne and Berlin as well as in Hamburg. The French
set up the *Südwestfunk* (SWF) at Baden-Baden. The Americans, used
more to a decentralised system, organised four stations — *Radio Bremen*
(RB), *Radio Frankfurt, Radio Stuttgart and Radio München.* They did
not attempt to introduce American-style commercial stations, possibly
because of the derelict state of the German economy at that time. All
the West zonal radios were soon operating almost entirely with German
staff, for both practical and political reasons. The British were the first
to relinquish legal control of their broadcasting organisation on 1
January 1948. A British adviser did, however, remain. Under the Allied
Press and Broadcasting Law of September 1949 the Allied High
Commission (a body replacing the military governors) had access to
the media on request. The same law prohibited the publication of
material detrimental to the Allies' interests. The High Commission
reserved the right to determine whether new broadcasting stations
should be set up or not. The High Commission also appointed itself to
be the guardian of the freedom of West Germany's mass media. This
situation ended in 1955 when West Germany became a fully sovereign
state.

   Article 5 of the *Grundgesetz*, referred to above, was the only
mention made of broadcasting; special legislation regulating radio, and
later television, was not thought to be necessary. The pattern of radio
corporations established by the Allies has remained the basis for
broadcasting in the Federal Republic. Changes have, nevertheless, taken
place. In 1954 North Rhine-Westphalia seceded from the NWDR and
set up the *Westdeutscher Rundfunk* (WDR) at Cologne. The other three
Länder — Hamburg, Lower Saxony and Schleswig-Holstein — within the
original NWDR region concluded a new agreement to establish the
Norddeutscher Rundfunk with headquarters in Hamburg. After *Sender
Freies Berlin* (SFB) was founded in West Berlin in 1953, the old NWDR

station there was handed over to the new organisation. When the Saar returned to Germany in 1957 the *Saarländischer Rundfunk* (SR) was created at Saarbrücken. West Germany and West Berlin then had nine broadcasting corporations and these have remained – *Bayerischer Rundfunk* (BR, Bavarian Broadcasting Corporation, formerly *Radio München*), *Hessischer Rundfunk* (HR, originally *Radio Frankfurt*), NDR, RB, *Süddeutscher Rundfunk* (SDR, originally *Radio Stuttgart*), SFB, SR, SWF and WDR. All these corporations are members of the ARD (*Arbeitsgemeinschaft der öffentlich-rechtlichen Rundfunkanstalten der Bundesrepublik Deutschland*), which was originally established in 1950 to co-ordinate their activities and represent them at home and abroad.

Television

Germany inaugurated the world's first regular television service on 22 March 1935. The Berlin Olympic Games of 1936 were broadcast live from the *Fernsehsender Paul Nipkow*. The small television service was kept going until 1944 and, remarkably, a Franco-German service was broadcast from the Eiffel Tower from 1943 to 1944.

When a regular television service was inaugurated in the Federal Republic in December 1952, the ARD was given custody of it under the name *Deutsches Fernsehen*. A second nationwide television service was introduced in April 1964. This had followed a dispute between the federal government and the *Länder*, which the *Länder* won. They were awarded, by the federal constitutional court, the right to make programmes and generally run the service, though the Post Office carried the responsibility for maintaining the transmitters. The *Länder* combined to form the *Zweites Deutsches Fernsehen* (ZDF) which, unlike the ARD, is centrally organised from Mainz.

The *Deutsches Fernsehen* (DFS) has a standing programme conference with representatives from the nine member corporations to plan its programmes. Each individual corporation is required to provide a certain amount of agreed material. No one corporation is allowed to predominate in any given field at a regular time of each week or day. The DFS and the ZDF agree a programme pattern and representatives from both meet every month to work out the details. Most of the individual ARD corporations have third TV programmes which are mainly educational or regional in flavour. The BR, for instance, runs a *Telekolleg* which has certain similarities to the British Open University broadcasts but is not meant to provide instruction up to degree level.

In addition to what could be called their normal 'co-operative competition' with each other, the ARD and the ZDF work together on the *Vormittagsprogramm* (before-noon programme) which is broadcast daily from 10.0 a.m. until 1.30 p.m. (until 10.50 a.m. on Sundays). This programme is aimed at viewers in the German Democratic Republic, most of whom can receive West-German TV. ARD and ZDF contribute equally to this, providing mainly repeats of their respective outputs and highlighting items of particular significance for inter-German relations or of particular interest to East German viewers. It is convenient to mention here two other West German broadcasting services aimed at listeners outside the Federal Republic. These are the *Deutsche Welle* (DW), a short-wave radio station giving a world service, and the *Deutschlandfunk* (DLF), a long-wave radio station providing programmes for European listeners. The DW is financed out of the federal budget, the DLF mainly by the ARD. The DW broadcasts mostly in languages other than German; the major part of the DLF output, on the other hand, is in German. Both are seen as political and cultural ambassadors of the Federal Republic. West Germany is also host to the private American organisation, Radio Free Europe, which broadcasts in all the East European languages with a strongly political emphasis. Its output has been a source of some controversy in the West and of great annoyance and anger to the politicians of the Soviet bloc. Finally, RIAS, Radio in the American Sector, was founded by the United States Information Service in West Berlin in November 1945. It too has not been beyond controversy in the West as its highly political purpose is aimed largely at the East German population. At least half of its daily output is music. However, by winning listeners through popular music programmes RIAS hopes to influence them politically.

Apart from trying to gain friends and influence people beyond its borders through DW, DLF and its broadcasts to the GDR, West German television collaborates extensively with other West European television services. This collaboration has always been especially close with Austria and Switzerland, where a common language makes such co-operation much easier. Like British television, the West German service imports a good deal of material from the United States, such as the popular detective series 'Cannon', 'Columbo' and 'Kojak', and series like 'Best Sellers'. British thrillers have been popular with West German viewers. All of these imports are dubbed. The American series which received the most comment was, of course, 'Holocaust' which exposed

Nazi persecution of the Jews by telling the story of a single German Jewish family. Shown in 1979, it caused a nationwide debate and revealed widespread West German ignorance of Nazi atrocities. West Germany is a major exporter of television material. This material goes to the rest of Europe and overseas. In 1965 a joint ZDF–ARD enterprise, Trans-Tel, was established to adapt and distribute West German television programmes to countries outside Europe. In the early 1970s it was exporting to over 80 countries; roughly one-third of these exports went to Latin America and as much again went to Asia. Africa took one-fifth of the total. The FRG is also a worldwide distributor of newsfilm through a large newsfilm agency, DPA-ETES. Finally, the West Germans belong to EBU, which promotes co-operation between the television organisations of Western Europe.

Broadcasting: Finance and Control

West Germany's broadcasting corporations are financed from licence fees and from advertising revenue. The federal post, which is in part responsible for the transmitters and other equipment, collects the monthly licence fee, claiming appropriate reimbursement from the corporations for its services. The licence charges are standard in all the *Länder*, as are the rules regarding exemptions. Between 5 and 7 per cent of licence holders are exempted from their fees. Only about 12 per cent of the television service's income was derived from commercial advertising in the early 1970s. At the same time about 6 per cent of income for the radio service came from this source. Advertising follows neither the US nor the British pattern. First of all, there is no advertising on Sundays and national holidays. Secondly, it is restricted to the time before 8.0 p.m. The maximum time allowed on any one day is 25 minutes. There are great differences in the numbers of licence holders between the larger and the smaller corporations. *Radio Bremen* had just over 275,000 in 1974 while the WDR had over 5.5 million. For this reason there exists a system of equalisation payments. This is administered by the financial equalisation committee (*Finanzausgleichsgremium*). The ZDF is the only corporation not involved in this equalisation programme.

All the West German broadcasting corporations, except for the two in Berlin, have two main organs of control: the broadcasting council (*Rundfunkrat*) and the administrative council (*Verwaltungsrat*). The first is meant to represent the public and is made up of representatives from the *Land* government, the *Land* parliament, the churches, higher education, the schools, youth and sports organisations, trade unions, chambers of commerce, the press and local government. In the case of the NDR and the WDR the *Länder* parliaments elect the broadcasting councils, each party receiving the proportion of seats it has in the parliament. The administrative council, as its name suggests, supervises more directly the running of the corporation and is a much smaller body. It is made up of several members elected by the broadcasting council by majority vote, and several other members — usually a prominent lawyer, academic and president of the *Land* bank. The administrative council of the ZDF consists of three members selected by the Prime Ministers of the *Länder*, five members elected by the broadcasting council and one representative appointed by the federal government. The head of the broadcasting corporation is the *Intendant* who is elected either by the two boards or, at ZDF for example, by the television council[1] alone, for five years. He can be re-elected. He is responsible for the entire programme output. He is directly responsible to the administrative council for his activities. He usually has a business manager and a technical manager working under him, the appointment of whom is agreed with the administrative council.

The composition of the broadcasting council would seem to point to wide democratic control and participation — more so than in Britain or France — but, inevitably, the various representatives are not always in close touch with public taste and sentiment. The representatives are certainly not representative of the age and sex structure of the FRG. Employers are much better represented than employees. On the ZDF television council, for example, there are only three trade union representatives: one from the DGB, one from the DAG, the independent white-collar union, and one from the DBB, the organisation of civil servants. This council has 66 members.

Over the years there has been a great deal of party strife in broad-casting. In the *Länder* where one party predominates, its representatives, in one guise or another, usually dominate the *Rundfunkrat*. This is so in the HR and at RB, where the Social Democrats dominate the scene, and in BR, SDR, SR and SWF, dominated by the Christian Democrats. In most of the other corporations, the *Intendant* is a member of one party, his deputy a member of the other. Party strife has reached such proportions that the CDU in Schleswig-Holstein have threatened to withdraw their *Land*, which they have controlled since 1949, from the NDR. At the other end of the Republic, the BR increasingly goes its own way, or rather the CSU's way. Perhaps the most notorious case of political interference in television was the hounding out of office of several executive producers of the NDR's current affairs programme, 'Panorama', in the late 1960s. The Christian Democrats found it too left for their taste.

Election broadcasts in the Federal Republic are regulated in a similar way to those in Britain. Time cannot be bought by rival parties as in the United States; it is allotted free and of right to the parties represented in the *Bundestag*. Both major parties have been allotted equal time in recent federal elections, with the third party, the FDP, getting rather more time than its representation in the *Bundestag* would suggest it was entitled to. The only other parties to get any time at all were those contesting all the constituencies throughout the Republic — namely, the NPD and the DKP.

Summing up the position of German television in the 1970s, the distinguished French observer of the West German scene, Alfred Grosser, after praising the achievements of the FRG's television, went on:

the Federal Republic has undergone a development in the 1970s which is unique in Western Europe. . . During times of relaxation of tension, the FRG is, however, the only country which is inwardly worried and therefore outwardly intolerant. The public employment prohibitions imposed by the authorities are merely a sign of a hardly justified insecurity which breeds intolerance. This insecurity is reflected within the television corporations by a new conformism, a fear of questioning. There can be no doubt that in the 1960s people indulged to excess in criticism of everything and anything. Now the pendulum has swung too far the other way. It has not swung so far, however, as to destroy the positive qualities of FRG television.[2]

Cinema in the 1970s

As in other West European countries, the number of cinema tickets sold in the FRG declined in the 1960s and 1970s. In 1965, 294 million were sold, ten years later only 113.5 million were sold.[3] The number of feature films produced actually fluctuated during this period, rising from 66 in 1963 to 121 in 1969, but then falling substantially for a number of years. The number of films on offer to the public has also fluctuated. It was 409 in 1963, dropping to 388 in 1973. Of these, in 1973, only 96 were of West German production, 13 were French, 28 of Franco-Italian origin, 29 were from Britain, and no less than 113 from the United States.

The West German film industry's main answer to the challenge of declining audiences and foreign competition was sex and sensationalism. However, during the later 1960s the younger generation of film directors broke away from this trend and attempted to restore the reputation of the German film to what it had been during the Weimar period. This was only possible due to the widespread commissioning of feature films by the television corporations and the generous subsidies available from public funds. The *Filmförderungsanstalt* (FFA) in West Berlin, established under legislation introduced in 1967, carries on this work as does the Ministry of the Interior. The yearly budget of the FFA has to be approved by the Minister for Economics. In 1977 the Ministry of the Interior subsidised 18 feature films, 5 other long films and 15 shorts. A further 17 film scripts qualified for ministry assistance. In addition, 50 cinemas out of approximately 3,000 in the FRG were granted awards on the basis of their programmes over the year. To qualify for subsidies films and scripts should be of high artistic merit and should not offend against the *Grundgesetz*, or the law, moral or religious feeling. To what extent this has resulted in a form of censorship and self-censorship it is difficult to judge. Good films have been made with, and without, official sponsorship.

There are many highly competent directors in the Federal Republic today; among the more noted younger ones are Rainer Werner Fassbinder, Werner Herzog, Alexander Kluge and Volker Schlöndorff. Inevitably they, and a number of the other better directors, are seen outside West Germany as a 'school' — a description which they would deny. However, the similarity of their experiences, their means and their market has led to similarities in their completed work. The older directors, Kluge for instance, born in 1932, remember their childhood in the Third Reich and adolescence in the early post-war years. The younger ones are really children of the economic miracle. Fassbinder, for example, was born in 1945. Kluge's *Abschied von Gestern* (*Farewell from Yesterday*), made in 1967, is often regarded as his best film and as a turning-point in the history of the post-war cinema in the FRG. It describes the failure of a young woman from East Germany to adapt to life in the Federal Republic. Kluge, who is critical of both East and West, questions the clumsy methods and patronising ways of the modern welfare system. This much praised film was made with a subsidy from the *Kuratorium Junger Deutscher Film*, an official fund which Kluge helped to create and which was financed by the *Länder* to help young film makers. The problem of women in modern industrial society was taken up again by Kluge in his *Gelegenheitsarbeit einer Sklavin* (*Occasional Work of a Female Slave*) which is about the growing self-awareness of a housewife who works as a part-time abortionist. This 1973 film caused both Kluge and the authorities many headaches, but in the end he retained his subsidy for it. Both these films by Kluge have highly topical themes and this is true of much of Fassbinder's output. In his *Angst essen Seele auf* he relates with great sensitivity the loneliness of the big city as well as the plight of the foreign workers in the FRG. This is done by showing the problems encountered by a young Algerian and an older German woman when they embark on a friendship. Schlöndorff has also dealt with topical themes, with women taking the lead. In *Die Ehegattin die Moral der Ruth Halbfass* (1971) we see the problems of a divorced woman trying to survive alone in a man's world. In *Die verlorene Ehre der Katharina Blum* (1975), adapted from a novel by Heinrich Böll, the young woman is hunted by the yellow press for harbouring a fugitive. The film also turns the spotlight on the massive powers of the police. The police and terrorism form the core of Fassbinder's *The Third Generation* (1979) about which one British reviewer commented:

> Distorted, trivialised, made histrionic, terrorism here becomes the last desperate bid for individualism in a cynically mechanised society where everyone — cop, robber or plain Joe Average — is at once manipulator and manipulated. Society's outlaws are here shown to be fashioned in its own image.[4]

In his films Werner Herzog tends to be drawn to the odd and unusual as a means of illuminating man's dilemmas. *Auch Zwerge haben klein angefangen* (*Even Dwarfs Started Small*, 1970) is, as the title suggests, about dwarfs. *Land des Schweigens und der Dunkelheit* (*Land of Silence and Darkness*, 1972) is the story of a deaf and blind woman played by a woman suffering from both afflictions off the screen. His *Nosferatu* (1979) is a visually extraordinary remake of an old German film about the vampire legend. His most recent success is *Woyzeck* (1979), based on Georg Büchner's 1835 play. The film features a fine performance by Klaus Kinski, in the title role, as the exploited soldier forced to perform humiliating menial services and submit to degrading medical experiments, in order to earn a meagre living for his mistress and their child. Other directors too have tackled the classics with success. Schlöndorff's *Der Junge Törless* (1966) is adapted from Robert

Musil's novel about a boy's reaction to his time at a paramilitary academy in the Austro-Hungarian empire. Fassbinder made *Effi Briest* (1975), again a woman's tale, from Theodor Fontane's novel of the same name. Finally, Schlöndorff made *The Tin Drum* (1979) from Günter Grass's book with the same title, which tells the story of a boy in pre-war Danzig. The film authentically recreates the atmosphere of that city.

In the 1970s a minority of West German directors achieved well-deserved international success with films dealing directly or indirectly with the daily reality of the FRG or exposing Germany's recent past. Although heavily dependent on public funds, they nevertheless managed to take up a cautioning, questioning, critical attitude to the FRG and its problems. To some extent, in so doing, they gave audiences outside the Republic insights into the reality of their own societies.

Theatre in the FRG

Though not strictly part of the mass media, the theatre remains a significant means of popular communication. This is more true in Germany than in most countries. Plays written for the theatre frequently find their way into the cinema or on to television, thus becoming part of mass communication. It is therefore appropriate to survey, briefly, the theatre scene in West Germany.

In 1977 there were 211 theatres, opera houses, concert and multi-purpose halls in use in the FRG.[5] Most of them were publicly owned either by the *Länder* or by the local authorities. The large number of theatres in Germany is, originally, the result of Germany's division until 1871 into small states, with each state believing its dignity required it to have a theatre, opera house or both. The other factor which gave rise to this situation was the existence of a relatively large educated class. Weimar Germany was renowned for its theatres, with names such as Max Reinhardt, Gerhart Hauptmann, Erwin Piscator and Bertolt Brecht claiming worldwide attention. Naturally, the Third Reich brought the *Gleichschaltung* of the theatre as it did the cinema and the other arts.

The collapse of Hitler's Reich hit the theatre in the same way as the cinema. Many theatres had been destroyed or damaged. What of the actors and directors? Many of them were accused because of the roles they had played or the honours they had received from the Nazis. Gustaf Gründgens, Heinrich George, Victor de Kowa and Werner Krauss were among the prominent actors who had difficulties convincing the occupying authorities that they had not willingly supported the Nazis. In most cases all was soon officially forgiven if not forgotten, especially by colleagues who had suffered under the Nazis. Talented emigré actors, directors and writers returned to settle down again in their homeland with varying degrees of success. Brecht and Piscator were among them. In terms of productions, the early post-war theatre found security in the classics — Goethe, Shakespeare (*The Merchant of Venice* only in Bochum in 1952), Schiller, Molière, Chekhov and Shaw. These authors, together with Brecht, have remained the bread and butter of the West German stage. As was only to be expected, modern plays from the four occupying powers were quickly introduced — Eugene O'Neill and Tennessee Williams, Jean Anouilh, Maxim Gorky, Christopher Fry and T. S. Eliot. Remarkably, Robert Ardrey's *The Beacon* (1939) was the most successful American stage play, with performances in 25 theatres. There were relatively few plays which sought to lay bare the nightmare of Nazism. The two most successful of those which did were Zuckmayer's *Des Teufels General*, discussed above, and Wolfgang Borchert's *Draussen vor der Tür* (*Outside in Front of the Door*). First performed in Zürich, Zuckmayer's piece was the most successful play in the post-war period. There were 3,238 performances of it in Germany between 1947 and 1950. Borchert told the story of Beckmann, an eternal outsider who returned from a Soviet PoW camp to find his parents dead and his wife living with another man. He became a symbol for his generation. This was Borchert's only play. His life was as tragic as that of his hero; he died shortly after the première of the play in Hamburg in 1947.

The period immediately following the currency reform of 1948 was not a very happy one for the West German theatre. Short of money, people put the theatre low on their list of priorities. In the 1950s and early 1960s there was once again a great improvement. In the changed economic climate, the theatres were filling up again. New theatres were being built to excite the imagination — the *Schauspielhäuser* of Bochum, Düsseldorf, Frankfurt, Hamburg, the *Stadttheater* of Bonn and Münster, the *Haus der Ruhrfestpiele* at Recklingshausen, the theatre complex at Cologne among many — but there seemed to be a dearth of German plays to produce in them. Instead, the theatre-going public was left to puzzle over the meaning of Beckett, Pinter and Ionesco. This was the heyday of the theatre of the absurd. The only contemporary German-language writers whose work was fashionable at this time were the Swiss Friedrich Dürrenmatt and the Austrian Fritz Hochwälder.

Britain had its 'angry young men' wave in the second half of the 1950s starting with John Osborne's *Look Back in Anger*, which was also staged in the FRG. West Germany's 'angry' wave followed in the 1960s. It is associated above all with Rolf Hochhuth, Heinar Kipphardt, Martin Walser and Peter Weiss. Their plays became part of what was known as the documentary theatre, in some ways following Brecht and Piscator. They often put historical events at the centre of the plays. Hochhuth in *Der Stellvertreter* (*The Representative*, 1963) examines the Pope's relations with the Nazis, Kipphardt's *In der Sache J. Robert Oppenheimer* (1964) centres on the Un-American Activities Committee's investigation of the H-Bomb scientist Oppenheimer. Weiss's *Die Ermittlung* (*The Investigation*, 1965) deals with the trial of Auschwitz guards in 1965. In some respects Walser's first play, *Eiche und Angora* (translated as *The Rabbit Race*, 1962), is the most directly critical of the FRG. It is an attack on the silent majority whose superficial political views change with the times, who first run with the Nazis, then become pacifist in 1945, only to change again with the economic miracle and rearmament. Alois, the anti-hero, falls foul of this majority because he is too serious and sincere and cannot change his allegiances as quickly as Gorbach, the successful businessman. The play offers little hope for the FRG, for Alois voluntarily goes into an asylum.

West Germany's mass media have carried on their predecessors' traditions of innovation and high technical standards. They enable the public they serve to obtain a wide range of opinions on the issues of the day as well as a wealth of information and a variety of entertainment. The media have faced a number of crises in their thirty-five years of development. The press exhibits unhealthy concentration of ownership and lack of political balance in certain areas. The radio and television services face both economic and political pressures which could radically alter them in the next decade. The cinema, heavily dependent on public funds and television contracts, could not for long run counter to a less tolerant climate in Bonn. Will 1980 prove to be a turning back, or will the industry go forward to build on its existing achievements?

Further Reading

Daiber, Hans. *Deutsches Theater seit 1945* (Stuttgart, 1976)
Hayman, Ronald. *The German Theatre* (London, 1975)
Manvell, Roger and Fraenkel, Heinrich. *The German Cinema* (London, 1971)

above, case law plays little part in the West German legal system, judges' decisions being binding only in the specific cases to which they refer.

West German courts do not use the jury system. Instead a system of lay judges or *Schöffen* is used in criminal cases. The *Schöffen* have no legal training and any citizen can, in principle, be called upon to discharge this honorary office for a period of four years. During this time he is expected to serve at trials for a specified number of days. His main duty is to listen to the case and to confer with the *Richter* on all circumstances affecting the guilt or innocence of the accused and the appropriate level of punishment.

Apart from the professional and lay judges, the other key figure in the West German judicial system is the *Staatsanwalt*, or state advocate, for whom there is no equivalent in the English system. A state advocate's office is attached to each court and is required by law to investigate and prosecute all punishable offences without regard to the persons involved. The principle underlying this requirement is to ensure universal equality before the law. The *Staatsanwalt* undergoes the same legal training as the *Richter* and he must work within the constraints of the law. Unlike the *Richter*, however, he is required to act on instructions from his superiors in the state advocate's office — e.g. he can be required against his own better judgement to prosecute, or to desist from prosecuting, a particular case, whereas the *Richter* cannot be subjected to pressure from his superiors to convict or to acquit but passes the judgement which he alone considers most appropriate within the law. It is important to note that the *Staatsanwalt* is not merely a prosecuting counsel whose task is to secure conviction and punishment for the accused. He is required to take into account all the circumstances and evidence relating to the crime, both incriminating and mitigating, and to present the objective truth of the case to the court as far as this is humanly possible. Adherents of the English legal system might well dismiss the notion of objective truth as being so elusive a concept as to impede rather than expedite the course of justice; on the other hand, it must be pointed out that the thorough preliminary investigation carried out by the *Staatsanwalt* largely eliminates the element of chance and coincidence which can sometimes affect verdicts in English courts.

Courts

The main branch of the legal system in the FRG is made up of the civil and criminal courts which occupy 10,000 of the country's 13,000 judges. Alongside these are:

1. the constitutional court (*Verfassungsgericht*), the work of which is described in Chapter Two;
2. the labour courts (*Arbeitsgerichte*), presided over by an equal number of judges and lay judges, the latter representing employers and employees, and dealing with disputes over dismissals, wage agreements, strikes, lock-outs, etc.;
3. the administrative courts (*Verwaltungsgerichte*) which arbitrate in disputes between citizens and the administrative authorities;
4. the social courts (*Sozialgerichte*), the task of which is to pronounce judgement in disputes arising from the implementation of the laws relating to pensions and other social benefits as set out in the *Sozialgestzbuch*;[1]
5. the financial courts (*Finanzgerichte*) dealing with the application of tax and customs law.

Each type of court is represented at the highest level by a federal court. These courts are the *Bundesgerichtshof* in Karlsruhe for civil and criminal cases; the *Bundesarbeitsgericht* in Kassel; the *Bundesverwaltungsgericht* in Berlin; the *Bundessozialgericht* in Kassel; and the *Bundesfinanzgericht* in Munich.

Apart from the supreme federal courts, jurisdiction is in the hands of the *Länder*. Taking the civil and criminal courts as a model, there are three tiers of jurisdiction in each *Land*:

1. the *Amtsgericht* (district court);
2. the *Landgericht* (*Land* court);
3. the *Oberlandesgericht* (*Land* court of appeal).

At present there are 773 *Amtsgerichte* in the FRG, to each of which is attached a number of *Richter* corresponding to the amount of work to be done. In a small country town one or two judges may be sufficient, whereas the *Amtsgericht* in a large city may have a staff of some thirty *Richter*. In simple cases the *Amtsgericht* is presided over by one judge who can pass a maximum sentence of twelve months' imprisonment. In more serious criminal cases, where a sentence of up to three years is envisaged, the *Richter* is assisted by two *Schöffen*. At the 93 *Landgerichte*, cases are heard by three judges and either three or six *Schöffen*, depending on the gravity of the criminal offence. The *Landgerichte* hear serious cases referred to them from the *Amtsgerichte* where a sentence exceeding three years is expected. The 19 *Oberlandes-gerichte* do not call upon the services of *Schöffen*, but are presided over by five *Richter* and hear appeals from the lower courts as well as cases of treason, genocide and serious attempts to pervert the course of justice.

Anglo-German Differences

Just as the structures of the legal systems in England and Germany differ considerably, so do the actual procedures in court. The best way of demonstrating this is to outline the basic procedure in a criminal case before a West German court and to draw attention to the most important points of difference. The first of these occurs before the case comes up for trial and is concerned with the role of the police. Whereas in England the police both detect the crime and prosecute the criminal, in the FRG the work of prosecution is taken over by the *Staatsanwalt* who, if necessary, may call upon the police to assist him in obtaining information, tracking down witnesses and similar operations. Thus, the criminal trial falls into two stages: the preliminary proceedings, which are conducted in private by the *Staatsanwalt*, and the main proceedings, which are held in open court. In serious criminal cases, and in cases where there is a danger of the accused absconding, interfering with witnesses or destroying evidence, the *Staatsanwalt* can keep the accused on remand (*Untersuchungshaft*) by obtaining a remand warrant signed by a judge. The maximum period of remand is normally six months, but this can be extended by application to the judge. During the preliminary proceedings it is the duty of the *Staatsanwalt* to collect all possible information on every aspect of the case, and in order to do this he will interview the accused and the witnesses for and against the accused, and will gather evidence from other persons who may be called in, e.g. the police and technical assessors. On the basis of these investigations the *Staatsanwalt* must then decide whether it is likely that a court would bring in a guilty verdict against the accused. If this seems probable he must prosecute, in which case the accused must be provided with a defence counsel either of his own choice or, failing this, appointed by the state. The law stipulates that defendants must have a defence counsel at the levels of *Landgericht* and *Oberlandesgericht*, but this is not compulsory at the *Amtsgericht* level. Criticism is frequently heard of the length of time the accused parties have to spend in remand before a decision is taken as to whether to bring the case to trial. It is felt by some that the judicial authorities could expedite the process considerably, but because of their powerful and entrenched position in society as administrators of the codified law they take no account of the hardship inflicted on mere human beings by long delays in bringing cases to trial.

The main proceedings before the court begin with an examination of the accused and his personal circumstances without reference to the specific charge. This examination may include questions about previous convictions — a practice which is not permitted in English courts of law. The right of the prosecution to introduce information of this kind during the main proceedings has been limited in recent years in order to protect the accused against harmful publicity and prurient public interest, so that previous convictions can now only be mentioned in open court if they have some direct bearing on the matter in hand. Clearly, these terms can be interpreted very widely and have greater relevance to crimes involving sex and violence than to most other categories. It is therefore not unusual for newspapers to report in detail a defendant's previous offences as mentioned in court before the trial proper is begun.

When the first examination is completed, the *Staatsanwalt* reads out the charge, after which the defendant has an opportunity to make a statement of his own referring to the charge. The court then sets about considering the case before it by examining the witnesses, hearing expert evidence and calling upon all other sources of information as it sees fit, both for and against the defendant. The defence counsel endeavours to bring all the mitigating circumstances clearly before the court, while the *Staatsanwalt*, as has been noted above, has to present both the incriminating and the mitigating evidence in order to assist the court to reach its verdict. Although the position of the defence lawyer has been strengthened in recent years, it is not comparable with that of the defence counsel in an English criminal trial. This is due to the fact that the West German court functions on the 'inquisitorial' principle, on the assumption that it is possible to construct a true version of events as a basis for an objective verdict, whereas the English court functions on the 'accusatorial' principle which matches the prosecution against the defence in a battle of forensic skill which decides the outcome of the case as it appears before the court. The German defence lawyer does not see his primary task as discrediting or confounding prosecution witnesses under cross-examination and thereby undermining the prosecution case, but as working within the terms of the charge brought by the *Staatsanwalt* so as to mitigate as far as possible the guilt of his client. When all the evidence has been considered and witnesses heard, the *Staatsanwalt* sums up the case and recommends a verdict to the court. This is followed by a plea from the defence counsel and the last word is left to the defendant himself who may make a statement on his own behalf. The judges then retire to confer on their verdict. If they are not unanimous a vote is taken among them: in civil cases a simple majority is required, but in criminal cases verdicts must be based on a two-thirds majority. Finally, the court is reassembled and the verdict is announced by the presiding judge.

Prisons

A reformed and unified law on the punishment of offenders for the whole of the FRG was introduced with effect from January 1977 to replace the previous legislation operated individually by the *Länder*. It lays down the rights and duties of prisoners and officials of the prison service, and is based on the principle of re-education for normal civilian life rather than on the concepts of guilt and punishment. In this respect, however, it falls short of the demands made by some penal reformers who point to the fact that over half the inmates of West German prisons are released after serving less than one year's imprisonment to face the vicious circle of unemployment, difficulty in finding accommodation and the danger of relapsing into a life of crime. They would therefore like to see legislation providing for full industrial wages for prisoners and the maintenance of pension and sickness insurance contributions, but these have so far been rejected by the *Länder* because of the escalating social insurance costs.[2] The prison population in West Germany is approximately 35,000 compared to 42,000 in the UK, but the physical problems of overcrowding in old buildings dating from the last century are very similar in both countries. In order to alleviate this problem the new penal code provides for the gradual reintegration of prisoners who are not regarded as dangerous into normal working life and the maintenance of contact with families through holidays on parole of up to a maximum of 21 days. A small wage is paid for work done in prison and contributions to the unemployment insurance scheme are maintained. The new legislation also covers compensation for victims of criminal violence.

Article 102 of the Basic Law states clearly: 'Capital punishment shall be abolished.' Without doubt the decision to include this prohibition in the constitution was influenced by the excessive use made of the death penalty by the National Socialist regime which carried out over 16,000 executions of German civilians in its twelve years in power, quite apart from its campaign of genocide during the Second Word War. Repeated opinion polls carried out in West Germany, often by popular newspapers, show that a majority of the population is still in favour of the death penalty for the worst crimes, and this tendency has become more marked with the rise of urban terrorism. Nevertheless it seems highly unlikely that any West German government would be willing to risk international opprobrium by amending the constitution to allow for its reintroduction.

All other types of punishment are dealt with in the *Strafgesetzbuch* which provides for a maximum term of 15 years' imprisonment for the worst offenders. Wherever possible, use is made of the system of suspended sentences in order to 're-socialise' the offender and alleviate the pressure on prisons. Fines are also imposed, according to the offender's ability to pay, up to a maximum of DM 10,000. Juvenile crime can be punished by a wide variety of measures ranging from simple prohibitions – e.g. a young offender might be forbidden by the court to frequent licensed premises – to fines and detention in a special institution for up to five years.

A record is kept of all sentences passed by the courts in the *Bundeszentralregister*, or central criminal register. These records are not available to the public, but citizens can apply to the registry for a certificate showing that they have never been convicted of any criminal offence. This document, known as a *Führungszeugnis*, is sometimes required when applying for a job, especially in the civil service. Entries in the central register are removed after a specified period according to the gravity of the offence in order to enable the offender to rid himself of the stigma of a criminal record and to start a new life.

Police

It has been noted above that the police in West Germany are not concerned with the prosecution of criminal cases, whereas the British police both detect and prosecute. This reflects the different historical development of the police in the two countries, in particular on the German concept which separates the state as the agent of prosecution from the police as the agent of detection and, in certain spheres, of administration. In fact, the term *Polizei* has a wider application in the

FRG than the corresponding term 'police' in Britain. The organisation of the police in Prussia was the most influential model until the National Socialist period, when normal standards of law and order collapsed, and the police were used for political ends against opponents of the regime. In 1945, however, the Western Allies reorganised the German police in their own zones of occupation according to their national views on the role and function of the police force. In the British Zone, for instance, the functions of the police were limited to the maintenance of law and order on the streets and the detection of crime. Its administrative function was abolished. In the US Zone there was a strong tendency to decentralise the police and to give more authority to local government in controlling the police force according to the North American pattern; while in the French Zone the police administrative apparatus was fully retained and certain police functions were allotted to the local *Bürgermeister*, or mayors, corresponding in some ways to the functions carried out by the *maire* in France. These differences have now been largely assimilated and the police have been organised to meet the specific requirements of the new West German federal state, though it is still true to say that the model of Prussian centralism has more influence in the north of the country than in the south, where more extensive powers are wielded at local level. There is no centrally controlled federal police force. Instead, each *Land* is responsible for its own police force under the over-all control of its Minister of the Interior. Each *Land* is party to administrative agreements with the *Bund* covering the concerted use of the police forces in case of national catastrophe, emergencies or severe political danger.[3]

Although the internal organisation and the nomenclature of the police differ slightly in each *Land*, there are certain basic principles observed. The main organisational division is between the *Schutzpolizei*, responsible for the general maintenance of law and order and averting possible dangers arising through disregard of the law, and the *Verwaltungspolizei*, which performs many administrative functions such as the issuing of passports and identity cards and the enforcing of regulations covering prices, trade, commerce, building permits and a range of other civil matters. This branch of the police is thus responsible for many of the tasks which in Britain would be allotted to the immigration authorities or to special local departments. It is interesting to note that there are several departments operated by the *Verwaltungspolizei* which have no equivalent in Britain and the existence of which is rooted in the different historical development of the two countries — for example, departments for registering the names and addresses of all residents in the area, together with all changes of address, arrivals and departures (*Einwohnermeldeamt*), and departments for the issue of personal identity cards (*Personalausweis*) which are compulsory for all West German citizens aged 16 and over. The *Schutzpolizei* is divided into a larger branch responsible for routine duties and a smaller section concerned with the detection of crime, the *Kriminalpolizei*; these correspond roughly to the uniformed and plain clothes branches in the British police. Members of the police force in the FRG, whether *Schutzpolizei* or *Verwaltungspolizei*, are all *Beamte*.

Apart from this main section of the police force, there are other specialist forces and departments which should be mentioned. Each of the *Länder* maintains in permanent barracks a paramilitary police force known as the *Bereitschaftspolizei*. This force is not equipped to undertake military duties, its main task being to support the *Schutzpolizei* on occasions where a strong police presence is deemed necessary. In this respect its function can be compared with the special forces of riot police maintained by other continental countries. The *Bereitschaftspolizei*, like the *Schutzpolizei*, is under the control of the Minister of the Interior who decides when and where it will be deployed. Unlike the *Schutzpolizei*, however, its training and equipment is standardised to federal requirements in all the *Länder*.

The protection of the frontiers of the FRG is in the hands of a special frontier protection force, the *Bundesgrenzschutz*, which is a federal organisation responsible to the federal Minister of the Interior. The *Bundesgrenzschutz* is responsible for protecting frontier installations within 30 km of the frontier, preventing illegal entry into the FRG, protecting airports and other points of entry, and patrolling the frontier between East and West Germany.

Verfassungsschutz

Two central departments exist at federal level to co-ordinate and direct specialist operations: the *Bundeskriminalamt* and the *Bundesamt für Verfassungsschutz*. The *Bundeskriminalamt*, or federal crime office, keeps crime statistics, evaluates information from the police in the *Länder* and carries out research into all aspects of crime. It co-ordinates detection campaigns undertaken by the *Länder* and is also responsible for liaison with foreign police forces through Interpol. The *Bundesamt für Verfassungsschutz*, or federal office for the protection of the constitution, is concerned with the detection of espionage, treason and sedition against the federal state. Some critics have recently expressed concern about the extensive use of computers by this and other federal agencies for the recording of information about individual citizens and regard it as a possible encroachment on civil liberties. On the other hand, the authorities are clearly faced with a difficult problem in tracking the elusive movements of terrorist organisations and their members, and are naturally keen to exploit the advantages offered by the computer in information storage and retrieval. It is not unlikely, however, given the thoroughness with which West German authorities collect information on their citizens, that the use of computers at federal level could develop into a major political controversy going well beyond the immediate issue of terrorism.

At the beginning of this chapter brief mention was made of some of the reasons for disquiet in the FRG at developments and trends in crime generally and at the apparent inability of the judiciary and the police to deal with them effectively. Foremost among these trends is the disturbing rise in all types of common crime which has afflicted most industrial societies in recent years. The rise in the West German crime rate has been even more spectacular than in neighbouring Western European countries, with the emphasis on brutality and violence by younger criminals. It is widely feared that the level of criminality will soon reach American levels and, as has been pointed out already, there is a strong feeling that harsher punishments should be introduced for crimes of violence. The mass circulation press, in particular the *Bild-Zeitung*, has taken a leading part in calling for harsher punishments and in drawing attention to outraged public feelings. Another alarming element in the pattern of crime in the FRG is the extent to which foreigners are involved in organised crime; this is partly due to the attraction of the FRG as a wealthy country offering rich pickings, and partly because the large population of foreign workers in West German industry provides an ideal background for criminal operations. Thus, a relatively high proportion of foreigners are convicted of violent crimes, while drug trafficking is largely in the hands of foreign gangs. For this reason a special department for the surveillance of foreigners in the FRG has been set up within the *Bundesamt für Verfassungsschutz*. It seems likely that this type of crime will continue to afflict the FRG severely, not least as a result of the Common Market provisions for the free movement of labour and the relative ease with which organised crime can operate across frontiers and thus evade detection.

Although violent crime receives sensational treatment in the press and thus claims most public attention, the so-called 'white-collar crime' has been recognised as a more serious long-term threat to the stability of the economic and financial structure of the country and to social and moral values in general. This kind of crime grew rapidly with increasing prosperity in the FRG during the sixties and came to the notice of the general public through a series of scandals involving the embezzlement of public funds in the *Länder.* It was estimated that astronomical gains were being made at the expense of both the private and public sectors of the economy, and fears were expressed that the FRG was coming to be regarded as the playground of Europe for white-collar crime. Considerable pressure was exerted on the government by the trade unions and the employers' associations to introduce legislation to combat this, and on 1 September 1976 the first piece of legislation on economic crime was introduced. This provides measures to curb the diversion of public funds, credit frauds, criminal bankruptcy and the manipulation of interest rates. Some *Länder* have also set up special departments in the office of the *Staatsanwalt* to handle this type of crime.

The public debate surrounding the trials of Nazi war crimes, some of which have dragged on for up to fifteen years at enormous expense, has in recent years been concerned with the problem of whether the statute of limitations for the prosecution of certain crimes such as genocide should be extended, and if so, for how long. Article 130 of the Basic Law states clearly: 'An act can be punished only if it was an offence against the law before the act was committed.' This sentence would have protected ex-concentration-camp officials and members of the SS from being brought to trial for murder and genocide after the statute had expired in 1979, but for the *Bundestag* vote of July 1979 that the limit should be extended indefinitely. Over the years since 1945 West German courts have dealt with approximately 85,000 cases of suspected complicity in war crimes, but 75,000 of these were acquitted for lack of evidence.

Spies and Terrorists

Another problem which affects Germany with particular severity is that of espionage, especially by agents of the GDR. The vulnerability of the FRG in this respect is apparent from a series of spectacular espionage cases in recent years, such as the arrest of Günter Guillaume, a personal aide to Chancellor Brandt (who resigned over the issue), and

the resignation of the Defence Minister Leber over a matter of internal
security. It is generally acknowledged by the security authorities that
such cases are but the tip of the iceberg, and the state of affairs was
well summed up by a headline in *The Economist*: 'Kennst du das Land,
wo die Spione Blühn?'[4] There have been numerous scandals in government offices and ministries in Bonn as various officials in key positions,
or secretaries with access to secret files, have been discovered to have
been working for the East German state security service for years. The
bitter accusations and counter-accusations of negligence which
inevitably follow such discoveries have become a regular and familiar
item in West German public affairs.

The most severe test to which the whole German legal and police
systems have ever been subjected is undoubtedly that of urban
terrorism throughout the decade since about 1970. The severity of the
test was intensified by the fact that the state was completely unprepared
for such an onslaught by violent and fanatical groups who ruthlessly
employed every means open to them to achieve their aims – unclear as
these aims are. In the case of Baader–Meinhof terrorists, for instance,
the law was faced with a completely new category of crime, while the
criminals themselves demonstratively refused to recognise the courts
and the judges. The problem was further compounded by the fact that
certain defence lawyers were discovered to be not only sympathetic
to the political aims of their clients, but also involved in their activities.
The question might well be raised as to how, under such circumstances,
the *Staatsanwalt* could ever penetrate to the 'objective truth' of the
matter and present it to the court in a balanced appraisal, and how a
judge could pass an appropriate sentence on unrepentant killers who
openly declare their aim to destroy the social order and to kill anyone
who tries to stop them. At the time of these trials and subsequently,
when prominent public figures were kidnapped or assassinated in the
open street, the government came under enormous public pressure to
introduce severe measures for dealing with terrorism. Several laws have
been passed to this end, but in the main the government acted
cautiously for fear of provoking a witch hunt. Whether these laws and
the lessons of the past decade will be sufficient to ensure that such
terrorist excesses can be curbed in future, or whether the FRG – the
model industrial welfare state – will again produce such violent groups,
remains to be seen.

Further Reading

Kommers, Donald P. *Judicial Politics in West Germany: A Study of the Federal Constitutional Court* (Beverly Hills, 1976)

Notes

1. See pp. 99–100 above.
2. Cf. p. 101 ff. above.
3. Cf. also pp. 38–9 above.
4. 'Do you know the land where the spies flourish?' – an adaptation of Goethe's famous opening line to Mignon's song: 'Kennst du das Land, wo die Zitronen blühn?'

9 WOMEN IN THE FEDERAL REPUBLIC

Women under the Kaiser

German women have been given a bad press generally. It is usually supposed that until recently, a few mannish exceptions apart, they followed the advice of their male overlords to stick to *Kinder, Küche* and *Kirche* (children, kitchen and church). In fact, the development of the emancipation of women in Germany was similar to developments in other advanced nations. The reasons for this movement towards female emancipation were also the same. More and more women were being drawn into the industrial process and thus gaining some measure of financial independence and a sense of their own worth. Secondly, the growth of political democracy led more and more women to conclude that, if men got the right to vote merely because they had reached a certain age, why should women not also enjoy that right. This was particularly so of the better-educated women who contrasted their lack of right to vote with the right to vote which was being bestowed on men less educated than themselves. Thirdly, in Germany as elsewhere, the two world wars speeded up a process which was already under way.

In Germany, by 1907 millions of women were engaged in earning money as Table 9.1 shows.

Table 9.1: Distribution of Labour Force German Reich 1907

	Women (millions)	Men (millions)
Agriculture	4.6	5.3
Industry and mining	2.1	9.1
Commerce and traffic	0.9	2.5
Public service and professions	0.28	0.79

Usually women were to be found in the lower-paid jobs, often doing unskilled or semi-skilled work. The prevailing ideology and the education system had equipped them to do little else. Germany was behind the United States, France, Britain, Switzerland and even Russia in its refusal to admit women to higher education. The first breakthrough came in southern Germany where Prussianism had less influence and where the Catholic Church was gradually coming to the conclusion that it would forfeit influence among women if it did not acquiesce in higher education for women. The first two German universities to admit women in all faculties were Freiburg and Heidelberg. Others then followed. In 1906 there were 254 women students at universities in the Reich, in the winter semester, 1908/9, there were already 1,077. By 1914 the number was 4,126. In 1908/9 Berlin had the highest number of women students (400), followed by Munich (134) and Göttingen (71). Most of these women were studying medicine. There were 334 in 1908/9. Of the others, three were students of theology, 31 were reading law and 709 philosophy. Most of the latter were undoubtedly destined for the teaching profession. In addition to these women reading for a degree, there were others who attended lectures without aiming at examinations. A big increase in the numbers of women students required better educational opportunities in the secondary schools, but this was to take time. Relatively few girls undertook academic courses leading to the *Abitur*. For most the emphasis was on 'feminine' subjects such as art, sewing, cookery and music. Even the heads of girls' schools were men and they wanted things to stay that way.

The advanced minority of women wanted not merely improved opportunities in education; they were conscious that there were many other wrongs which needed to be put right. At law women were the inferiors of men in all matters connected with sexual morality, marriage, children and property. Women's property, if they were married, was administered by their husbands. Women had no rights to pensions. Their job opportunities were so restricted that marriage was, by law, a reason for dismissing a woman from her job. Finally, women did not have the right to vote.

Many women felt that, if they won the right to vote, other rights would follow. As in Britain and the USA, the campaign for the vote got under way in earnest in the decade before 1914. The women's suffrage movement in one country inspired similar movements in others. Anita Augspurg, a well-known German suffragette, led 30 German women in a demonstration for women's suffrage in London's Hyde Park in June 1908. Sylvia Pankhurst, one of Britain's best-known suffragettes, toured Germany in 1914 spreading the message. German suffragettes expressed solidarity with imprisoned British female activists and protested to Prime Minister Asquith about their treatment. It is also interesting to recall that the founder of the first committee to promote women's suffrage in Britain — the Manchester Women's

Suffrage Committee – was set up in 1866 by an Anglo-German, Lydia Becker. Unlike their British comrades, German suffragettes risked prosecution in the early days of the movement as women did not have the right in certain parts of Germany to take part in political activity. This changed in 1908 when the Imperial Law on Association freed women activists throughout the Reich from legal restraints. This undoubtedly helped the SPD. It had long sought to organise women within its ranks. Its first women's organisation had been set up in Berlin in 1872 by Pauline Staegemann. In 1914, 174,754 of its 1,085,905 members were women. The SPD's leader, August Bebel, was tireless in his efforts on behalf of women and had written a highly successful book advocating women's emancipation, *Die Frau und der Sozialismus*, which can still be read with interest today. In 1908 the Social Democrats elected Luise Zietz to their executive committee and in 1911 they held their first international Women's Day. On this occasion the SPD formally approved the demand for women's suffrage. Anita Augspurg and some of the other leading middle-class suffragettes had been associated with the left-liberal *Fortschrittliche Volkspartei.* Others, like Lida Gustava Heymann, believed their best policy was action, independent of the 'men's parties'. But as the Kaiser's era was drawing to a close, the politicians of the right as well as the left began to see that women would eventually get the vote and that they should anticipate that event by organising them. The Centre Party did so before most others through the Catholic Church which founded a Catholic Women's League in 1903. Later the National Liberals encouraged women to support them and by 1912 there was even an 'Alliance of Conservative Women'.

German women appeared to have responded as enthusiastically as their menfolk to the outbreak of war in 1914. The war economy sucked ever greater numbers of women into the arms factories where the pay was relatively high. The main federation of German women's organisa-tions, the BDF, by this time under the leadership of Gertrud Bäumer steering a right-wing course, set up a 'National Women's Service' (*Nationaler Frauendienst*) in close co-operation with the Ministry of the Interior in Berlin. Women took on a variety of jobs previously done only by men. Only a few left-SPD women like Käte Duncker, Rosa Luxemburg and Clara Zetkin opposed the war and suffered imprison-ment for their agitation. Pacifists like Anita Augspurg and Lida Gustava Heymann also campaigned against the war with less severe conse-quences. The words of these brave women fell on deaf ears until mounting casualties and declining rations caused many other women to question the war.

Progress in the Weimar Republic

It was not until the collapse of the Kaiserreich that women got the right to vote in Germany. Under the pressure of events the last *Reichstag* of the Kaiser's Germany passed a resolution on political reform which included the right of women to vote on the same basis as men. Women voted for the constituent assembly of the Weimar Republic which confirmed women's suffrage on 12 November 1918. In this respect German women had moved ahead of their sisters in many other advanced nations. In the USA women got the vote in 1920, in Sweden in 1921, in France and Italy only after World War II. In Britain women only got the right to vote on the same basis as men in 1928. Australia (1902) and New Zealand (1893) and some of the Scandinavian states had already led the way on this issue. In the constituent assembly which met in Weimar in January 1919, 10 per cent of the membership − 41 deputies − were women. Subsequently, in the 1920s, the share of women in the *Reichstag* dropped to around 6 per cent, rising again to 9 per cent in November 1932.

As in other countries, most of the changes in the status of women in Germany brought about by the war could not be reversed. Superficially there were changes in dress, manners and leisure activities − women, for instance, took part to a greater extent than before in sport − and at a more fundamental level there had been great improvements in the job opportunities for women. It is true, of course, that women were, and were to remain, most heavily concentrated in the lower-paid jobs in textiles, clothing, food, drink and tobacco. However, in the 1920s, about one-third of white-collar employees were women. Women also retained a foothold in the metal industry. The shortage of men to some extent helped women; it also meant that many more women were forced out to work to earn a living. With more women employed, the trade unions sought to organise women workers. Trade union membership had reached a peak in 1920 but then declined for some years. In 1930, a bad time for trade unionism, about 14 per cent of trade unionists were women. The ties of the trade unions with the SPD and the Centre Party led to some improvement in the working conditions of women in the Weimar Republic. From 1927, for example, women could have up to twelve week's leave around their confinement, during which time maternity benefit was payable by the sickness funds, dismissal was illegal and, on returning to work, a nursing mother was to be allowed time for feeding her baby. In addition, measures for the protection of women workers, put aside during the war, were reintroduced.

German women were not responsible for the rise of National Socialism. Many working-class women, like their husbands, supported the SPD, KPD or, if they were Catholics, the Centre Party. As for those in the other social groups, they were more likely to support the Conservative parties before 1933. The NSDAP, in its ideology, its membership and, as far as one can see, its voters, was more of a 'men's party' than its rivals.

Regression in the Third Reich

The Nazi ideal of woman was that of a peasant woman, blonde and powerful of body, capable of bearing a large family, unadorned outwardly by make-up and unspoilt inwardly by the decadence which all too often passed for learning. This ideal had never existed and the Nazis were unable to get very far in realising it except in a few paintings of the time. At the superficial level they were helped to some extent by international trends. Hemlines went down in the 1930s and the image of woman became that of a slightly more sober and subdued character than in the 1920s. Nazi efforts to get women to stop smoking and using cosmetics had little impact. They could and did, by government action, reduce the number of students, including women, but it was much more difficult to remove women from factory, office, shop and school. Out of 95,807 students at 23 universities in 1930–31, 17,183 were women. In 1936–37 the number of female students had dropped to 7,832 out of a total of 48,558. Thus women were hit more than men by the government's policy of curtailing higher education. In Germany's ten technical universities the reduction in the number of women students was even more marked.

Table 9.2: Enrolments at German Technical Universities

	1931–32	1936–37
Total students	22,540	10,928
Women	1,948	325

By way of comparison, in 1938–39, out of a total of 50,002 students at British universities, 11,634 were women.

Given the Nazi view of the place of women in society, it could be expected that the opportunities for women pursuing a career in the professions would be strictly limited. In fact, the Nazi impact on professional women was not as great as anticipated. If women were virtually excluded from the legal profession and the higher reaches of the civil service, the situation had not been so different before 1933. In the Weimar Republic the majority of professional women had been in teaching and medicine, two professions which the Nazis recognised as needing large female components. The percentage of women in the medical profession actually rose from 5 per cent in 1930 to 6 per cent in 1934 and 7.6 per cent at the beginning of 1939, when there were 3,650 women medical practitioners in Germany.

Under the Nazis all welfare work on behalf of women was carried on by the women's section of the Labour Front (*Arbeitsfront*) headed by Gertrud Scholtz-Klink. The Labour Front had replaced the trade unions. At first the Nazis encouraged women to give up paid employment in exchange for becoming housewives and mothers. The legislation introduced to protect women in industry marginally assisted in this direction. More important were the marriage loans introduced for women who were prepared to give up work outside the home. Later on, as Germany prepared for war and labour was becoming scarce, in 1937, the idea of the wife's obligation to give up her job was dropped. The percentage of women in the industrial labour force had fallen from 29.3 per cent in 1933 to 24.7 per cent in 1936. In 1939 it rose to 27 per cent at a time of full male employment. Even before the outbreak of war women were starting to deliver the post, and to work on trams, buses and trains, and even in banking and insurance. Medals and allowances continued to be given to women who produced large families, but this ideal was now competing with the need for labour. For a variety of reasons full-scale conscription of women into industry was not resorted to. During the war, due to the shortage of male candidates, women were once again given greater scope in the science and technological faculties of universities. Hanna Reitsch, the test pilot, became a symbolic figure. In a dramatic way she seemed to represent the small but growing number of women engaged in professions for which the Nazis thought women were ill fitted by temperament. However, the hospital, the *Wehrmacht* office, the postal round, and the field and factory, rather than the airfield, were the typical spheres of activity for German women between 1939 and 1945.

Women in the Economy After 1945

Sadly, the typical image abroad of German women in 1945 was, at best, of chains of women clearing rubble and, at worst, of women concentration camp personnel removing the bodies of their victims under the supervision of stunned-looking 'tommies'. On the whole German women were regarded as a plain, and hard, bunch. By 1948 their image was to change a little for the better as the photographs appeared of the West Berlin housewife under blockade, struggling to cook a hot meal for her family by candlelight in a semi-derelict flat. By the 1950s, Hollywood was playing its part in improving the image of German women by introducing non-German audiences to Hildegard Knef, Romy Schneider and, later, Christine Kaufmann and by continuing to expose Marlene Dietrich. Although, strictly speaking, not really Germans, Alida Valli and Ursula Andress must also have helped. Back in the real world the majority of German women had put up with considerable hardships between 1945 and 1950. For a time the food situation was worse after the war than it had been during the war. Millions of Germans had lost their homes completely or were living in damaged homes. Official West German estimates put German war losses, 1939–45, military and civilian, at around 5.8 million killed or presumed dead. Most of them were men. Millions of women, therefore, faced the future without likelihood of marriage or remarriage. For some women there was the additional difficulty of not knowing whether their partner would return. In 1962 the fate of 1,279,000 German servicemen had still not been cleared up. Well over one million civilians were missing, though many of these were women. There were also over one million severely disabled war victims.

All these circumstances meant that women were forced out of their traditional home-orientated roles and into commerce and industry. This was not easy because many of them lacked training and skills and faced, in the early years, considerable competition for jobs. In 1950 there were 1.5 million registered unemployed persons in West Germany. This represented 10.3 per cent of the insured labour force. The figure certainly under-represented the number of women who did not qualify for unemployment benefit but who were seeking work. By 1960 only 237,000 were registered as unemployed (1.2 per cent). During these years the number of women employed grew steadily. In 1950, 4,168,000 women were employed. By 1956 the number had grown to 5,982,000 and in 1960 there were 6,876,000 women in employment. In 1962 the 7,247,000 employed women represented over one-third of the labour force. The number of women employed continued to rise in the 1960s reaching 9,631,000 in 1969 out of a total labour force of 26,854,000. This trend continued throughout the 1970s. In April 1978 there were 10,159,000 women employed out of a total workforce of 26,952,000. Of these women the majority were married and 3,476,000 had children under 18. This represented 41.6 per cent of women with children under 18. In 1979, many of the traditional characteristics of female labour could still be noted. There were still many women in agriculture (they actually formed a majority), in the textile industry and generally in lower-paid work. However, women had made rapid progress in banking and insurance and in the white-collar sector in general. In terms of their status, we find the situation shown in Table 9.3.

Table 9.3: Status of Women in Economy of FRG

	Women		% of total (men and women)	
	1969	1977	1969	1977
Self-employed	586,000	475,000	20.5	20.6
Helping in family business	1,630,000	967,000	83.9	86.3
Beamte	215,000	363,000	15.1	16.3
White-collar employees	3,683,000	4,694,000	48.9	51.3
Workers	3,419,000	3,139,000	27.6	28.4

These figures indicate the progress made and the long way still to go along the road to some kind of equality for women with men in the higher-status jobs. One would, for instance, have expected more women with the *Beamte* status by 1979.

Even among the white-collar employees, women usually held the more routine positions. As in other countries, many women take a break in the early years of raising a family and find it too late by the time their children are independent to get anything more than routine work. Those who would like to return when their children are still under school age find there is little provision for nursery places. In this respect their situation is similar to that of mothers with young children in Britain, and compares unfavourably with that in the neighbouring GDR. Of course, not all women want to be senior executives but, if there were fewer burdens on the mother and more training opportunities, it seems likely more women would rise higher.

In 1976, about 40 per cent of married women had full-time jobs. Women made up roughly 37 per cent of the total workforce. Their earnings were about half those of men. According to *Die Zeit* (16 June), in 1978 only 90 of West Germany's 5,000 managers were women. What of the future? Progress is likely to continue but not to be rapid. Figures on the numbers of youngsters taking apprenticeships reveal that fewer girls than boys embark upon such training and those who do are fairly concentrated in the more traditional female occupations.

With so many more women working outside the home, with the increasing use of the contraceptive pill and the greater availability of abortion, it is only to be expected that birth rates are declining. Since 1972 West Germany has joined those European states which are 'dying'. Since that year the number of deaths each year has exceeded the number of births.

Table 9.4: Number of Births and Deaths 1966—77

Year	Births	Deaths
1966	1,050,345	686,321
1969	903,456	744,360
1970	810,808	734,843
1971	778,526	730,670
1972	701,214	731,264
1973	635,633	731,028
1974	626,373	727,511
1975	600,512	749,260
1976	602,851	733,140
1977	582,344	704,922

Education and Sport

It is said in West Germany that the most underprivileged group so far as education is concerned are Bavarian, Catholic, working-class girls. For a variety of reasons the working class is poorly represented higher up the education ladder and education facilities in Bavaria tend to be poorer than in other parts of the Federal Republic. Nowhere do girls in West Germany get the same opportunities for education as do boys. No doubt the attitudes of parents remain an important factor. Though the number of girls gaining the *Abitur* has gone up over the years, up to 1979 far fewer girls than boys got this all-important certificate. This is a prime reason why, by the end of the 1970s, women were still not as well represented as men at West German universities. On the positive side, it will be noted that the percentage increase in the number of

Table 9.5: Enrolments at Universities in FRG (Germans only)

Winter	Total university students	Women
1960–61	199,456	46,080
1964–65	248,294	59,633
1968–69	290,593	73,522
1977–78	862,056	299,763

female students was greater than the percentage increase in the student body as a whole. However, if we look at the distribution of women students according to subject we find that the traditional pattern had been largely maintained. Few women, even in 1979, were studying law, architecture, chemistry, physics, agriculture or engineering. On the other hand, women were well represented in modern languages and subjects likely to take them into teaching as a career. Women had also made further progress in medicine.

Even though sport in Germany was originally closely associated with defence and national prestige and therefore not considered of interest to women, women had made a considerable contribution to German sport before 1945. In the 1920s and 1930s the achievements of German women in sport compared favourably with those of British and French women. At the Amsterdam Olympic Games of 1928 German women gained gold medals in athletics, fencing and swimming. In athletics there were only five events for women. Linda Radke of Germany won the 800 metres, an event in which many of the competitors showed signs of distress. It was subsequently dropped because it was believed to be too strenuous for women. Helen Mayer, who took the gold in the individual foil, the only women's fencing event, won every match throughout the competition. In the women's 200 metres' breaststroke Hilde Schrader won the gold for Germany. Partly because of cost, Germany (and many other countries) were not so well represented at the Los Angeles Olympics in 1932. The American women swept the board in most of the events. On their home ground in 1936, and with far more official backing, Gisela Mauermeyer won the discus and Tilly Fleischer took the gold for the javelin. In gymnastics German women won the team gold. In the Olympics since 1956 German women have been prominent once again. In the period up to 1980 East German women had a far greater impact than their West German sisters, but the West Germans too have had their successes. One outstanding performer was Heidi Rosendahl who, at Munich in 1972, came back in decisive fashion after being injured in Mexico (1968) where she had been

Table 9.6: Awards of *Deutsches Jugendsportabzeichen* by Sex

	Boys	Girls
1967	54,083	47,499
1968	50,342	45,258
1969	43,767	40,977
1975	42,641	49,546
1976	46,589	53,044
1977	60,987	67,190

expected to take the gold in the pentathlon. In Munich she won the gold in the long jump, took the silver in the pentathlon and played the vital part in enabling West Germany's women to win the 4 x 100 metres' relay. Equally impressive at Munich was Ulrike Mayfarth who, only 16, greatly improved on her best previous performance to win the gold in the high jump. How things are changing for the better in women's sport can be gauged by reviewing the figures for the numbers of young men and women achieving the *Deutsches Jugendsportabzeichen*, a nationally recognised award requiring achievement in five sports' activities.

At the adult level of this award, *Deutsches Sportabzeichen*, men still far outnumber women in 1977 — 65,953 as against 19,878. Yet here too figures over a considerable period indicate the increasing interest of West German women in sport and the determination of an increasing number to excel.

Marriage and the Family

Even in the 1950s Germans used to smile when they saw British soldiers stationed in Germany carrying their wives' shopping baskets or pushing their prams. To many Germans, men and women, such activities appeared slightly unmanly. Certainly in the home, German men at that time appeared to take a more traditional view of the relations between the sexes than did British men. Officially, of course, men and women were, and are, equal. This was even the case in the Weimar constitution, Article 119 of which declared that marriage was based on the equality of the sexes. The Basic Law of the Federal Republic (Article 3) laid down that: 'Men and women shall have equal rights.' Existing laws which ran counter to Article 3 were to lose their validity after 31 March 1953. In June 1957 an equality of the sexes law — *Gesetz über*

*die Gleichberechtigung von Mann und Frau auf dem Gabiet des
bürgerlichen Rechts* – was passed. More legislation followed which
came into force on 1 July 1977. It was based on the principle of the
equal place of man and woman in marriage in the sense of a real
partnership. It regards marriage as a private arrangement between man
and wife as equal partners. The two partners decide on the way they
shall carry out their domestic and professional responsibilities. The
husband is no longer regarded as the custodian of the family finances.
Both have equal responsibilities for any children. They can use either
the husband's name, or the wife's, or a combination of both. Divorce
will be granted merely because of the breakdown of the marriage – not,
as before, on the basis of the guilt of one or other of the parties. If
both parties agree, divorce becomes effective after one year of
separation. If only one party seeks the divorce, three years of separation are necessary before the divorce will be granted. The partner who
is financially better off must assist the partner unable to earn a
livelihood. In most respects the 1977 law was merely catching up with
what very many younger Germans thought the relations between the
sexes should be. The actual working of this law has been widely
criticised. It can make divorce very expensive for the man even if he is
getting divorced because of the infidelity of his wife. The divorce figures
indicate the changing attitude to marriage over the post-war period.

Table 9.7: Divorces in FRG 1950–76

1950	86,341	1970	76,711
1955	48,860	1975	106,932
1960	49,325	1976	108,363
1965	59,039		

As in other advanced industrial societies, the rising divorce rates run
parallel with the decline in membership of the churches and falling
church attendances, which are recorded annually by the churches
themselves. Most West Germans still pay the traditional church tax
which is deducted from wages and salaries. As elsewhere, women in the
FRG remain more committed to the churches than do their menfolk.
Between 1969 and 1976 membership of the Catholic Church in the
FRG fell from 28.7 million to 26.9 million. In the same period
Evangelical Church membership declined from 29.2 million to 26.9
million. The population as a whole rose from 60.6 million in 1970 to
61.4 million in 1976.

Despite the trend in recent years towards greater equality between the sexes and the legislation to promote such equality, change has been slower in the home. A survey carried out in the mid-1970s, published in *Der Spiegel* (17 February 1975), revealed that women, even those with professions outside the home, still did most of the housework. Of the housewives interviewed, 90 per cent claimed they made the beds, 89 per cent prepared the meals, 83 per cent cleaned their homes, 82 per cent kept the windows clean, 70 per cent did the washing up, 62 per cent did the shopping and 55 per cent were responsible for cleaning the shoes. If they had a garden men were more likely to keep it tidy. About 55 per cent of West Germans lived in flats at that time, compared with 18 per cent in Britain. Notwithstanding the lack of assistance in the home, most West German housewives did not express any desire to return to their previous employment. Those without children showed the least enthusiasm to go out to work (13 per cent). Of those with one child, 25 per cent wanted to go out to work, as did 38 per cent of those with two children. Of those with three or more children, 36 per cent would have welcomed work outside the home. Perhaps this lack of enthusiasm for being 'gainfully employed' resulted in part from the fact that most women had been involved in doing routine, relatively poorly-paid work, before getting married. Though attitudes were changing, in 1975 Germans of the Federal Republic remained fairly conservative in their views about the roles of men and women.

How one interprets such figures will depend on one's view of marriage and its place in modern society. There will be little disagreement, however, with the proposition that the rising crime rates are a cause for concern; and the growth of female criminality is a part of women's emancipation which few will welcome. The West Germans are suffering from this in just the same way as other advanced industrial societies.

Table 9.8: Criminal Convictions in the FRG

	Total men and women	Women only
1970	643,285	84,337
1974	699,198	94,235
1976	699,339	103,354

Unfortunately, the *Statistisches Jahrbuch* of the Federal Republic, from which these figures are taken, does not give details of the type of crimes committed by the convicted women. Other sources, however, indicate that women are involved in many of the crimes of the consumer society such as shoplifting and fraud. More worrying is the relatively large number of young women involved in terrorist activity. Ten of the top 16 terrorists on the wanted list after the murder in September 1977 of Hanns-Martin Schleyer, President of the employers' organisation, were women. Among the two best known — or notorious — were Ulrike Meinhof and Gudrun Ensslin, the daughters, respectively, of a museum curator and a Lutheran pastor. Then there were Ina Siepmann, the daughter of a chemist, and Angela Luther, the daughter of a well-to-do Hamburg lawyer. These young women, and others, were engaged in every kind of terrorist activity from bank robberies and jail breaks to kidnapping and hijacking. They claimed to be Marxists working for a new, socialist order of society in which there would be no more exploiters or exploited. It was to be a new order unlike any existing socialist model. They were a sad little breakaway from the student revolt of the 1960s. When other student rebels took new hope from the victory of Brandt in 1969 and joined, or returned to, the SPD, they saw the new regime as merely the alternative party of industrial capitalism. They felt the masses could only be awakened from their slumbers and the 'repressive freedom' of the Federal Republic exposed by constant confrontation with the authorities. Their wave of angry violence reached its peak in 1977 with the murder, in three separate incidents, of Schleyer, Siegfried Buback, Chief Federal Prosecutor, and his driver, and Jürgen Ponto, Chairman of the Dresdner Bank. They also hijacked a Lufthansa airliner with 86 passengers and crew on board. Ensslin and Meinhof killed themselves in prison.

There has been much speculation about the significance of the women terrorists. It is worth remembering that the evidence so far indicates that they made their entry into the world of political violence through the influence of men with whom they had close relationships. There does not appear to be anything peculiar to German women's rights' activists which makes them prone to urban terrorism. These women are very much a tiny minority of a minority. Everywhere women are becoming more concerned about political issues, and it is natural that some of them will end up on the violent fringe of politics. If anything, this violent fringe has made the achievement of further social and political progress more difficult.

As we saw in Chapter 3, West Germany looks a long way off electing a woman as Chancellor, for women in the two main parties have not used their considerable numbers to ensure that more women are selected as candidates for the *Bundestag*. However, the Federal Republic is by no means backward compared to its neighbours in this respect. The elections to the European Parliament in 1979 provided some useful comparisons on the place of women politicians in Western Europe.

Table 9.9: Female Representation in the European Parliament 1979

Country	Seats	Women	%
Belgium	24	2	8
Denmark	16	5	31
FRG	81	12	15
France	81	18	22
Ireland	15	2	13
Italy	81	11	14
Luxembourg	6	1	17
Netherlands	25	5	20
United Kingdom	81	11	14

German women have captured many citadels since Pauline Staegemann set up the SPD's first women's organisation in Berlin in 1872; they still have many more to conquer.

Further Reading

Brandt, Willy (ed.). *Frauen heute – Jahrhundertthema Gleichberechtigung* (Cologne, 1978)

Evans, Richard J. *The Feminist Movement in Germany 1894–1933* (London, 1976)

Helwig, Gisela. *Zwischen Familie und Beruf Die Stellung der Frau in beiden deutschen Staaten* (Cologne, 1974)

Stephenson, Jill. *Women in Nazi Germany* (London, 1975)

10 THE ARMED FORCES

Origins

On 12 November 1955 at the Ermekeil Barracks in Bonn, the first 101 soldiers of the *Bundeswehr*, the FRG's armed forces, received their commissions. They ranged in rank from two three-star generals, Adolf Heusinger and Hans Speidel, to five NCOs (*Oberfeldwebel*). The ceremony took place on the 200th anniversary of the birth of Gerhard Scharnhorst, a fact mentioned by Defence Minister Theodor Blank. This reminder of the Prussian general of the Napoleonic era possibly sent a chill down the spines of any Allied representatives present, but it need not have done so. Scharnhorst was not the exponent of an army based on blind obedience; rather he attempted to drag the Prussian army out of its feudalistic ways and turn it into a thinking, disciplined and well-organised force. Armies need tradition and Scharnhorst could, without too much whitewash, be written up as part of a positive strand in German military history. Like the Prussian Army which fought at Waterloo, the *Bundeswehr's* first 101 were rather an austere lot. In fact most of them were still without uniforms. Heusinger and Speidel, in their American-style uniforms, lacked the swank and swagger displayed even by many of the German officers at the various surrender ceremonies in May 1945. Such fine distinctions were lost on wide sections of opinion in all parts of Europe. There was dismay that Germans should once again be carrying arms. The rearmament which appeared so unlikely in 1945, when the Germans were not even allowed to manufacture toy aircraft, was the result of the Cold War between the Soviet Union and the West. Ironically, the worst period of East–West confrontation was over when on 8 June 1955 Herr Blank took the oath as the FRG's first Defence Minister. Blank had, of course, been going about his task exploring the defence situation for Adenauer since 1950; and West Germans had been armed in the little-publicised *Bundesgrenzschutz* since 1951. This body had recruited most of its officers from the *Wehrmacht* rather than the police, and many of them subsequently joined the armed forces. Germans had also served in the uniformed, and lightly armed, Allied service units before 1951. These units, which guarded Allied installations, carried out maintenance work and so on, had the advantage of keeping together suitable military cadres against the day Germany, or rather the FRG, got the green light to go ahead with rearmament.

Strength and Expenditure

The first training company of the *Bundeswehr* was organised on 1
January 1956. Later in the same month Chancellor Adenauer greeted
the approximately 1,500 volunteers at the Andernach Barracks. This
occasion, 20 January 1956, has been designated the birthday of the
Bundeswehr. This American-equipped force had grown to 66,000 men
by the end of the year − 9,572 of them were volunteers from the
Bundesgrenzschutz, most of them had previous military service. After
some initial hiccups the FRG's forces grew rapidly. By 1960 they
numbered 270,000, rising to 403,000 three years later. Expansion then
slowed reaching 462,700 in 1969. Development in the 1970s is shown
in Table 10.1.

Table 10.1: Armed Forces FRG, France and UK

	1973	1979
FRG total	475,000	495,000
France	503,600	509,300
UK	361,500	322,890

The West Germans showed themselves more reluctant than the British,
or for that matter the East Germans, to recruit women for the armed
services, but changing attitudes and difficulties in recruiting men caused
the Defence Ministry to review the situation. By the mid-1970s
around 49,000 women were employed by the armed services. The
Signal Corps alone employed 3,370. The Medical Corps is also gradually
building up its *woman*power. Few of these women are actually classed
as soldiers. In addition to nearly 500,000 men and women in uniform,
the Defence Ministry employs a large force of civilian employees to
administer and service the *Bundeswehr*. About 47 per cent of the
armed forces are conscripts.

Virtually all the West German armed forces are assigned to NATO −
a condition insisted upon by the Western powers after the failure to set
up a European Defence Community in 1955. Today West Germany
boasts the strongest land and air forces in Western Europe, and is
second in NATO only to the United States. Its navy is mainly of a
coastal defence type made up of modern (non-nuclear) submarines,
destroyers, fast frigates, patrol boats and minesweepers.

West German official publications stress the entirely defensive nature of the FRG's armed forces. As the *Weissbuch 1975/76* puts it:

> The Federal Republic of Germany has renounced the production
> and ownership of strategic offensive weapons in its own land and has
> agreed to international control of its armed forces by the West
> European Union. The *Bundeswehr* has no atomic, chemical or
> biological weapons. It has not available to it long range strategic
> war planes and missiles. There is no national general staff with
> operational leadership tasks. The great majority of the fighting units
> will be led, in wartime (*Verteidigungsfall*), by NATO commanders.
> The *Bundeswehr* has only a limited transport capacity. Because of
> this and because of the geographical situation of the depots, the
> fighting units can only be supplied inside federal territory. All this
> makes clear that the *Bundeswehr* − its personnel, material and
> supply technology − and the possibilities of its leadership, are not
> capable of a strategic offensive.

All this defence costs West Germany a lot of money. It is true that
compared with earlier times the FRG is spending less on defence than
did its predecessors. In 1907, for example, Germany used 33 per cent
of its tax revenue for military purposes. In 1977 the Federal Republic
spent 'only' 19 per cent of its revenue on defence. Nevertheless, the
FRG spends more on defence than any other NATO country except
the USA. This is also true of its *per capita* defence expenditure.
However, the Federal Republic has consistently spent less on defence
than have Britain and some other countries when such expenditure is
measured as a percentage of gross domestic product − in other words,
its effective ability to pay.

Arms Industry and Exports

For some years after rearmament got under way, the Federal Republic
was not in the arms trade to any significant extent. This was because
its defence industries had not made up the leeway lost after the war
when they were prohibited from manufacturing arms. Secondly, West
Germany's defence sector was fully stretched filling orders for the
Bundeswehr − often making American equipment under licence.
Thirdly, it was thought that for political reasons the FRG should keep
out of this trade. In recent years the mood has changed considerably.
The West Germans frequently express dissatisfaction over lack of

Table 10.2: Military Expenditure as a Percentage of Gross Domestic Product

	1957	1967	1976
USA	9.9	9.4	5.4
FRG	4.1	4.3	3.4
France	7.3	5.0	3.9
UK	7.2	5.7	5.1

orders from the United States for the FRG's defence industries. The West Germans have, for a long time, been supplying Greece, Portugal and Turkey — all NATO members — with a variety of armaments. The same is true of Israel and at least 17 African and Asian states. Nor has South America been neglected as an outlet for arms deliveries. The FRG has sold, among other things, submarines to Argentina, Brazil, Ecuador and Venezuela, helicopters to Indonesia, the Philippines and Sudan, frigates to Nigeria, and patrol boats to Ghana and Malaysia. West Germany still accounts for less of the total world trade in arms to the Third World than do some of its allies, including the United States. Between 1970 and 1976 the Federal Republic was responsible for 1 per cent of total arms exports to the Third World. In the same period Britain and France accounted for 9 per cent each of such exports. Italy was responsible for 2 per cent. From 1965 onwards West Germany has also been exporting tanks and other military equipment to the advanced NATO states such as Belgium, the Netherlands, Norway and Italy. Despite this much increased, though still limited, export of defence hardware, West German industry is not convinced it is getting its share of markets abroad and criticisms have been made over the years about the lack of initiative in this direction on the part of the FRG's service diplomats.

One of the disturbing aspects of the West German arms trade is the increasing use of former officers to lobby in Bonn and elsewhere for arms orders. During the formative years of the West German armed forces such orders were easy to come by, but later, as the *Bundeswehr* neared the target set for its expansion, orders became more difficult. Foreign firms, too, have sought to use the expertise of former West German officers to gain orders. Even in the early days former *Wehrmacht* officers who had not found a place in the new armed forces were sometimes involved in representing firms seeking defence contracts. Among the best known was General Adolf Galand, the

World War II flying ace. In the 1970s, a considerable number of former high-ranking *Bundeswehr* officers were active as lobbyists. Among the generals were: Johannes Steinhoff, former head of the West German air force, working for the aircraft firm Dornier; another former head of the FRG air force, Werner Panitzki, representing Europavia; Friedrich Schlichting, formerly deputy head of the air force, employed by Messerschmitt-Bölkow-Blohm (MBB); August Hentz, formerly commander of the 2nd air force division, engaged as Bonn representative of Boeing; Uwe Köster, employed by the US aircraft corporation Grumman; Kurt Gieser, engaged by BASF; Bernd Freiherr von Freytag-Loringhoven, on the payroll of Philips; Albert Schnez, former army chief, working for Kühne and Nagel. The West German navy contributed Admiral Erich Topp, formerly deputy commander of the *Bundesmarine*, who used his expertise on behalf of Deutsche Werft AG. Below these and other generals were a considerable number of former officers of lesser rank, engaged by the same and other firms seeking defence contracts. Former top civil servants have also been employed by firms in pursuit of defence work. Where big money is involved, sooner or later there will be corruption. In the FRG a number of cases have come to light. At the end of the 1960s Karl E. Ende, a former top civil servant working for the Defence Ministry, was exposed for having taken money from a tachometer firm. The clouds of the Starfighter affair still hang heavily over Bonn. The full story will probably never come to light. It is certain only that important files dealing with the procurement of this Lockheed aircraft disappeared from the ministry archives, and that civil servants did give confidential information to Lockheed.

The big orders in the 1980s are for the MRCA Tornado aircraft and the close support and battlefield reconnaissance Alpha Jet G-91 — MBB, Fokker, BMW, Dornier, AEG-Telefunken, MTU, Zeiss, Rhein-metall, Faun, Leitz, Porsche, Rheinstahl-Wenschel, Siemens and MAN, have all secured their part of the prize. Next among the big orders is the Leopard II tank which will be produced by Krauss-Maffei (Flick) and Krupp. Other big orders are planned to re-equip artillery units and refit naval vessels. So far only the aircraft industry is heavily dependent on defence contracts.

The growth of the West German arms industry should not be exaggerated. Although over 10,000 firms are directly involved in armaments contracts, and perhaps four times that number are indirectly involved on subcontract work, the contracts are so widely distributed as to avoid unhealthy dependence on this source of income. However, it remains to be seen to what extent Bonn politicians can resist using defence contracts for job creation should the bleak prophecies for the world economy in the 1980s come true.

Constitution and *Bundeswehr*

When considering the setting up of new armed forces, the West German politicians were very cautious, both because of the bad experience of the Weimar Republic with its armed forces, the *Reichswehr*, and because of the need to appease public opinion both at home and abroad. For this reason the commander-in-chief of the armed forces was not, as in the Weimar Republic, the President, but the Defence Minister responsible to the *Bundestag*. In times of war the Chancellor takes over responsibility for the armed services. Like other ministers, Defence Ministers in the FRG tend to be long serving. Up to 1980 there have been seven: Theodor Blank (CDU), to 1956; Franz Josef Strauss (CSU), 1956–62; Kai-Uwe von Hassel (CDU), 1963–66; Gerhard Schröder (CDU), 1966–69; Helmut Schmidt (SPD), 1969–72; Georg Leber (SPD), 1972–78; Hans Apel (SPD), 1978. Of these probably Strauss, followed by Schmidt, had the most influence.

The highest-ranking member of the *Bundeswehr* is the *Generalinspekteur* who is responsible to the Defence Minister. The *Generalinspekteur's* position, as defined by Hans Apel on 7 December 1978, is one of chief military adviser to the Minister. He does not have the power to issue orders on his own behalf. Under him are three deputies responsible for the army, navy and air force respectively. The permanent Defence Committee of the *Bundestag* is the parliamentary friend and watchdog of the armed services. Its special representative is the *Wehrbeauftragter* (Defence Commissioner) whose activities are discussed separately below. As part and parcel of the attempt to create democratically oriented armed services, the *Soldatengesetz* (Soldiers' Law) of March 1956 laid down that soldiers have the same rights as other citizens, limited only by the demands of military service. Thus, unlike the soldier in the Weimar Republic, the West German soldier can join a political party, be elected to local, regional or federal parliaments, and even be a member of a trade union. He cannot go on strike. Under Article 35 of the same law, NCOs and soldiers in each unit of the *Bundeswehr* elect, for a minimum period of three months, a representative and two deputies. The representative (*Vertrauensmann*) contributes to the development of 'responsible co-operation between superiors and subordinates' and the creation of an atmosphere of 'comradely trust' in his unit. He has the right to be heard when making proposals in the fields of welfare, career advancement, off-duty social life, and questions about the life of the unit. This institution has been attacked as undermining military discipline but there is no evidence of this. It is an institution which was not unknown in Germany before the war. The Weimar Republic, under the *Wehrgesetz* of 23 March 1921, regulated an institution which had evolved in German military units at the end of the 1914–18 War. It was abolished under Nazi legislation of 21 May 1935. Under the *Soldatengesetz* soldiers are freed from the obligation to obey an order which is degrading. It is their duty not to obey any order which would lead them to commit a crime. Unlike other states, including the German Democratic Republic, the FRG does not have any system of military courts. Crimes committed by servicemen are tried in the normal courts.

Conscription and Conscientious Objection

Conscription was introduced in the Federal Republic under the *Wehrpflichtgesetz* (Defence Duty Law) of 21 July 1956. It has been subject to modifications since then. Conscripts are obliged to serve 15 months, the same as Italians, but three months longer than the French and Belgians. Denmark, with nine months' service, has the shortest compulsory military service of any NATO state. In Britain, of course, there is no national service. On the other side of the Elbe, East Germans are required to serve 18 months, and they get off lightly compared with their Warsaw Pact colleagues, except, that is, for the Rumanians. National service has never been very popular in the FRG and seemed to grow less popular over the 1960s and early 1970s. Between 1956 and 1961 just under 15,000 West Germans, including 240 servicemen, applied to be registered as conscientious objectors. Over 4,500 were recognised, none of whom were soldiers. The number of draftees wanting to be registered as objectors reached 4,489 in 1962 (2,842 were recognised), and then fell for the next two years to 2,777 in 1964 (2,593 recognised). The number then rose year by year throughout the 1960s, more than doubling between 1967 and 1968 – from 5,963 to 11,952 (the number of those recognised rose only from 4,739 to 5,588). In 1970 over 19,363 applied and 9,351 were recognised. Interestingly, the number of servicemen applying increased every year from 162 in 1962 to 3,184 in 1970 (in the later year, 1,906 of them were recognised). According to the official Defence Ministry *Weissbuch* for 1975—76, the annual number of applications to be recognised as a conscientious objector had levelled off at around 35,000. The *Weissbuch* claimed there was a greater preparedness on the part of young men to do their military service. However, the number has gone on rising. In 1977, over 70,000 applied to be recognised. What happens to conscientious objectors in the Federal Republic? Certainly the FRG has more liberal provision for them than most other states. They are required to do appropriate directed work for 18 months. The relatively liberal treatment of objectors in West Germany is due to the initial widespread opposition to rearmament and the need to compete with East Germany. It is significant that in the German Democratic Republic conscientious objectors are treated more humanely than in the other Warsaw Pact states. In the Federal Republic the objector has to convince a four-member examining board of his sincerity. The only grounds that are recognised are reasons of conscience — that is, a rejection of war as such on ethical, ideological or religious grounds. The candidate's application will be rejected if he simply objects to fighting particular opponents or in particular situations. Having convinced the board, the objector is then usually put to work as a medical orderly in hospitals, especially those dealing with mental patients, the severely physically handicapped or the very old. With the growing number of objectors, there has developed a problem of finding them suitable alternative service. An attempt by the government to simplify the procedure granting recognition was taken by the Christian Democratic opposition to the constitutional court. The court accepted the opposition's plea and the law was rescinded. Interestingly, a public opinion poll conducted in 1979 indicated that 54 per cent of the West German population recognise the right to conscientious objection.

The *Wehrbeauftragter*

The *Wehrbeauftragter* of Defence Commissioner in the FRG follows the Scandinavian model. Sweden had a Defence Commissioner or *Militieombudsman* between 1915 and 1968. Now a more general *ombudsman* investigates complaints from the three services. Norway established such an office in 1952 and it is still in existence. The West German Defence Commissioner is appointed, according to the *Gesetz über den Wehrbeauftragten* of 26 June 1957, by the President of the *Bundestag* after election by the federal parliament. The appointment is for five years and may be renewed for a further term. The *Bundestag* can direct its President to relieve the Defence Commissioner of his duties. Under Article 16 of the Law, the Defence Commissioner is under the administrative control of the *Bundestag* President. He is responsible to the federal parliament, and is required to submit an annual report to that body. The federal parliament and its Defence Committee can demand at any time the attendance of the Commissioner, who is clearly regarded as the servant of the *Bundestag*. To emphasise this his office is in the *Bundeshaus* (the federal parliament building) in Bonn. However, he also has independent premises elsewhere in the capital. The *Wehrbeauftragter* has a staff of over 60, eleven or so of them lawyers, to assist him in carrying out his duties.

Article 2 of the 1957 Law sets out the main functions of the Defence Commissioner. He must investigate specific matters on the instructions of the federal parliament or its Defence Committee. Further, acting on information from members of the *Bundestag*, members of the *Bundeswehr*, or other sources, he is obliged to examine.

> circumstances which lead him to believe that there has been a breach of the soldiers' basic rights or an infringement of the principles of 'Innere Führung'. He shall inform the *Bundestag* of the outcome of his enquiries either in a special report or within the scope of his annual report.

In order to carry out this work, 'He may at any time visit any troops, headquarters, administrative agencies and establishments of the armed forces without prior notice.' He also enjoys the right to attend any disciplinary tribunals — even in closed session — in matters pertaining to his area of responsibility. Federal, *Länder* and local authorities are required to assist him.

Under Article 7 of the 1957 Law, every serviceman has the right to direct requests or complaints to the Defence Commissioner. 'No person shall be reprimanded or discriminated against on the grounds of his having applied to the Commissioner.' Article 8 states that anonymous complaints and accusations will not be dealt with. Judged by the number of requests for help he has had, the *Wehrbeauftragter* has proved the need for such an office. In 1961, there were nearly 4,000 requests for his assistance. The number rose to nearly 6,000 in 1963. In the mid-1960s, there was some falling off of requests, but in the last years of the decade big increases were recorded. In 1970 the

Wehrbeauftragter got 7,142 requests. In the last few years there has been some levelling off: 1976, 7,319; 1977, 6,753; 1978, 6,234. Normally, there are about 200—300 requests which are about matters not within the competence of the Commissioner, and usually there are two or three — in 1978 actually ten — which are anonymous. It is interesting to examine where the requests for investigation came from:

Table 10.3: Originators of Submissions to *Wehrbeauftragter*

	1977	1978
Soldiers of the *Bundeswehr*	4,437	4,395
Soldiers' families	347	338
Former soldiers	551	513
Members of the *Bundestag*	70	48
Other deputies (*Länder*, etc.)	5	8
Other private persons	163	142
Organisations	36	16
Visits to the troops by Commissioner	27	41
Press reports	22	28
Special occurrences	811	408
Draftees who have not yet served	162	148
Other sources	77	56
Total	6,708	6,141

In both the years in question, the great majority of the requests or complaints were made by, or on behalf of, conscripts — 2,506 in 1977, and 2,020 in 1978. In both years nearly 500 concerned reservists.

What do West German soldiers complain about? In 1975, 62.5 per cent of the complaints were connected with pay, promotion, leave and living conditions. There were, however, a significant number of complaints dealing with 'basic rights' such as freedom of opinion, infringement of human dignity, constitutional rights and so on. In both 1977 and 1978 the Defence Commissioner — since 1975, Karl Wilhelm Berkhan — cited a number of cases, as examples of many others, in which the dignity of service personnel had been infringed. Many involved 'initiation ceremonies' at which recruits were beaten or otherwise degraded by drunken NCOs, soldiers were subject to severe oral abuse by company commanders and recruits were used as 'targets' by NCOs firing blanks or airguns, or so-called training marches or survival courses which resulted in brutality towards servicemen. The Commissioner also expressed his worries about the abuse of alcohol in the armed forces, a view supported by the highly responsible *Die Zeit* (29 June 1979). Of course, it must be remembered that, precisely because West Germany has a Defence Commissioner, the kind of situations mentioned above are more likely to come to light than in some other NATO armed forces.

Just how successful Herr Berkhan has been in resolving complaints it is difficult to be sure. In 1975, for instance, the Defence Commissioner claimed success in 1,826 cases and partial success in a further 467, and admitted failure in 3,084. The results in the final 1,529 processed, some from the previous year, were unclear.

Controversies about *innere Führung*

Ever since the *Bundeswehr* was established in 1955 there has been controversy about the office of the Defence Commissioner and the closely associated problem of the intellectual-spiritual orientation of the armed forces, its so-called *innere Führung*. Many right of centre politicians saw the Defence Commissioner right from the start as a tool of pacifists, leftists and Social Democrats who would undermine military discipline. This helps to explain why it took eighteen months to appoint the first incumbent, and why the first two Commissioners were military men. Both of them resigned after criticisms. The first, General Grolman, withdrew after a personal scandal; the second, Admiral Heye, after attacks on him for merely doing his duty. Heye, a wartime Vice-Admiral and former Christian Democratic member of the *Bundestag*, expressed the view that the *Bundeswehr* was becoming a 'state within the state'. In his 1965 report the Admiral exposed severe cases of brutality including loss of life, and asked the question, 'Do the majority of the officer corps today acknowledge the democratic institution of the Defence Commissioner? I entertain well-founded doubts.' Under the Admiral's successors[1] controversy about the *Wehrbeauftragter* subsided for a time but arguments continued about the *innere Führung*. First formulated by General Wolf Graf Baudissin, this vague concept has been reformulated from time to time. Gerhard Schröder, as the responsible minister, stated (5 May 1969) that the essentials of this concept embraced: the paramountcy of political as against military leadership; the incorporation of the armed forces into the democratic community; the protection of the individual's rights regardless of his status as a soldier; the respect of every soldier's dignity regardless of his duty to obey orders; the law of nations as an integral part of the military domain; the image of the citizen in uniform or rather the citizen as a soldier. These basic tenets are reduced to two dimensions — modern management and moral armament. The first of these means recognition of the armed forces more as a progressive corporation in a service industry than as an old-fashioned hierarchical body based on mere obedience to superior authority. Obedience there must be, but also discussion, understanding and participation. The second dimension means recognition of the ideological, the 'hearts and minds' aspect of warfare. It requires the education of the soldier to a sense of obligation towards the democratic society in which he lives and a readiness to defend it against any external or internal threat. All too often this was translated in practice into simplistic anti-Communism, with only a brief, superficial look at Germany's National Socialist past. With so many officers involved in that past, this was perhaps inevitable.

The last of the *Bundeswehr* generals who had been generals under Hitler left the service in 1968, but their successors had been officers in the *Reichswehr* and the *Wehrmacht*, so their ideas had been formed before the 'citizen-in-uniform' concept became the *leitmotif* of the German military. In the late 1960s, the old guard hit back against the *innere Führung.* In 1966 the highest officer of the armed forces, *Generalinspekteur* Heinz Trettner, air force chief Werner Panitzki and General Günther Paper attacked what they considered excessive civilian control of the *Bundeswehr* and made a gesture by resigning. In 1969 General Hellmut Grashey, the deputy to the army chief, attacked the Defence Commissioner and the *innere Führung*, claiming it had only been accepted originally to appease the SPD. His line was endorsed by General Heinz Karst, chief education officer of the army. At the end of 1969 General Albert Schnez, head of the army, demanded changes in West German society as well as in the *Bundeswehr.* His 'reforms' would have meant changing three articles of the Basic Law and 30 federal laws, all in the direction of a more authoritarian state and armed forces. In 1970 eight young lieutenants, graduates of the Hamburg Army Officers' School II, issued a counterblast in a more liberal direction. But in December 1970 came the 'captains' revolt'. A group of 30 captains of the 7th Panzergrenadier Division stationed at Unna, Westphalia, issued a pamphlet which, among other things, attacked the 'citizen-in-uniform' concept. Defence Minister Helmut Schmidt tried to talk the young officers round and to minimise, at least in public, the differences between their views and those of the government. He took the same line as Schnez, causing anger among many of his own colleagues, but sent Grashey into early retirement. Karst apparently asked for, and received, the same treatment, in 1970. In the same year the last post sounded for 22 generals and admirals, which *Die Zeit* (1 May 1970) saw as, in part, the removal of officers whose mentality was not in accordance with that of the Defence Minister. This was undoubtedly a welcome development.

Of the 182 air and army generals and 27 admirals in 1977, most had experienced the war as junior officers, a few only as schoolboys. For example, the youngest air force general was Horst Jungkurth who was only eleven in 1945. General Wust, somewhat more typical (*Generalinspekteur*, 1977–78), was eighteen when the war broke out. He served as an air force intelligence officer. In 1959 Harald Wust was still only a major in the new West German air force. Born in Kiel, Wust was the first air force officer to be placed in charge of the *Bundeswehr*. As a man who has spent his entire career in a technological service, Wust was no doubt fully behind government attempts to improve both the specialist and the general education of the armed forces. Whether the setting up of special *Bundeswehr* higher education establishments, rather than using civilian universities, was a good move either to achieve this object or to help the integration of the services into society is open to question.

General Wust was forced to retire in 1978 because of alleged shortcomings in connection with a spy scandal. He had been criticised on all sides by the *Bundestag* Defence Committee. His successor is Türgen Brandt. Once again the politicians had shown that they could discipline the military. However, the annual reports of the Defence Commissioner indicate there is no cause for complacency about the dedication to democratic norms of Bonn's professional soldiers.

Further Reading

Bredow, Wilfried von. *Die unbewältigte Bundeswehr* (Frankfurt/M, 1973)

Grimm, Siegfried. . . . *der Bundesrepublik treu zu dienen* (Düsseldorf, 1970)

Hasslein, Bernd C. and Duve, Freimut. *Die unbewältigte Vergangenheit der Bundeswehr Funf Offiziere zur Krise der Inneren Führung* (Hamburg, 1977)

Jahresberichte des Wehrbeauftragten des Deutschen Bundestages (Bonn, annually)

Mechtersheimer, Alfred. *Rüstung und Politik in der Bundesrepublik*
    (Bad Honnef, 1978)
Waldman, Eric. *The Goose Step is Verboten* (New York, 1964)
Zoll, Ralf (ed.). *Wie infegriert ist die Bundeswehr?* (Munich 1979)

Note

1. Matthias Hoogen (1964–70) and Fritz-Rudolf Schultz (1970–75). Hoogen
was a former CDU member of the *Bundestag*. Schultz, a much-decorated wartime
tank commander, was an FDP *Bundestag* member.

11 FOREIGN POLICY

The Social Democrats were widely tipped as the party which would emerge with the biggest single vote in the first federal elections in 1949. As it turned out, the Christian Democrats were 400,000 votes ahead of their main rivals – not a great deal. If the votes of the West Berliners had counted, the SPD would have commanded more votes in the *Bundestag* than the CDU/CSU. Alternatively, had the states still holding considerable numbers of German prisoners of war – mainly workers in uniform – been a little more generous, it is perfectly possible that the SPD would have won. In this case Schumacher would have stood a good chance of being elected Chancellor with the help of the left of the CDU, the remnants of the *Zentrum* and some other small groups. Something similar happened in neighbouring Austria where socialists and Catholics were in a 'grand coalition' throughout this period. Would German history have been different? This is perfectly possible. Schumacher would have been more determined than Adenauer to put German reunification at the top of his 'foreign' policy priorities. He would have been less ready to integrate the Federal Republic into Western organisations, and would have made another serious attempt to get a four-power agreement over Germany. It is not entirely certain he would have failed.

So much for speculation. The reality is that Konrad Adenauer became Chancellor and he had a totally different analysis of the situation confronting Germany. As early as October 1945 he had concluded that there would be an East–West division of Europe along the river Elbe. He had also concluded that Western Europe, including Britain, must be united in order to survive. This was, in part, because he had not anticipated continued American involvement in Europe. By the time he had become Chancellor he was more convinced than ever of the rightness of his conception and happy to see the unanticipated United States' presence in Western Europe.

The first major change in American policy towards Germany after the war, designed to treat Germany more as a partner, less as a conquered state, was made public in the Stuttgart speech (September 1946) of James Byrnes, the US Secretary of State. Byrnes argued,

> Germany must be given a chance to export goods in order to import enough to make her economy self-sustaining. Germany is part of

Europe and recovery in Europe, and particularly in the states adjoining Germany, will be slow indeed if Germany with her great resources of iron and coal is turned into a poorhouse.

American policy quickly changed with this in mind. The merging of the British and American Zones at the end of 1946 was one step on this road, the granting of Marshall Aid was another. The speeding up of German self-government was also an intrinsic part of this recovery programme.

Regaining Sovereignty

The Federal Republic was set up on the basis of the Washington resolutions of April 1949 which replaced the military government of the Western Zones with an Occupation Statute (*Besatzungsstatut*). This meant that the Federal Republic was not allowed to have diplomatic or consular relations with foreign states nor was it able to join international organisations. The Allies also retained important reserve powers over the West German economy and over any proposed legislation. The Petersberg Agreement of 22 November 1949 removed some of these restrictions. The Federal Republic became eligible to join international bodies and it was allowed consular relations with other states. In January 1950 the Federal Republic sent consul-generals to Washington, London and Paris. As a result of the New York conference of the US, British and French Foreign Ministers of September 1950, the Federal Republic got the right to speak for all Germans, in East Germany as well as West. It also gained the right to engage in foreign relations and to set up paramilitary police formations. Both the Petersberg Agreement and the New York conference led to less Allied control of the West German economy. In March 1951 the shadow Foreign Ministry was officially established as the *Auswärtige Amt* and Dr Adenauer became Foreign Secretary as well as Chancellor. The Federal Republic joined the OEEC in October 1949 and the Council of Europe, as a full member, in May 1951. It was rapid progress indeed! There was however, another side to all of this. The Federal Republic was obliged to do certain things in return for this progress towards full sovereignty. It had agreed to become a member of the International Ruhr Authority in November 1949 which looked like agreeing to extensive and permanent foreign control of Germany's most important industrial region. Also, Dr Adenauer had agreed to acquiesce in France's aim of separating the Saar from Germany. The French started to detach this important coal and steel area from Germany in 1945. They subsequently set up a puppet state controlled by them in which pro-German parties were banned. When the Saar voters were presented in 1955 with a referendum on Europeanisation Dr Adenauer urged them to vote in favour of such a development. In fact a substantial majority rejected it in favour of a return to Germany. Chancellor Adenauer had also been prepared to accept an inferior status for Germans in a European Army, an army which would be within a European Defence Community (EDC). The so-called Bonn Treaties (*Bonner Verträge*) of 26 May 1952 were part of the reward for agreement by the West Germans to rearm. The treaties, or contractual arrangements, were signed by Adenauer and the three Western High Commissioners. The treaties ended the occupation regime, laid the basis for the re-establishment of (West) German sovereignty, relaxed restrictions on the West German economy, and bound the Allies to work for German reunification. They were supposed to become operative when the Paris Treaty (27 May 1952), setting up the EDC and signed by Adenauer, came into force. A European Army would have been difficult to create and it is doubtful whether it would have satisfied the Germans for long. The West Germans were lucky that the French National Assembly rejected the EDC treaty in August 1954, This meant that the Western Powers were forced to think again and they decided to allow the FRG to establish its own national armed forces, the *Bundeswehr*, integrated into NATO. The legal and international framework of this was another Paris Treaty signed on 23 October 1954, placing the regulation of defence partly under national responsibility and partly under the West European Union (WEU) – a defence pact involving France, Britain, the Benelux states and later Italy and the FRG – and NATO. The WEU controlled the size and armaments of member states' forces. When this Paris Treaty was ratified by the Federal Republic and became operative in May 1955, West Germany had fully regained its sovereignty.

On 1 January 1957 the Saar became part of the Federal Republic. It appeared to many of his supporters that Konrad Adenauer was truly a miracle worker, yet, as we have seen, he had contributed little or nothing to this situation. The Social Democrats had been the main opponents of French plans to detach the Saar from Germany. They had also opposed rearmament and the Ruhr Authority. This Authority had been abolished when the Coal and Steel Community, in which FRG, France, Italy, Belgium, the Netherlands and Luxembourg were equal members, was formed in 1951. The strong opposition of the SPD to all these measures of Western integration had no doubt helped Adenauer to win concessions from his new American and West European partners. But the Social Democrats were to get no recognition from the electorate for their pains. The revolt in East Germany in June 1953, which was put down by the Soviet armed forces and about which the Western Powers could do little, further convinced Adenauer that his original conception of a Western-integrated state was correct. It proved to be a trump card in the election of 1953, an election at which Adenauer was given strong American backing. It is known that the Soviet leadership was in crisis at this time and was contemplating dismantling the German Democratic Republic in favour of reunification. In these circumstances a Social-Democratic-led government would have had a greater chance of pursuing a fruitful dialogue. How did Adenauer see relations with the Soviet Union?

Hallstein Doctrine

Konrad Adenauer expected to get little from the Soviet Union and agreed with those Americans, notably John Foster Dulles, American Secretary of State, 1953–59, who favoured 'negotiations from strength'. When the Soviet Union proposed a neutralised, united democratic Germany with its own defence forces in March 1952, Adenauer's attitude was entirely dismissive. The Western Powers took the same view. To them the neutralisation of Germany would entail unacceptable risks. Nevertheless, when the Soviet leaders issued an invitation to Adenauer to visit Moscow to discuss the establishment of diplomatic relations, the Chancellor accepted. Stalin had died in 1953 and the new Soviet leaders, Bulganin and Khrushchev, had indicated a strong desire to relax East–West tension, distancing themselves from many of Stalin's earlier policies. The visit took place in September 1955. It resulted in the establishment of diplomatic relations and the release by the Soviet Union of nearly 10,000 Germans serving sentences in the USSR for war crimes. Adenauer made it quite clear on his return that the improved relations with the Soviet Union did not mean any change in the FRG's Western orientation nor did it imply any recognition of the East German regime or the Oder–Neisse frontier between the German Democratic Republic and Poland. In some respects the Federal Republic took a tougher line on East Germany. On 9 December 1955 the so-called Hallstein Doctrine was officially announced. Dr Walter Hallstein was the State Secretary in the Foreign

Ministry. The 'doctrine' attributed to Hallstein meant that the FRG
would break off diplomatic relations with all countries which recognised
the German Democratic Republic, and would refuse to enter into
diplomatic relations with any Communist country except the Soviet
Union. The doctrine was enforced against five states. In 1956 the FRG
recalled its Chargé d'Affaires from Damascus on learning that Syria had
agreed to the opening of a Consulate by the GDR. Diplomatic relations
were broken off with Yugoslavia in 1957 when that country recognised
the GDR. Relations were resumed at the beginning of 1968. In 1963
West Germany broke off relations with Castro's Cuba when his regime
decided to recognise the GDR. Relations with Cuba have since been
restored. The doctrine was still being applied in 1969 when the Federal
Republic suspended its relations with both Cambodia and South Yemen
when these states decided to have full relations with the GDR. Both
these cases were before Brandt took over as Chancellor. He was,
however, Foreign Minister. In one other case, that of the United Arab
Republic, the Federal Republic cut off economic aid after a visit by the
East German leader, Walter Ulbricht, in 1965. Cairo did not recognise
East Berlin. But Egypt and nine other Arab states broke off diplomatic
relations with Bonn.

Relations between the Federal Republic and the USSR took a turn
for the better when Anastas Mikoyan, the Soviet First Deputy Prime
Minister, visited Bonn in April 1958 to sign Soviet—West German trade
agreements and a consular convention. After this relations deteriorated
once again as the Berlin crisis built up.

Berlin Crisis

In November 1958 Khrushchev issued an ultimatum to the Western
Powers over Berlin. This involved the ending of four-power control of
Berlin — a product of wartime agreements and the Potsdam Conference
of 1945 — with West Berlin becoming a demilitarised Free City. The
four powers — the Soviet Union, USA, Britain and France — would
guarantee its status. Under a separate agreement, East Germany would
guarantee access to West Berlin from West Germany in return for an
undertaking that there would be no 'subversive activity' from West
Berlin directed against the GDR. If the Western Powers did not come to
an agreement about this within six months the USSR would simply
recognise the GDR's right to exercise full sovereignty by land, water and
air over the approaches to West Berlin. Western agreement would have

meant recognising the East German Republic, weakening the political
links between West Berlin and the FRG, and leaving West Berlin
dependent on paper guarantees rather than the physical presence of
Western troops in the city. Exactly why Khrushchev started to demand
this change at this time is not clear. No doubt he was feeling more
confident with Soviet space successes. On the other hand, the GDR
seemed to be reaching some sort of stability and was, therefore, in less
need of a change in the status of West Berlin. In the three years
1957–59 the number of people leaving the GDR for the West was
reduced year by year until, in 1959, it was at its lowest level since 1950.
Whatever the reasons for the Khrushchev ultimatum, there was no
chance of the Western Powers agreeing to his proposals. The Foreign
Ministers of the four powers did, nevertheless, meet at Geneva in May/
June 1959, talking a great deal but agreeing on very little other than
that future negotiation would be necessary to reach an agreement. The
scheduled heads of government conference in Paris in May 1960 broke
down at its very beginning in consequence of a strong Soviet protest
against American reconnaissance flights by U-2 aircraft over the USSR.
In June 1961 the Soviet leader explored the German situation with the
new US President, John F. Kennedy, in Vienna. Once again no firm
agreements were reached but at least the two powers were discussing.
Meanwhile the SPD opposition in Bonn had been active formulating its
own plans. On 18 March 1959 it announced its 'Plan for European
Security and German Reunification'. This forsaw a stage-by-stage
reunification with both German states having parity during the interim
period. Free elections would come at the end of a lengthy period of
convergence. The whole agreement would be guaranteed by the four
powers, who would also draw up a peace treaty with the two states.
This made a good many concessions to the East German–Soviet
position which favoured German reunification by way of a
'confederation' of the two German states. The Plan was unrealistic in
that the Western Powers, who had not been consulted, did not like it.
In any case, all such plans met with complete rejection by the West
German government which refused over and over to have anything to
do with the GDR authorities and simply sought reunification through
free elections, leaving the new all-German government free to choose
whether it wished to be a member of NATO or not. The West Germans
seemed to offer the Soviets very little either in respect of saving face, or,
even more important, in respect of their military security. By May 1960
the SPD had given up its Plan and was offering Dr Adenauer a joint
approach to foreign, defence and all-German problems. This did

not prevent Walter Ulbricht, East German head of state, from presenting his German Peace Plan to the East German parliament in July 1961. It contained the proposal for a German Peace Commission consisting of representatives of the two German parliaments and governments, with the task of reaching agreement on all-German proposals for a peace treaty and on 'a goodwill agreement aiming at an immediate improvement of their relations'. It saw the future Germany as a neutralised state guaranteed by the four powers and within existing frontiers. It also contained the controversial proposal for a free city of West Berlin until German reunification had been achieved. It recognised the holding of free, secret and democratic elections for an all-German parliament. Clearly, given the leadership of Dr Adenauer in Bonn, the Plan had no chance of even being investigated.

The Berlin crisis had reached its climax at 2.30 a.m. on 13 August 1961 when the East German authorities sealed off the sector boundaries between East and West Berlin. Apart from verbal protests, there was little the Western Powers appeared able to do, although they did see to it that uniformed Allied personnel could still drive through East Berlin unhindered. The East German measures indicated the poverty of the regime. Khrushchev and his East German colleagues had so frightened the East German population into thinking something was brewing that the considerable number of refugees, leaving because of renewed collectivisation measures, was turned into a flood. The crisis also exposed the poverty of the aged Chancellor's inflexible attitude to East Germany, Germany's frontiers and the Soviet Union. The reduction of support for his party in the 1961 elections showed that at least some West German voters had come to this conclusion.

Help for Israel and Friendship with France

One step which helped to establish West Germany's respectability in the Western world and also eased its path, especially in the United States, was the agreement between the FRG and Israel on restitution. It was concluded in Luxembourg on 10 September 1952. Under this agreement the FRG agreed to pay Israel 3,000 million marks for the expenses incurred in integrating the Jewish victims of Nazism who had sought refuge in Israel. The FRG also put aside 450 million marks to help Jewish victims of National Socialism living outside Israel. Separately from this, the FRG gave Israel military assistance until 1965. Diplomatic relations had to wait until May 1965 and Bonn's anger with

Egypt and Ulbricht's visit there, and cost the Federal Republic relations with most Arab states.

On 25 March 1957 the Treaty of Rome was signed setting up the European Economic Community. Its title was more modest than the ambitions held for it by most of its founders who saw it as the nucleus of a future European state. Built on the foundations of the Iron and Steel Community — FRG, France, Italy and the Benelux states — it aimed at a customs union within three or four years, and an integrated common market in the longer term. West Germany's five partners allowed the FRG a significant concession regarding East Germany. Trade between other member states and the GDR was to be regulated in accordance with existing agreements between the two Germanies. In the event of reunification the situation would be re-examined. With Britain not even applying for membership, the prospects for West Germany as a leading, if not the leading, state improved. The Germans were sensible enough to realise that they must keep a 'low profile' at this time and, once de Gaulle took over France in 1958, Adenauer faced a leader of similar stature to himself. There could have been considerable friction between the two men — Adenauer was no military man, he took a far more positive view of the United States and NATO, and he may have thought there was no room for two prima donnas in Western Europe. In reality things turned out rather differently. Franco-German relations took on a new intimacy. The two leaders met 16 times in two years. They had much in common as men and their political interests coincided. Adenauer and de Gaulle were both autocratic democrats, both were old men — Adenauer at 82 was 14 years senior to de Gaulle — both were Catholics, both had been impressed by the tragic consequences of Franco-German rivalry, and both were sceptical about Britain. They belonged to that part of the older generation in France and Germany who resented Britain's ability to come out on top in two world wars while their countries had been deeply humiliated. Adenauer was with de Gaulle in rejecting British entry into the EEC in 1962–63. With the USA looking increasingly for *détente* with the USSR — especially after 1957 — it was less attractive to Adenauer. This was even more so once Kennedy became President in 1961. De Gaulle went so far as to take France out of NATO. There is no evidence that Adenauer contemplated such a move for the FRG, but he was Gaullist to the extent that he wanted increasing German influence in the higher councils of NATO in accordance with the FRG's growing economic and military power. Significantly, eight days after de Gaulle had announced (14 January 1963) that he would veto Britain's entry, the Franco-German treaty of Friendship was signed in Paris. The treaty was achieved partly at Britain's expense, but it was the Russians who protested about it. They saw it as an attempt by West Germany to get nuclear weapons as France had become a nuclear power in 1960. Adenauer had been forced by his colleagues to accept a preamble to the Franco-German Treaty which laid down that the treaty would not militate against German commitments to the Western Alliance. It was only to be expected that once Erhard replaced Adenauer as Chancellor in 1963, the 'Bonn–Paris axis' would become less effective. Erhard and his Foreign Minister Gerhard Schröder, who had also served, rather obediently, under Adenauer, were both orientated more towards the United States (and Britain) and its interest in *détente*. De Gaulle was, however, too willing in his relations with the Soviet Union and Eastern Europe for their taste. In 1964 he sent a parliamentary delegate to East Berlin, an act which offended Bonn. He also flirted with the Kremlin leaders. Erhard realised that the world was not what it had been in Adenauer's heyday, but he pursued a more cautious policy *vis-à-vis* the East. He looked for modest openings in Yugoslavia, Rumania, Poland and even Hungary and Bulgaria. He did, however, stick to the inherited policy of the Hallstein Doctrine, no recognition of the GDR and no recognition of the Oder–Neisse frontier. He showed some flexibility in regard to Berlin, allowing Willy Brandt, as Governing Mayor, the chance successfully to negotiate a local agreement with the GDR allowing West Berliners to visit their relatives in East Berlin at Christmas 1963 and on four occasions in 1964.

Brandt: Origins of *Ostpolitik*

The Grand Coalition of Kiesinger and Brandt took a few more hesitating steps in the direction of developing an *Ostpolitik* as well as repairing its *Westpolitik*. In January 1967 diplomatic relations were established with Rumania, and a year later they were re-established with Yugoslavia. In August 1967 a trade agreement with Czechoslovakia led to trade missions being established in Prague and, by the Czechs, in Frankfurt. Chancellor Kiesinger had some nice things to say about the achievements of the East German people and proposed certain practical improvements in relations between East and West Germany. The East Germans refused to be drawn, demanding full diplomatic recognition. Progress could only be slow. The East Germans prevailed as much as they could on their allies to secure recognition of the GDR before entering into diplomatic relations with Bonn. At home Kiesinger had to be mindful of the suspicion of Franz Josef Strauss, who was also in the government, towards any overtures to the Soviet bloc. The Warsaw Pact invasion of Czechoslovakia in August 1968 halted all further progress in this direction. Here matters stood until after the coming to office of the Brandt government in 1969.

On 21 October 1969 Herr Brandt was elected Federal Chancellor by the *Bundestag* and a week later he made a statement outlining his policy towards the GDR. As earlier West German governments had done, he rejected international recognition of the GDR by the Federal Republic but, and this was a new departure, he recognised the GDR as a separate state. He offered the East Germans 'negotiations at government level without discrimination on either side, which would lead to contractually agreed co-operation'. The East German Chairman of the Council of Ministers (head of government), Herr Stoph, found in Brandt's statement a 'hint at a more realistic assessment of the situation created in Europe as a result of the Second World War'. Various other moves then followed, including the presentation of a draft treaty on GDR–FRG relations by Walter Ulbricht, GDR head of state. Brandt and Stoph met in the East German town of Erfurt, amid scenes of great popular enthusiasm, on 19 March 1970. The two heads of government then met again in West Germany at Kassel on 21 May 1970. In April a postal agreement was signed and in the same month the Bonn government announced measures to help the GDR export more to the FRG. The so-called 'safe conduct' law of 1966, under which certain East German politicians could visit the FRG without facing prosecution, was repealed as a gesture to the Democratic Republic. After prolonged negotiations between the FRG and the USSR, a treaty on the renunciation of force was signed in Moscow on 12 August 1970. The treaty had the full approval of Bonn's allies. Under Article 3 the two states undertook to respect the territorial integrity of all states in Europe within their existing frontiers, including the Oder–Neisse line and the frontiers between the GDR and the FRG. The treaty set the scene for other treaties. In December followed the treaty with Poland, Article 1 of which declared that the two states agreed that the Oder–Neisse line 'shall constitute the Western State frontier of the People's Republic of Poland'. Once again the Western Powers communicated their agreement with the treaty. On the day the treaty was initialled, the Polish government issued a statement announcing measures to allow the repatriation of ethnic Germans to the Federal Republic. The four powers reached agreement on Berlin on 3 September 1971. The main

points of this were Soviet recognition of the close ties between West
Berlin and West Germany and its guarantee of the unimpeded
movement of people and goods between West Berlin and the FRG. The
Soviet Union also promised improved opportunities for West Berliners
to visit East Berlin and the GDR. In return the Western Powers agreed
(once again) under Article 4(a) that the Western sectors 'continue not
to be a constituent part of the Federal Republic of Germany and not to
be governed by it'. This was not really a concession by the Western
Powers as they had maintained this position since 1949. But it was
unwelcome to the West Germans. Under Article 4(b) the Federal
Republic could no longer elect its President in West Berlin or have
sessions of the *Bundestag* there. Another Soviet gain was the right to
have a consulate-general in West Berlin. West Germany was allowed a
permanent liaison agency. In the case of the Berlin Treaty it appears
that neither the Russians nor the Americans were as enthusiastic about
coming to an agreement as were the West Germans. For one thing, the
Russians had some difficulties with Walter Ulbricht until his forced
retirement as Party Secretary in May 1971. The Soviets became more
amenable once they saw the rapidly changing relations between the
United States and China. The Americans, for their part, did not wish to
be accused of improving relations with Peking at the expense of those
with Moscow.

Even more dramatic than the earlier treaties was the so-called
Grundvertrag (Basic Treaty) between the FRG and the GDR. This was
signed on 21 December 1972. Both parties agreed to renounce force, to
develop good neighbourly relations on the basis of the aims and
principles of the UN Charter, to respect each other's sovereignty, to
work for disarmament and to solve the practical and humanitarian
problems between the two states. On the basis of the treaty the two
states agreed to exchange permanent representatives in 1974. In a letter
to the East German government the Chancellor reaffirmed that the
treaty did not contradict the FRG's aim to work for the right of self-
determination of the German people and German reunification. In
1973 there were other great strides forward in *Ostpolitik* with the
establishment of full diplomatic relations between West Germany and
Finland, Czechoslovakia, Hungary and Bulgaria and the admission of the
two German states into the United Nations. The signing of the
Helsinki Agreement by the states of Eastern and Western Europe,
Canada and the United States in 1975 was made possible by *Ostpolitik.*

A number of other agreements were achieved between the two
German states in the second half of the 1970s. Under the Postal Accord

of March 1976 considerable improvements were made to the inter-German postal service. Services are charged at inland rates. The two states signed a border agreement on 29 November 1978 under which they agreed the exact course of over 90 per cent of their joint frontier. They could not agree on the frontier along the river Elbe. East Germany claimed a frontier following the centre of the river bed, West Germany claimed its territory extended to the eastern bank of the river. Two traffic agreements were also signed in 1979. Despite this progress, relations between the FRG and the GDR were at times strained over East German restrictions on West German journalists working in the Democratic Republic, over the GDR's continued strengthening of its frontier with the FRG, and over the GDR's treatment of its dissidents and those wishing to emigrate. The GDR authorities accused the FRG of interfering in its internal affairs and of failing to recognise the Democratic Republic as a sovereign, independent and foreign state. West Germany stuck to its view that the two German states were not foreign to each other.

The critics of the Brandt government, and they were not only in West Germany, claimed that the FRG had given away a great deal and got very little in return. It is true that West Germany had given up some of its most fundamental tenets of policy regarding its right to speak for the whole of Germany, the rejection of the Oder–Neisse line, the position of West Berlin and the non-recognition of the GDR. However, the Federal Republic had been able to do little on most of these matters. Even on the non-recognition of the GDR, where it had had notable success, the situation was changing in favour of the East Germans. Moreover, by clinging to these tenets the Federal Republic greatly reduced its influence in Eastern Europe and remained under suspicion in East and West that it still harboured dangerous resentment if not actual aggressive designs. Brandt greatly increased the Federal Republic's moral stature, at least among those nations which had been involved in the Second World War. *Ostpolitik* also made life more difficult for the hard-line faction in the GDR. It is amazing that it took the West Germans so long to see this. The recognition of the GDR did nothing to lessen the ties between the Germans of the GDR and those of the FRG. On the contrary, Brandt could rightly argue that for millions of Germans *Ostpolitik* had made life easier. The two million people of West Berlin can now visit East Berlin and the GDR without too much difficulty. The three million or so former GDR citizens who left East Germany 'illegally' between 1949 and 1971 are able to visit their relatives without danger of being arrested. Roughly 6.5 million

West Germans living in the frontier areas can now cross into the frontier area of the GDR where they have friends, relatives and, in some cases, even property. These are just some of the more important gains from *Ostpolitik*. Finally, some critics harboured the suspicion that Brandt was in some way weakening or neglecting the FRG's friendship with the USA and the EEC in order to pursue *Ostpolitik*. This was not so. Brandt did not forget *Westpolitik*. He worked hard, for instance, for an extension of the EEC to include Britain, and he retained his conviction that the FRG needed to keep the USA interested in its fate.

The FRG and the United States

The West Germans continue to regard the alliance with the United States, as Chancellor Schmidt has put it, as 'the bedrock of our security'. They also regard the United States as a valuable market and a source of cultural and intellectual enrichment. There have been differences in the 1970s between the two states. There is the continuing problem for the United States (and Britain) of the cost of stationing troops in the Federal Republic. Also, the United States was worried about the possible adverse effects on its trade due to the extension of the EEC in 1973. The two states have not completely seen eye to eye over the continuing crisis in the Middle East. Both remain friendly towards Israel but the West Germans, like the British, feel they must not appear to be too closely associated with Israel at the expense of their ties with the Arab world. Like the other Western states, they got their calculations wrong over Iran, unable to see the Shah's regime in all its ugliness.

The Federal Republic of Germany has made a remarkable evolution in world affairs since 1949. From a state not empowered to carry on foreign affairs, it has developed into one of the top powers in 1979. In economic, political and military terms, it is overshadowed only by the United States and the Soviet Union. In some respects Japan is ahead of it in economic terms, but certainly not in political influence. The FRG owes this evolution to its spectacular economic success, the needs of the three Western Powers in the 1950s and, not least, to the shrewd diplomacy of its leaders, especially Adenauer and Brandt.

Further Reading

Baring, Arnulf. *Aussenpolitik in Adenauer's Kanzler-Demokratie*
    (Munich, 1969)
Cate, Curtis. *The Ideas of August* (London, 1979)
Kaiser, Karl. *German Foreign Policy in Transition* (London, 1968)
Landauer, Carl. *Germany: Illusions and Dilemmas* (New York, 1969)
Morgan, Roger. *The United States and West Germany 1945–1973*
    (London, 1974)
Prittie, Terence. *Konrad Adenauer* (London, 1972)
———. *The Velvet Chancellors* (London, 1979)
Tilford, Roger (ed.). *The Ostpolitik and Political Change In Germany*
    (London, 1976)

1918   11 November, armistice signed by Germans, bringing World War I to an end.

1919   19 January, elections to constituent assembly to draw up constitution for German Republic. 11 February, Friedrich Ebert (SPD) elected President. 28 June, Versailles Peace Treaty signed by Hermann Müller (SPD) and Johannes Bell (Centre) for Germany.

1921   Harding replaces Wilson as President of USA.

1923   Great inflation in Germany with 1 dollar exchanging in September for nearly 99 million marks. French occupy Ruhr to force reparations. November, Hitler attempts putsch in Munich without success. Coolidge US President.

1925   Hindenburg elected President of Germany on death of Ebert.

1929   Wall Street crash. Young Plan on German reparations agreed. Hoover US President. Stalin gains supreme power in USSR.

1930   14 September, in Reichstag elections Nazi vote leaps from 2.6 per cent in 1928 to 18.3 per cent, making NSDAP second party behind SPD with 24.5 per cent. KPD up from 10.6 per cent to 13.1 per cent, Centre gains 11.8 per cent.

1932   31 July, in Reichstag elections Nazis emerge as biggest single party with 37.4 per cent of vote, SPD 21.6 per cent, KPD 14.6 per cent, Centre 12.5 per cent. In 6 November election four main parties got: Nazis 33.1 per cent, SPD 20.4 per cent, KPD 16.9 per cent, Centre 11.9 per cent.

1933   30 January, Hitler appointed Chancellor by Hindenburg. In USA Roosevelt becomes President. 27 February, Reichstag fire. 5 March, in unfree elections Nazis gain 43.9 per cent, their Conservative allies (DNVP) 8 per cent, SPD 18.3 per cent, KPD 12.3 per cent, Centre 11.2 per cent. 2 May, trade unions banned. 23 March, Enabling Act giving Hitler dictatorial powers without the votes of the SPD or the (banned) KPD.

1935   Saar returned to Germany after plebiscite on 13 January. Conscription reintroduced in Germany. Nuremberg anti-Semitic laws passed.

1936   Remilitarisation of Rhineland by Germany. Germany gives military assistance to Franco rebels in Spain. Olympic Games held in Berlin.

1938   February, Austria annexed by Germany. 28 September, Munich Agreement between Germany, Britain, France, Italy hands over Sudetenland of Czechoslovakia to Germany.

1939   March, rest of Czechoslovakia taken by Germany. 25 May, Anglo-Polish Treaty signed. 23 August, Hitler–Stalin Pact agreed. 1 September, Germany attacks Poland. 3 September, Britain and France declare war on Germany.

1940   April, Germany attacks Denmark and Norway. May, Germany attacks Holland, Belgium, Luxembourg, starts offensive against Anglo-French forces. May–June, Dunkirk evacuation by British.

1941   22 June, Germany attacks USSR. 4 December, German assault halted outside Moscow. 7 December, Japan attacks US fleet at Pearl Harbor. Germany declares war on USA. 3 September, SS start gassing in Auschwitz.

1942   30–31 May, first 1,000 bomber raid on Germany hits Cologne.

1943   January–February, German 6th Army surrenders at Stalingrad. 7 September, Italy surrenders after overthrow of Mussolini. Day-time raids by Allies on Germany.

1944   6 June, D-Day landings in France. 20 July, bomb plot against Hitler. V-weapons hit London.

1945   February, Yalta conference of Roosevelt, Stalin and Churchill. 14 February, Dresden bombed. 2 May, Russians capture Berlin. Death of Roosevelt, replaced by Truman. 8 May, end of war with Germany. Labour win election in Britain. August, A-bombs used against Japan, Japan surrenders.

1946   SED set up in Soviet Zone. 16 October, Nazi war criminals executed at Nuremberg.

1947   January, British and US Zones merged. Later French Zone joins them.

1948   London six-power conference recommends integration of West Germany into Western Europe. Western currency reform is followed by Berlin blockade. September, convocation of Parliamentary Council to draft West German constitution.

1949   April, Washington Agreement. May, Basic Law of FRG ratified by *Länder* except Bavaria. 23 May, proclamation of Basic Law. August, election to *Bundestag*, Adenauer elected Chancellor. October, German Democratic Republic (GDR) proclaimed.

1950   Outbreak of Korean War.

1951   Conservatives replace Labour as government in Britain.

1952   German Treaty.

1953   Death of Stalin. 17 June, rising in GDR. Elections to 2nd *Bundestag*. Eisenhower becomes US President.

1954   Paris Treaties signed.

1955   FRG regains sovereignty. *Bundeswehr* set up. Austrian State Treaty leads to withdrawal of four powers. Adenauer visits Moscow.

1956   Hungarian Revolution. Suez operation mounted. KPD banned in FRG.

1957   January, Saar returned to Germany. 15 September, CDU/CSU win absolute majority in election to 3rd *Bundestag*. 4 October, Russians launch first artificial earth satellite.

1958   January, treaties establishing EEC and Euratom come into force. May, de Gaulle forms government in France leading to 5th Republic.

1959   May, four-power conference on Germany in Geneva ends in deadlock. July, Heinrich Lübke (CDU) elected West German President replacing Theodor Heuss (FDP). November, special congress of SPD at Bad Godesberg agrees new programme.

1960   DFU founded. Land collectivised in GDR.

1961   13 August, Berlin Wall erected. Kennedy takes over as US President. CDU/CSU win 4th *Bundestag* election with reduced majority.

1962   October, *Spiegel* affair involving Defence Minister Franz Josef Strauss.

1963   15 October, Adenauer retires, Erhard becomes Chancellor. 22 November, Kennedy assassinated, is replaced by Johnson as US President.

1964   Khrushchev removed as CPSU Secretary, Brezhnev takes over. Labour win election in Britain. NPD set up.

1965   CDU/CSU win election to 5th *Bundestag* with increased majority. FRG establishes diplomatic relations with Israel.

1966   December, Grand Coalition of CDU/CSU and SPD formed with Kiesinger as Chancellor and Brandt as Foreign Minister. November, NPD gains admission to parliaments of Hessen and Bavaria.

1967   January, diplomatic relations between Rumania and FRG agreed. Recession and increasing unemployment in FRG. NPD in elections gains admission to parliaments of Schleswig-Holstein, Rhineland, Lower Saxony, Bremen. June, Arab—

Israeli War. For first time in history of FRG negative growth of real social product.

1968   FRG and Yugoslavia renew diplomatic relations. NPD wins seats in Baden-Württemberg parliament. Emergency powers' constitution agreed by *Bundestag*. Student 'revolt' in Paris and FRG. 21 August, Warsaw Pact states invade Czechoslovakia. 27 October, DKP formed as follow-up to KPD. Autumn, full employment in FRG virtually restored.

1969   5 March, Heinemann (SPD) elected President of FRG with FDP help. 28 September, elections to 6th *Bundestag*, CDU/CSU still biggest party but SPD–FDP form government, Brandt Chancellor. Nixon becomes US President.

1970   Meetings of Brandt and Stoph in Erfurt and Kassel. 12 August, signing of Renunciation of Force Treaty by FRG and USSR. December, Brandt visit to Warsaw. Conservatives win election in UK.

1971   New *Betriebsverfassungsgesetz* agreed by *Bundestag*. Ulbricht replaced by Honecker in GDR.

1972   SPD emerges as biggest single party in elections to 7th *Bundestag*. September, Olympic Games held in Munich. October, diplomatic relations with China agreed by FRG. 21 December, Basic Treaty between FRG and GDR signed.

1973   January, Britain, Denmark, Ireland join EEC. September, FRG and GDR admitted to UNO. October, Israeli–Arab War followed by oil crisis. December, Prague–Bonn Treaty. Unemployment up in FRG.

1974   2 May, permanent representatives of FRG in East Berlin and GDR in Bonn begin their work. 6 May, resignation of Brandt, Schmidt elected Chancellor. 15 May, Scheel (FDP) elected President. Labour replace Conservative government in Britain. Nixon resigns as President of USA, is replaced by Gerald Ford. December, unemployment in FRG 4.2 per cent as against 2.2 per cent a year earlier.

1975   February, unemployment in FRG rises to 5.2 per cent. 30 April, end of Vietnam War. 1 August, 35 states sign Helsinki Agreement on Security and Co-operation in Europe. December, unemployment in FRG down to 4.8 per cent.

1976   October, elections to 8th *Bundestag*, CDU/CSU largest party once again but not enough seats to dislodge SPD–FDP coalition.

1977   September, kidnapping of Dr Hanns-Martin Schleyer. January, Jimmy Carter inaugurated as US President.

1978   February, reorganisation of West German Cabinet after resignations of five ministers. May, more anti-terrorist measures agreed by *Bundestag*. June, resignation of Werner Maihofer as Minister of the Interior.

1979   Conservatives regain office in Britain. May, Karl Karstens (CDU) inaugurated as Federal President.

1980   October, SPD–FDP coalition wins federal election to 9th *Bundestag*:

Turnout 88.7%

% of votes cast		seats in *Bundestag*
CDU/CSU	44.5	226
SPD	42.9	218
FDP	10.6	53
Greens (ecology)	1.5	–
DKP	0.2	–
NDP	0.2	–

INDEX OF NAMES

224 Index

SUBJECT INDEX